AQA History

AS
Unit 2

...land:

The Struggle for Supremacy, 1529–1547

Rebecca
Carpenter
Series editor
Sally Waller

OXFORD
UNIVERSITY PRESS

OXFORD
UNIVERSITY PRESS

Great Clarendon Street, Oxford, OX2 6DP, United Kingdom

Oxford University Press is a department of the University of Oxford.
It furthers the University's objective of excellence in research, scholarship,
and education by publishing worldwide. Oxford is a registered trade mark of
Oxford University Press in the UK and in certain other countries

First published by Nelson Thornes Ltd in 2009

British Library Cataloguing in Publication Data
Data available

978-1-4085-0303-4

10 9 8 7 6 5 4

Printed in China

Acknowledgements

Illustrations: David Russell Illustration and Angela Knowles
Page make-up: Thomson Digital

Although we have made every effort to trace and contact all
copyright holders before publication this has not been possible in all
cases. If notified, the publisher will rectify any errors or omissions at
the earliest opportunity.

Links to third party websites are provided by Oxford in good faith
and for information only. Oxford disclaims any responsibility for
the materials contained in any third party website referenced in
this work.

Contents

Introduction

The publisher has worked hard to ensure that this book offers you excellent support for your AS course and helps you to prepare for your exams. You can be confident that the range of learning, teaching and assessment practice materials has been checked and is closely matched to the requirements of your specification.

How to use this book

The features in this book include:

Timeline

Key events are outlined at the beginning of the book. The events are colour-coded so you can clearly see the categories of change.

Learning objectives

At the beginning of each section you will find a list of learning objectives that contain targets linked to the requirements of the specification.

Key chronology

A short list of dates usually with a focus on a specific event or legislation.

Key profile

The profile of a key person you should be aware of to fully understand the period in question.

Key term

A term that you will need to be able to define and understand.

Did you know?

Interesting information to bring the subject under discussion to life.

Exploring the detail

Information to put further context around the subject under discussion.

A closer look

An in-depth look at a theme, person or event to deepen your understanding. Activities around the extra information may be included.

Sources

Sources to reinforce topics or themes and may provide fact or opinion. They may be quotations from historical works, contemporaries of the period or photographs.

Cross-reference

Links to related content within the book which may offer more detail on the subject in question.

Activity

Various activity types to provide you with different challenges and opportunities to demonstrate both the content and skills you are learning. Some can be worked on individually, some as part of group work and some are designed to specifically 'stretch and challenge'.

▇ Question

Questions to prompt further discussion on the topic under consideration and are an aid to revision.

▇ Summary questions

Summary questions at the end of each chapter to test your knowledge and allow you to demonstrate your understanding.

Study tip

Hints to help you with your study and to prepare for your exam.

Practice questions

Questions at the end of each section in the style that you may encounter in your exam.

Learning outcomes

Learning outcomes at the end of each section remind you what you should know having completed the chapters in that section.

▇ Web links in the book

Because the publisher is not responsible for third party content online, there may be some changes to this material that are beyond our control. In order for us to ensure that the links referred to in the book are as up-to-date and stable as possible, the web sites provided are usually homepages with supporting instructions on how to reach the relevant pages if necessary.

Please let us know at **schools.enquiries.uk@oup.com** if you find a link that doesn't work and we will do our best to correct this at reprint, or to list an alternative site.

Introduction to the History series

When Bruce Bogtrotter in Roald Dahl's *Matilda* was challenged to eat a huge chocolate cake, he just opened his mouth and ploughed in, taking bite after bite and lump after lump until the cake was gone and he was feeling decidedly sick. The picture is not dissimilar to that of some A-level history students. They are attracted to history because of its inherent appeal but, when faced with a bulging file and a forthcoming examination, their enjoyment evaporates. They try desperately to cram their brains with an assortment of random facts and subsequently prove unable to control the outpouring of their ill-digested material in the examination.

The books in this series are designed to help students and teachers avoid this feeling of overload and examination panic by breaking down the AQA history specification in such a way that it is easily absorbed. Above all, they are designed to retain and promote students' enthusiasm for history by avoiding a dreary rehash of dates and events. Each book is divided into sections, closely matched to those given in the specification, and the content is further broken down into chapters that present the historical material in a lively and attractive form, offering guidance on the key terms, events and issues, and blending thought-provoking activities and questions in a way designed to advance students' understanding. By encouraging students to think for themselves and to share their ideas with others, as well as helping them to develop the knowledge and skills they will need to pass their examination, this book should ensure that students' learning remains a pleasure rather than an endurance test.

To make the most of what this book provides, students will need to develop efficient study skills from the start and it is worth spending some time considering what these involve:

- Good organisation of material in a subject-specific file. Organised notes help develop an organised brain and sensible filing ensures time is not wasted hunting for misplaced material. This book uses cross-references to indicate where material in one chapter has relevance to material in another. Students are advised to adopt the same technique.

- A sensible approach to note-making. Students are often too ready to copy large chunks of material from printed books or to download sheaves of printouts from the internet. This series is designed to encourage students to think about the notes they collect and to undertake research with a particular purpose in mind. The activities encourage students to pick out information that is relevant to the issue being addressed and to avoid making notes on material that is not properly understood.

- Taking time to think, which is by far the most important component of study. By encouraging students to think before they write or speak, be it for a written answer, presentation or class debate, students should learn to form opinions and make judgements based on the accumulation of evidence. These are the skills that the examiner will be looking for in the final examination. The beauty of history is that there is rarely a right or wrong answer so, with sufficient evidence, one student's view will count for as much as the next.

Unit 2

Unit 2 promotes the study of significant periods of history in depth. Although the span of years may appear short, the chosen topics are centred on periods of change that raise specific historical issues and they therefore provide an opportunity for students to study in some depth the interrelationships between ideas, individuals, circumstances and other factors that lead to major developments. Appreciating the dynamics of change, and balancing the degree of change against elements of continuity, make for a fascinating and worthwhile study. Students are also required to analyse consequences and draw conclusions about the issues these studies raise. Such themes are, of course, relevant to an understanding of the present and, through such an historical investigation, students will be guided towards a greater appreciation of the world around them today, as well as develop their understanding of the past.

Unit 2 is tested by a 1 hour 30 minute paper containing three questions. The first question is compulsory and based on sources, while the remaining two, of which students will need to choose one, are two-part questions as described in Table 1. Plentiful sources are included throughout this book to give students some familiarity with contemporary and historiographical material, and activities and suggestions are provided to enable students to develop the required examination skills. Students should familiarise themselves with the question breakdown, additional hints and marking criteria given below before attempting any of the practice practice questions at the end of each section.

Answers will be marked according to a scheme based on 'levels of response'. This means that the answer will be assessed according to which level best matches the historical skills displayed, taking both knowledge and understanding into account. All students should have a copy of these criteria and need to use them wisely.

Table 1 *Unit 2: style of questions and marks available*

Unit 2	Question	Marks	Question type	Question stem	Hints for students
Question 1 based on three sources of c.300–350 words in total	(a)	12	This question involves the comparison of two sources	Explain how far the views in Source B differ from those in Source A in relation to…	Take pains to avoid simply writing out what each source says with limited direct comment. Instead, you should try to find two or three points of comparison and illustrate these with reference to the sources. You should also look for any underlying similarities. In your conclusion, you will need to make it clear exactly 'how far' the views differ
Question 1	(b)	24	This requires use of the sources and own knowledge and asks for an explanation that shows awareness that issues and events can provoke differing views and explanations	How far… How important was… How successful…	This answer needs to be planned as you will need to develop an argument in your answer and show balanced judgement. Try to set out your argument in the introduction and, as you develop your ideas through your paragraphs, support your opinions with detailed evidence. Your conclusion should flow naturally and provide supported judgement. The sources should be used as 'evidence' throughout your answer. Do ensure you refer to them all
Question 2 and 3	(a)	12	This question is focused on a narrow issue within the period studied and requires an explanation	Explain why…	Make sure you explain 'why', not 'how', and try to order your answer in a way that shows you understand the inter-linkage of factors and which are the most important. You should try to reach an overall judgement/ conclusion
Question 2 and 3	(b)	24	This question is broader and asks for analysis and explanation with appropriate judgement. The question requires an awareness of debate over issues	A quotation in the form of a judgement on a key development or issue will be given and candidates asked: Explain why you agree or disagree with this view	This answer needs to be planned as you will need to show balanced judgement. Try to think of points that agree and disagree and decide which way you will argue. Set out your argument in the introduction and support it through your paragraphs, giving the alternative picture too but showing why your view is the more convincing. Your conclusion should flow naturally from what you have written

Marking criteria

Question 1(a)

Level 1 Answers either briefly paraphrase/describe the content of the two sources or identify simple comparison(s) between the sources. Skills of written communication will be weak. *(0–2 marks)*

Level 2 Responses will compare the views expressed in the two sources and identify some differences and/or similarities. There may be some limited own knowledge. Answers will be coherent but weakly expressed. *(3–6 marks)*

Level 3 Responses will compare the views expressed in the two sources, identifying differences **and** similarities and using own knowledge to explain and evaluate these. Answers will, for the most part, be clearly expressed. *(7–9 marks)*

Level 4 Responses will make a developed comparison between the views expressed in the two sources **and** own knowledge will apply to evaluate and to demonstrate a good contextual understanding. Answers will, for the most part, show good skills of written communication. *(10–12 marks)*

Question 1(b)

Level 1 Answers may be based on sources or on own knowledge alone, or they may comprise an undeveloped mixture of the two. They may contain some descriptive material which is only loosely linked to the focus of the question or they may address only a part of the question. Alternatively, there may be some explicit comment with little, if any, appropriate support. Answers are likely to be generalised and assertive. There will be little, if any, awareness of differing historical interpretations. The response will be limited in development and skills of written communication will be weak. *(0–6 marks)*

Level 2 Answers may be based on sources or on own knowledge alone, or they may contain a mixture of the two. They may be almost entirely descriptive with few explicit links to the focus of the question. Alternatively, they may contain some explicit comment with relevant but limited support. They will display limited understanding of differing historical interpretations. Answers will be coherent but weakly expressed and/or poorly structured. *(7–11 marks)*

Level 3 Answers will show a developed understanding of the demands of the question using evidence from **both** the sources **and** own knowledge. They will provide some assessment backed by relevant and appropriately selected evidence, but they will lack depth and/or balance. There will be some understanding of varying historical interpretations. Answers will, for the most part, be clearly expressed and show some organisation in the presentation of material. *(12–16 marks)*

Level 4 Answers will show explicit understanding of the demands of the question. They will develop a balanced argument backed by a good range of appropriately selected evidence from the sources and own knowledge, and a good understanding of historical interpretations. Answers will, for the most part, show organisation and good skills of written communication. *(17–21 marks)*

Level 5 Answers will be well focused and closely argued. The arguments will be supported by precisely selected evidence from the sources and own knowledge, incorporating well-developed understanding of historical interpretations and debate. Answers will, for the most part, be carefully organised and fluently written, using appropriate vocabulary. *(22–24 marks)*

Question 2(a) and 3(a)

Level 1 Answers will contain either some descriptive material which is only loosely linked to the focus of the question or some explicit comment with little, if any, appropriate support. Answers are likely to be generalised and assertive. The response will be limited in development and skills of written communication will be weak. *(0–2 marks)*

Level 2 Answers will demonstrate some knowledge and understanding of the demands of the question. They will either be almost entirely descriptive with few explicit links to the question **or** they provide some explanations backed by evidence that is limited in range and/or depth. Answers will be coherent but weakly expressed and/or poorly structured. *(3–6 marks)*

Level 3 Answers will demonstrate good understanding of the demands of the question providing relevant explanations backed by appropriately selected information, although this may not be full or comprehensive. Answers will, for the most part, be clearly expressed and show some organisation in the presentation of material. *(7–9 marks)*

Level 4 Answers will be well focused, identifying a range of specific explanations backed by precise evidence and demonstrating good understanding of the connections and links between events/issues. Answers will, for the most part, be well written and organised. *(10–12 marks)*

Question 2(b) and 3(b)

Level 1 Answers may **either** contain some descriptive material which is only loosely linked to the focus of the question **or** they may address only a limited part of the period of the question. Alternatively, there may be some explicit comment with little, if any, appropriate support. Answers are likely to be generalised and assertive. There will be little, if any, awareness of different historical interpretations. The response will be limited in development and skills of written communication will be weak. *(0–6 marks)*

Level 2 Answers will show some understanding of the demands of the question. They will either be almost entirely descriptive with few explicit links to the question **or** they contain some explicit comment with relevant but limited support. They will display limited understanding of differing historical interpretations. Answers will be coherent but weakly expressed and/or poorly structured. *(7–11 marks)*

Level 3 Answers will show a developed understanding of the demands of the question. They will provide some assessment, backed by relevant and appropriately selected evidence, but they will lack depth and/or balance. There will be some understanding of varying historical interpretations. Answers will, for the most part, be clearly expressed and show some organisation in the presentation of material. *(12–16 marks)*

Level 4 Answers will show explicit understanding of the demands of the question. They will develop a balanced argument backed by a good range of appropriately selected evidence and a good understanding of historical interpretations. Answers will, for the most part, show organisation and good skills of written communication. *(17–21 marks)*

Level 5 Answers will be well focused and closely argued. The arguments will be supported by precisely selected evidence leading to a relevant conclusion/judgement, incorporating well-developed understanding of historical interpretations and debate. Answers will, for the most part, be carefully organised and fluently written, using appropriate vocabulary. *(22–24 marks)*

Introduction to this book

The nature of Tudor monarchy

Unlike monarchs of today, 16th century rulers possessed real power, but their powers were not unlimited. The power of the Church, and the existence of a parliament made up of nobles and representatives of the shires and boroughs, ensured that the King could not do just as he pleased.

- It was accepted that the King was appointed by God as defender of his subjects' property. The spiritual well-being of his subjects, however, lay in the hands of the Catholic Church. This was the Christian Church, in which all English people grew up. It had its own hierarchy, courts and taxation system and was loyal to the Pope, in Rome, who was the head of the Catholic Church.

- The King was expected to seek advice from councillors who were drawn from the nobility, from lawyers and from the Church. They formed the Council, an executive body which also provided advice on matters of law and order and foreign policy. Informal advice and guidance would also be sought from the men who served the King in his private apartments; this was known as the Privy Chamber. The most important person here was the Chief Gentleman of the Privy Chamber, who often also held the post of Groom of the Stool at the same time.

- The King was expected to pay for the ordinary expenses of government from rents paid by tenants of crown lands and through customs duties. Customs duties were paid on all goods passing through English ports. Taxation was not regular and was usually raised for the defence of the country or for a war. Parliaments granted one or more fifteenths and tenths as subsidies; these were based on an assessment of wealth or income to be paid in specified instalments.

- The King could issue proclamations but he could secure laws only through parliament. A proclamation was an order sent out to royal officials by the King. Anyone who went against a proclamation would be committing a crime, but only laws passed through parliament could carry the death sentence for those who disobeyed.

The English social hierarchy

The structure of English society was based on a belief in the 'Great Chain of Being', headed by God and the angels in heaven, whereby each social group had a fixed, predetermined role in society. Below the King came those who helped him direct society: the lords spiritual (archbishops and bishops) and lords temporal (nobles or 'magnates'). They were followed by the gentry, within whose ranks there were knights with the title of 'Sir' and esquires, who were gentlemen who bore arms but had not been knighted. Most of the gentry held land; some were **retained men**, serving a noble, and others were engaged in other occupations such as practice of the law. Beneath them came the ordinary people, known as

Key term

Retained men: men who voluntarily contracted and obliged themselves to provide a certain number of soldiers for their nobleman.

the 'commonality'. This included a wide range of labourers from highly skilled craftsmen to peasants and beggars. Finally, the chain of being stretched down to animals and plants.

By the 16th century, this hierarchical structure contained a good deal of flexibility. Its seeming rigidity had been broken down by the growth of commerce and trade, as well as an expansion of the opportunities for educated men, for example in royal service. A middle ranking group had emerged, particularly in the growing towns where well-off citizens, often merchants, might assume local power and influence.

The King's court

Henry VIII's court comprised members of the nobility, who were often attended on by the sons and daughters of the minor nobility and gentry. The court was not based in any one place, but travelled around and no matter where it was, the King's favour was all important. Court nobles might be members of the King's Privy Council, in which they would provide formal advice on matters of state, but also, if favoured, play a additional role in the King's Privy Chamber. In return for governmental and military service in times of war, such nobles might also receive patronage from the King in terms of additional land, property and positions. A nobleman's land gave him an important role in local government where he was expected to keep order and administer justice. Furthermore, there was always the chance that he might augment his income from wealthy individuals seeking to advance their own positions within the local area. Some might even pay him money to influence the King. One of Henry VIII's favourites was Charles Brandon, whom he made Duke of Suffolk.

Fig. 1 *An early portrait of Henry VIII as a young man by Holbein*

 Key profile

The Duke of Suffolk

Charles Brandon (1484–1545) was close to Henry in age and interests. He held a number of key offices and was rewarded with titles and land. Their relationship deteriorated following Suffolk's unauthorised marriage to Henry's sister Mary. Frances Grey was a child of this marriage who was the mother of Lady Jane Grey, Queen for nine days.

The King's parliament

The nobility were also members of the upper house of parliament, the Lords, and often had influence in the lower house, the Commons. The House of Commons was made up of approximately 300 elected members from the shires (counties) and from the boroughs, and those elected from the shires were very often the younger sons of nobles or gentry; most were elected unopposed. Members from the boroughs tended to be drawn from the merchant class or lawyers. Of the two houses, however, the House of Lords was more important. In it sat between 45 and 55 nobles, as well as 27 abbots, priors and bishops from the Church. Parliament was called infrequently, usually when the King wanted money to finance war. Generally parliament was reluctant to finance war as it meant raising a tax from its members' own property, whether they were commoners, nobles or churchmen. Legislation passed by the infrequently called parliaments would mainly concern the localities. The passing of legislation was rare: in the four centuries before the calling of parliament in 1529 the statutes passed ran to 1,092 pages; in the next 18 years the statutes passed covered 1,042 pages.

■ Key terms

Common law: legal rights which had been established over many years by custom and practice but were not written down.

Tithes: these were sometimes known as 'first fruits and tenths'. People were required to give a tenth of specific produce such as corn, fruit, vegetables, milk and cheese. Where profits were made from trade and industry a tenth of this also had be given to the clergy. Tithes were used to support the clergy.

■ Exploring the detail

The Wars of the Roses

The conflicting claims of the House of York and House of Lancaster for the throne of England resulted in a prolonged period of domestic upheaval. The instability was further exacerbated by the minority and mental instability of Henry VI. The conflict led sporadically to battles and skirmishes and three significant usurpations. A final usurpation in 1483 culminated in the battle of Bosworth (1485) when Henry, Duke of Richmond defeated Richard III. Henry VII united the Houses of York and Lancaster by marrying Elizabeth, the daughter of Edward IV.

■ Cross-reference

The family tree of **Edward III's descendants** can be found on page 40.

■ Did you know?

England was one of the oldest Catholic countries, having converted from paganism by the 7th century.

As well as acts passed by parliament, the country was ruled by **common law**. Custom was often used to define law rather than laws being written down. Legal ownership and legal processes were very important to ensure that property was protected.

■ The relationship between Church and state

In the 15th century the Church in England was part of the much wider Catholic Church, a powerful and wealthy Church, with property greater than any king's. The Catholic Church had its own structure, its own legal system and its own system of taxation. It exerted its authority over the country through the cathedrals in cities, priories in towns, monasteries in the countryside and parish churches in local areas.

England thought of itself as part of 'Christendom', and the kings of Christendom looked to the head of the Church – the Pope in Rome – for their authority to govern. The Pope was elected by the Church cardinals and, in the 16th century, was almost always chosen from an influential Italian family. His prestige and powers were enormous, particularly since he could draw up laws which applied to all of Christendom, but his authority in England, where negotiations had achieved greater powers for the monarchy, was somewhat weaker than his position in France and Spain.

Church law was known as canon law. It covered the beliefs of the Church, its teachings and its practices, and the Pope acted as the final arbiter in cases based on canon law. The interpretation of canon law within England depended on the archbishops of Canterbury and York. Each of these two archdioceses had its own parliament, known as Convocation. In practice, the Convocation of Canterbury, which met at Lambeth Palace in London, was the more powerful, while that in York was little more than a rubber-stamping authority for what was decided by Canterbury.

Beneath the archdioceses came the dioceses, headed by bishops, and beneath them were the parishes, each with its own priest but owing its loyalty to a bishop and to Rome. All those who were responsible for the running of the Church and taking Church services were known as clergy. Some positions carried a great deal of power as bishops controlled large areas of land and collected taxes from them. Most of the higher clergy had taken degrees at Oxford or Cambridge and were able to read the Bible and conduct services in Latin.

However, the lesser clergy were not always educated men. Furthermore, in some cases a priest would be responsible for a number of parishes and would employ anyone who had learnt some Latin verses, quite often with little understanding, to take services for him in the parishes he couldn't attend.

The parishes were the basic administrative units of the English Church but they were also the immediate communities in which people lived and with which they would have identified. Everyone was a parishioner in one of the 9,000 parishes into which England was divided. In the parish church they would be baptised, get married and eventually be buried. They would attend services on a weekly basis, as they were required by Church law to do every Sunday. They would also pay **tithes** – a 10 per cent tax on all agricultural produce and income.

The clergy who carried out canon law were known as the Ordinaries. They were mainly concerned with matters which would be classed as heresy – acts against the beliefs and teaching of the Church. Minor cases might incur fines, but what every Christian feared was excommunication. Excommunication meant being cast out of the Church and the salvation it offered. This was very serious. Not only could an individual not attend a church service, obtain forgiveness for sins or participate in the Mass, but he or she was also condemned to hell after death.

By the beginning of the 16th century the Church was facing criticism for what were considered to be corrupt practices, such as selling positions within the Church and for being too involved in matters of state. Monks who observed very strict rules and withdrew themselves from the temptations of the world were less subject to attack, but the Church's failure to provide proper spiritual care, for example by allowing uneducated clergy in some parishes, was obvious to all.

Some scholars sought out the original texts of Christian teaching and practices in order to try to purify religious practices. A small number of people secretly shared ideas which challenged the very beliefs on which the Catholic faith was based. As early as 1515 the boundaries of the rights and responsibilities of the King and Pope were the subject of discussion in scholarly circles.

> ■ **Cross-reference**
> You can find details of the **Church hierarchy** on page 15.

Cardinal Wolsey

From 1514 the most important person in the government of England, apart from Henry VIII himself, was Thomas Wolsey, Henry's chief minister. Wolsey's pre-eminence continued until 1529. It was a surprising position for a man not born of the nobility but as the son of a butcher.

There has been much unresolved debate between historians about the relationship between Henry VIII and Cardinal Wolsey, but it is possible to be clear about the key outcomes of their partnership in terms of the policies followed.

■ Wolsey successfully managed foreign policy, which enabled Henry VIII to play a prominent role in Europe despite the limitations of England's military resources. The rivalry between the two major powers – France and the Holy Roman Empire – was exploited by Wolsey. His policy was at its most successful in 1518 with the signing of the Treaty of London, giving England diplomatic ascendancy in Europe.

■ As Lord Chancellor, Wolsey controlled the legal system. The Lord Chancellor sat in the House of Lords and was responsible for law and justice. While it has been argued that he used the court of Star Chamber, a court of the Privy Council which had been authorised by Henry VII to 'punish divers misdemeanours', to further his own interests, Wolsey's greater reliance on written law as opposed to common law increased the power of the monarch over that of the nobility.

■ Wolsey also attempted to restrict the power of the nobility in influencing the King through the Eltham Ordinances of 1526. The Eltham Ordinances were ostensibly an attempt to regularise the finances and administration of the Privy Chamber, but in reality they enabled Wolsey to appoint his own placemen as the gentlemen most closely charged with serving the King's personal needs.

Since Cardinal Wolsey had demonstrated his skills in foreign and domestic affairs, as well as holding a prominent role within the Church, it is not surprising that Henry VIII turned to him to produce a solution to his most serious problem – the search for an annulment of his marriage to Catherine of Aragon. Wolsey's failure to achieve this was the result of his compromised position as both Henry's first minister

Fig. 2 *A Victorian representation of Cardinal Wolsey. In what ways does the portrait emphasise Wolsey's self-importance?*

and the Pope's ***legatus a latere***. It was not helped by his close links with the French court, the growing criticism of his lifestyle and his alienation of the traditional elements of the English court. He was accused of putting his allegiance to the Church of Rome before his allegiance to the King and fell from power in 1529. His fall precipitated the changes which resulted in the struggle for royal supremacy in Church and state.

Key profile

Cardinal Wolsey

Thomas Wolsey (1471–1530) was born in Ipswich and graduated from Oxford University at the age of 15. He advanced through the Church, becoming Bishop of Lincoln. By 1513 his organisational abilities had brought him to Henry's attention. Henry's growing dependence on his skills and knowledge is evidenced by Wolsey's acquisition of positions. He became both Archbishop of York and Chancellor of England. The Archdiocese of Canterbury had already been given, but Wolsey was made Cardinal and created *legatus a latere*, the latter enabling him to act on the Pope's behalf in negotiations. Wolsey demonstrated none of the virtues expected of the clergy, living in great luxury and indulgence. After his failure to procure an annulment for Henry's marriage he was disgraced and removed from office.

Henry's position at the start of 1529

By the mid-1520s Henry VIII could rightly claim that his position was stronger than that of his father. He had governed a country without internal strife since 1509. He had established England's position in Europe through diplomatic links and shown that England was a worthy military ally. For many ordinary people in England the standard of living was high and the quality of life of the gentry and nobility was enhanced by the growth in literacy and the printing press. Yet for Henry there was a major problem which was more important than all his achievements – the lack of a male heir. Although he had a daughter, Mary, born to him by his wife Catherine of Aragon, for various reasons he believed he could only secure the succession with a legitimate son.

Although Mary was being educated by Catherine of Aragon to a level never experienced by a princess before, most English people believed that, at best, Mary could be no more than the wife of a foreign prince. The fear of civil war should Mary inherit was very real and made Henry's position in 1529 very insecure.

- In 1525 France questioned the legitimacy of his daughter Mary. This was because Henry had had to receive a special papal dispensation to allow him to marry Catherine, who had previously been betrothed to his brother Arthur, who subsequently died. While this may have only been a diplomatic ploy by the French to put pressure on Henry, it increased Henry's anxieties.

- Henry had executed the Duke of Buckingham for treason in 1521 for appearing to claim a right to the throne, but there were still a significant number of males who could claim a right to the throne should Henry not produce a male heir. These included the three sons of the Countess of Salisbury, Buckingham's son (Henry Stafford), Edward Courtenay, Earl of Devon, and even the sons of the Duke of Norfolk. Should Henry VIII only produce a daughter the Tudor line might be usurped.

- Henry did have an illegitimate son, Henry Fitzroy, who was created Duke of Richmond, but an illegitimate son would not be recognised by the nobles as a rightful heir.

By the 1520s Henry VIII had begun to take mistresses, one of whom was Mary Boleyn. There was much suspicion that Mary had been manoeuvred into Henry's view by her uncle the Duke of Norfolk, who was the most important duke in the kingdom. He was an enemy of Cardinal Wolsey and jealous of the power which Wolsey exerted over Henry. It would seem that Norfolk and his cousin Sir Thomas Boleyn used first Mary, and, when Henry tired of her, her sister Anne, to gain influence with Henry. Mary Boleyn was very submissive but Anne was both more attractive and more able to hold out for what she and her relations wanted. While Norfolk wanted to engineer the downfall of Cardinal Wolsey, Anne wanted to be queen. Henry VIII was mesmerised by Anne, who he believed could offer him what his current queen, Catherine could not – a son.

In the years 1529–47, the English Church and state were to undergo massive change, and much of this was set in motion by this desperate desire for a male heir. From this came the separation of the Church of England from the Catholic Church and the focus of power over people's lives, property and souls from an 'outside' Church into the hands of the King. The process by which this was achieved was entirely legal in that it was discussed and authorised by parliament. The power of the monarch was further enhanced through the dissolution of the monasteries. This not only gave Henry power and wealth but also brought him into conflict with groups of people within England and countries remaining faithful to Rome. While all actions were taken in the name of the King, Henry was dependent on the advice and activities of members of the Privy Council in these developments, and different factions of the nobility and chief ministers were instrumental in the political and religious changes which took place. The relationship between, and the powers of, the Church and the state were significantly different in 1547 from what they had been in 1529.

■ Timeline

Blue: marital/dynastic issues; Green: political events; Red: religious events. Note that at this period these factors were very much interlinked.

1526	1527	1528	1529	1530
Anne Boleyn favoured by the King Henry tells Catherine he is seeking a divorce	Pope taken prisoner by Charles V		Fall of Wolsey Reformation parliament called Act to remove benefit of clergy	Thomas Cromwell joins the King's Council Charge of Praemunire against the clergy Papal court meets at Blackfriars to hear the divorce appeal

1535	1536	1537	1538	1539
More and Fisher executed Cromwell appointed vicegerent Visitation of religious houses begins Statute of Uses	Lincolnshire Rising Pilgrimage of Grace Act for the Dissolution of the Lesser Monasteries Catherine of Aragon dies Anne miscarries a male child Anne Boleyn executed Act of Succession declares Mary and Elizabeth illegitimate Henry Fitzroy dies Henry marries Jane Seymour Act of Ten Articles	Bigod rising Execution of those involved in Pilgrimage of Grace Council of North reorganised Birth of Edward Prince of Wales Death of Queen Jane Bishops' Book published	France and Holy Roman Empire sign Treaty of Nice Larger monasteries encouraged to surrender to the crown Arrest of White Rose claimants Henry excommunicated by the Pope Royal injunctions against worship at shrines and pilgrimages	More larger monasteries surrender Act for the Dissolution of the Greater Monasteries Publication of the Great Bible in English Act of Six Articles

1546	1547
Anglo-French truce – agreement over lease of Boulogne Denny made Chief Gentleman Henry's will drawn up Anne Askew burnt for heresy	Earl of Surrey executed Death of Henry VIII

1531

Cromwell promoted to inner council

Convocation agrees to payment of £100,000

Pope orders Henry not to remarry

Henry dismisses Catherine from court and establishes court with Anne

1532

More resigns as Chancellor

Act to remove annates

Supplication of the Ordinaries

Submission of the Clergy

Anne created Marchioness of Pembroke

French support gained for marriage

1533

Act in Restraint of Appeals

Henry marries Anne Boleyn

Anne crowned Queen

Birth of Princess Elizabeth

Thomas Cranmer made Archbishop of Canterbury

1534

Act of Succession

Act for Abolition of Peter's Pence

Act of Supremacy

Treason Act

Thomas More and Bishop Fisher imprisoned

Thomas Cromwell appointed principal secretary

Pope declares marriage between Catherine and Henry valid

Elizabeth Barton hanged

Act of Supremacy makes Henry Head of the Church of England

Houses of Observant Friars closed

1540

Fall of Cromwell

Statute of Wills passed

Henry marries Anne of Cleves

Marriage to Anne annulled

Henry marries Catherine Howard

English Bible placed in every parish church

1541

Progress to York

Catherine Howard arrested for adultery

Abolition of Shrines

Abolition of Holy Days

1542

War against Scotland

Execution of Catherine Howard

Planned marriage of Edward and Mary Queen of Scotland

1543

All English law extended to Wales

Anglo-Imperial Alliance against France

Treaty of Greenwich signed with Scotland (later rejected by Scots)

Henry marries Catherine Parr

Plot against Cranmer foiled

King's Book published

Transubstantiation defended

Reading of Bible prohibited to those below rank of gentleman

1544

Henry VIII joins army in Calais

Boulogne seized

Charles V makes peace with France

English litany introduced into churches

1545

French invasion threat

Sinking of the Mary Rose

English army defeated by the Scots

Chantries Act

King calls for religious unity in parliament

1 The Church in England on the eve of the Reformation

1 The state of the Church in 1529

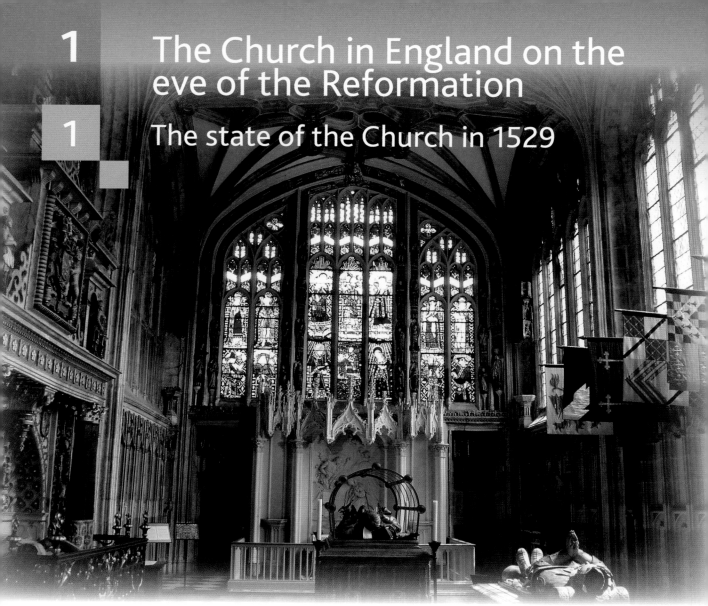

Fig. 1 *The Beauchamp chantry chapel in St Mary's Church, Warwick. How did the Beauchamps emphasise their importance?*

In this chapter you will learn about:

- the possessions and wealth of the Church in England in 1529

- the influence of religion in people's lives and in particular the doctrine taught by the Church

- the structure of the Church and the Church hierarchy in England

- the extent of anti-clericalism within England in 1529.

A humble peasant stepping inside a parish church in 1529 would be walking into a different world: the stained glass windows would change the light, the atmosphere would be thick with the smell of incense, and the walls would be richly painted, often with paintings of heaven which only the godly could hope to enter and the horrors and torments of hell where they might go should their lives be sinful.

The people of England were expected to obey not only the King's laws, but also ecclesiastical laws, and anyone who broke these could find himself in a church court. Of the two powers, Church and King, the latter, who was rarely, if ever, seen outside the small circle of the nobility, was the more remote. The Church on the other hand was a real physical presence in each parish and each parishioner would know the priest. Catholicism not only provided the outward structures of community life; it also provided a framework controlling how an individual thought, reasoned and behaved. Much of this would be drawn into question by the events of Henry VIII's Reformation of the 1530s.

Activity

Research task

Visit a parish church close to where you live which dates back to before the 16th century. Identify how much remains from the pre-Reformation era (i.e. pre-16th century) and how much has changed. Often details such as this are given in the guidebook.

Church fabric and wealth

The parish church

The parish church would have been the most magnificent building that most people would ever enter. Most were built of stone, unlike houses, which tended to be basically wooden structures. The church was strictly divided by a screen into the areas where ordinary people could go and the area reserved for the choir and the clergy. **Masses** for the souls of the dead

Key term

Mass: the most important service in the Catholic Church. During the Mass the priest prays and blesses the bread and wine as Jesus had done at the Last Supper. Roman Catholics believe that this act transforms the bread and wine into the body and blood of Christ. This is known as transubstantiation.

Fig. 2 *A parish church in the 16th century*

Tower

1. 15th century additions to 14th century tower
2. 15th century west door
3. Gargoyle or water spout

Nave

4. 15th century Perpendicular clerestory
5. 12th century Transitional arcade
6. Arch-braced tie-beam roof
7. Norman font
8. Late 13th century arcade
9. Sanctus bell
10. Doom painting
11. Door to rood loft
12. Rood screen
13. Pulpit
14. Lectern

Chancel

15. Organ
16. Choir and stalls
17. Hammerbeam roof
18. Door to vestry
19. Communion rail
20. Sanctuary
21. 15th century Perpendicular east window
22. Altar
23. Piscina
24. Squint
25. Tomb
26. Priest's door
27. Late 14th century chancel
28. Parclose screen

Aisle

29. 14th century seating in Decorated south aisle

Porch

30. 15th century additions to Decorated porch

Key terms

Purgatory: the place where, in the Catholic faith, the souls of the dead are punished and suffer, according to their degree of sin, until they are sufficiently pure to go to heaven. The amount of time a soul spends in purgatory is determined by good works done while alive and prayers said for a person after they are dead.

Chantry: the name given to an individual or a group of people joining together to provide funds to hold Masses for their souls after they died.

to reduce their time in **purgatory** could be chanted in Latin in **chantry** chapels throughout the day. Candles would be lit around statues to the Virgin Mary, the mother of God, and to local saints.

For wealthy people, the church was not only a place to worship; it provided an opportunity for people to impress other members of the community with their wealth and piety, and perhaps for the wealthy to lessen their time in purgatory by displaying evidence of their devotion and good deeds. Parish churches were always willing to receive gifts of gold and silver, vestments, altar cloths, service books and processional banners. All would be given in the name of the donor and this would be recorded as an indication of their generosity. A very large gift could even have the giver's name recorded in stone. In some cases communities would join together: a good example of such generosity was the £305, an astronomical amount at the time, which was given by the people of Louth to pay for a lavish new spire.

Each parish and its clergy were part of a larger unit of the Catholic Church: a diocese which was administered by a bishop. In turn each diocese was part of an archdiocese under the auspices of an archbishop. There were two such archbishops in England: York and Canterbury. Of these, Canterbury was the much larger and consequently the wealthier. Individual bishops had significant financial resources, including the rents on land held by the Church, and it was common for monarchs to reward their non-noble councillors such as Thomas Wolsey with positions within the Church.

The monasteries

Some monasteries individually, and even more as a group, were extremely wealthy and had great economic as well as political power. While

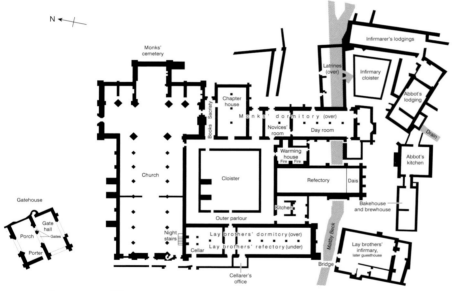

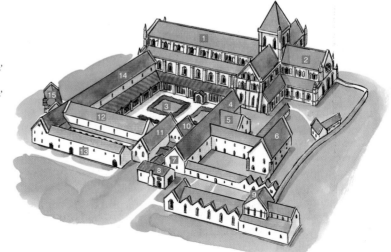

Key

1. Nave
2. Choir
3. Cloister
4. Dormitory
5. Chapter house
6. Monks' latrines
7. Day room
8. Meat kitchen
9. Abbot's lodging
10. Warming house
11. Refectory
12. Kitchen
13. Lay brothers' latrines
14. Lay brothers' dormitory
15. Barn

Fig. 3 *Two typical Cistercian monasteries in the early 16th century: Roche Abbey (plan) and Byland Abbey (drawing)*

individual monks had to swear a vow of poverty, institutions had often become very rich through gifts of land, silver, gold and other treasures given by those who hoped to obtain spiritual support in return. The financial assets of the monasteries had been acquired over a long period of time and through a variety of means. Members of the nobility and gentry might have made gifts as an act to demonstrate their beliefs, or to pay for a number of Masses to be said for them when they died to reduce their time in purgatory. Property of one kind or another had also been acquired as men and women were accepted into religious institutions. Many monasteries had extensive possessions by the 16th century and the importance of the monastic lands cannot be overstated. Such monasteries could be major producers of wool, and some were also renowned for the selective breeding of sheep to improve productivity. Their lands might produce food not just for the monasteries but for the wider market. Some were also producers of iron and were experimenting with different methods of production to increase output and improve quality. Although by the 16th century there were a number of smaller monasteries whose number of monks and wealth had gradually declined since the upheaval of the Black Death, the wealthier and more productive monasteries made an important contribution to the rural economy.

A closer look

Roche Abbey, Yorkshire

Roche was part of the order of the Cistercians who, despite their original ideal to live simply by the fruits of their own labour, had acquired a variety of possessions, such as arable and pastoral land, woodland, mills and fisheries, to sustain a self-sufficient community. Roche was a medium-sized house. The abbey's holdings stretched across the five counties of Yorkshire, Nottinghamshire, Derbyshire, Lincolnshire and Lancashire. Most of Roche's possessions were concentrated within a 15 mile radius of the abbey, and a number of these lay within five miles of the house.

Did you know?

Large rural monastic houses were known as abbeys and urban houses were most commonly known as priories.

Cross-reference

The **Pilgrimage of Grace** is discussed in Chapter 6.

The larger monasteries and abbeys played a significant role in the community. Robert Aske, who led the Pilgrimage of Grace, made much of

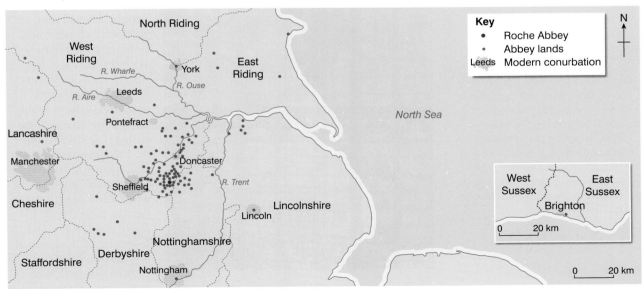

Fig. 4 *The lands of Roche Abbey in the early 16th century*

■ **Cross-reference**

Cardinal Wolsey and his influence are described in the Introduction.

Fig. 5 *The buildings which are still in use by the monks at Cîteaux, France. This monastery was the mother house of the Cistercian abbeys in England*

■ **Cross-reference**

For more on the **ritual and liturgy** of the Church, look ahead to page 23.

Key term

Original sin: this is the concept that everyone is born in sin and relates back to when Adam sinned in the Garden of Eden by disobeying God and eating the forbidden fruit given to him by Eve. As a result of this action, God punished Adam and his descendants, banishing them from Paradise until their sin had been redeemed.

the support given by the monasteries and abbeys to travellers in the Pennine area. The support given to communities was much more diverse than simply giving religious guidance: monasteries were at the forefront of the fight against disease and were able to provide some elementary health care. Monks provided education to the sons of the nobility and gentry and in towns help was given to the poor and needy. Even in the isolated rural monasteries food was distributed to the poor who gathered at the gate to be fed.

The smaller monasteries had a less obvious role to play. Indeed, there was some feeling (shared by other 16th century bishops across Europe) that such monasteries were a drain on the community and that their wealth might be put to better use in the financing of schools or priests for the wider community. Cardinal Wolsey, for example, had dissolved 29 small religious houses in the 1520s to fund the formation of a grammar school in Ipswich and a college at the University of Oxford. However, such dissolutions were on a small scale and the continuation of monasteries as important institutions within England seemed secure.

From the 11th century every house in England paid an annual tax of one penny to Rome. The giving of the money took place on midsummer's day and was known as Peter's Pence after the first Bishop of Rome, St Peter. In addition to this money the Pope had the right to tax the clergy; however, Henry VIII had gained the right for the clergy of England to be exempt from paying this tax and instead he collected it himself. It has been estimated that in the 1520s Rome received approximately £4,500 per year in taxation and religious fees from England whereas Henry VIII was amassing £12,500 per year from the Church.

■ Religious doctrine and practice

Fig. 6 *The Doom window at Fairford in Gloucestershire. It was intended to inspire the congregation with the glories of heaven but also to make them fear the vision of hell*

There has been much debate as to what people actually believed. It is difficult to look into people's minds, but it is possible to understand how they worshipped.

In the 16th century people believed that they were sinners: not only were they born with **original sin**, but during their lives every time they disobeyed God's laws they would acquire more sin. They feared that they would be condemned by these to the eternal fire of hell. They could, however, be saved from being sent to hell on their deaths by doing good works and by earning 'indulgences' as a result of which they would go first to purgatory. Their time in purgatory could be shortened, not only by the good works they had done, but also by those who were still alive praying for them and saying Masses for them.

Central to a person's chances of going to heaven and shortening the time spent in purgatory was the role played by the priest. The priest would hear the confessions of those who lived in his parish and would forgive the sins which they had committed. These might include lying, stealing, envy, jealousy, or adultery. The priest might give the person a penance – a punishment for their sins. Punishments might include saying prayers using rosary beads for a small sin or, for a major sin, the requirement to go on a pilgrimage to the shrine of a saint. The main function of the priest was the saying of the Mass. Masses would be said in the church a number of times a day. Mostly the parishioners would watch the service, but on Easter Sunday they would take part. The high point of the Mass was when the priest prayed over the bread and wine and transubstantiation occurred, whereby they became the body and blood of Christ. Only the priest was able to drink the blood, but on Easter Sunday the parishioners were able to eat the body of Christ, in the form of a wafer known as the host.

In addition to the parish Mass, the priest would say Masses for the dead. These Masses were held in chantry chapels. The nobility and the gentry would often have their own chapels in a church where the dead would be buried in tombs and Masses said for the souls of the dead. Poor people, who could not afford to build their own chapels and to pay for a priest, would belong to a chantry guild. This was similar to having a life insurance policy. Most of the money invested would pay for Masses to be said for the dead, but in some guilds money would also be used to support those who were left behind.

In the minds of the less educated peasants and townspeople it was sometimes difficult for a distinction between religious ritual and belief, as dictated by the Church, and superstition and the supernatural, as spread by gossip and fear, to be maintained. Some 'religious' practices had dubious authenticity and it was all too easy for the God-fearing lower orders to attribute success and misfortune to divine intervention.

> Awareness of the Supernatural was very much part of everyday life. Miracles were regularly proclaimed. The finding of lost possessions, recovery from sickness, resumption of egg-laying by hens were all attributed to saintly intervention. God, the devil and their respective supporters were believed to be busily at work in the world.
>
> **1**   Rosman, D., *From Catholic to Protestant: Religion and the People in Tudor England*, 1996

Ecclesiastical organisation

While the Catholic Church had a clear structure and identity, it was closely linked with that of the monarchy and nobility. The King and his government were also dependent on the Catholic Church in a number of important ways. Key to the monarch's legitimacy was the coronation, which took place in Westminster Abbey.

No kings questioned the teachings of the Church before the 16th century. Indeed, they were keen to demonstrate their allegiance to the beliefs of the Catholic Church. Monarchs were eager to make gifts of silver and gold to the church. One of the most high-profile acts of Henry VII had been the construction of the lady chapel at Westminster Abbey, which also housed his family's tombs. The Beauchamp chapel at St Mary's, Warwick, demonstrates that the nobility too defined themselves by their religious beliefs.

Activity
Thinking point

Why might the supernatural be part of everyday life? Why might the Church encourage these views?

Exploring the detail
The seven sacraments

There were seven sacraments by which people received the grace of God:

- baptism – when children were cleansed of original sin
- confirmation – when young people became members of the Church and could take Mass
- marriage – when two people were joined together by the priest
- ordination – when a man became a priest
- last rites – when the dying were anointed with holy oil before they died
- penance – when a person confessed their sins to a priest
- the Mass – when the priest carried out a re-enactment of the Last Supper of Christ.

The papacy

• God's representative on earth

The secular clergy

Roman curia

• administered the church

Cardinals

• senior churchmen
• elected popes

Archbishops

• senior churchmen in each country

Bishops

• regional leaders of the church

Parish priests

• ministered to each congregation
• special rights kept them apart from the laity

Fig. 8 *The structure of the Church in England at the beginning of the 16th century*

■ Did you know?

At the coronation the Archbishop of Canterbury anointed the monarch with holy oil and gave him the symbols of kingly authority – the orb and sceptre. He placed the crown on the monarch's head. Without this ceremony the monarch could not claim that he had the authority to rule.

■ Cross-reference

For the **fall of Cardinal Wolsey**, refer back to the Introduction.

Fig. 7 *A procession of the clergy and nobility in 1512. How are the two groups linked?*

The Catholic Church was a central part of politics. Abbots and bishops sat in the House of Lords alongside the nobility. As well as deciding on legislation at this stage, they were instrumental in advising the King. Henry VII had used Archbishop Morton and Bishop Richard Fox as key advisers. They had been selected for their knowledge of, and training in, the law. It was also useful that Henry could use the wealth of the Church to reward them and to give them prestige. Henry VIII's dependence on Cardinal Wolsey was further reinforced by his links with Rome. However, the Cardinal's divided loyalties between his role as the King's first minister and his position as an ambassador of the Pope were to be his undoing.

Henry VIII, in common with his predecessors, was dependent on the Church as a means of social control and support. Wall paintings in churches were a very visible threat of what might happen to those who sinned and the Ten Commandments provided a clear statement of what the godly should do and not do. The importance of giving to the poor was constantly stressed; many of the poor in a parish were able to be supported in times of hardship by gifts of food and clothing from the wealthier members of a community.

Membership of Christendom provided kings of England with links to the wider network of Christian monarchs. The Treaty of London of 1518, which secured 'universal' peace between the countries of Europe, was claimed as a diplomatic success by both Wolsey and Henry VIII but was also the result of the negotiations undertaken by the Pope's representative, Cardinal Campeggio.

> Every new King hastened to bolster his position by buying the support of the church, funding lavish building projects and courting leading churchmen. The English Church remained a pair of independent provinces with their own parliaments, courts and legal systems; working hand in glove with the monarch, but confident of their own ultimate integrity.
>
> **2** Murphy, V., in MacCulloch, D. (ed.), **The Reign of Henry VIII: Politics, Policy and Piety**, 1988

Monastic orders

'Monastery' is a term used to describe religious houses. In the 16th century people would have been much more familiar with the use of 'abbey' or 'priory' or 'nunnery'. When Henry VIII became king in 1509 there were more than 850 such institutions in England. They varied in size, in location and in the religious order to which they belonged. Large rural monastic houses were known as abbeys and urban houses were most commonly known as priories. In many ways the location of the institutions was determined by the type of role they undertook. The rural abbeys were places of prayer and learning, often with large land-holdings, whereas monks who lived in the towns in priories worked within the community; in addition to their prayers they would help the poor and the sick. Such institutions were valued also for their architecture and for their contribution to learning and art through the production of illuminated manuscripts. The libraries of the religious houses contained the vast majority of the books in the country; only the colleges of Oxford and Cambridge universities had similar libraries.

Within monasteries there were monks with distinct roles and a very clear hierarchy. The abbot was the monk who was in charge of the abbey. Monks were moved by their order between different monasteries as they took on different roles and most abbots would have entered a monastic order as a novice in their youth and have undertaken a number of responsible roles before becoming abbot. Those who rose to this position usually had a great deal of financial ability as well as being respected for their spirituality within the monastery. They also needed to be able to socialise with members of the nobility and gentry, who frequently stayed or dined in the guest houses of abbeys on their journeys.

A religious life was often seen as an acceptable future for a younger son, or a daughter for whom there was insufficient money to be established in society. Often these monks were known as choir monks because they took a full part in the services of the monastery. Roles which monks could undertake in monasteries could involve working in the infirmary or in the library, producing illuminated manuscripts, or being responsible for the silver and sacred possessions which had been given to the monastery. Lay brothers were monks who took partial vows but who did not have sufficient financial support to enable them to become full monks. They undertook religious duties but also helped in more manual tasks which were necessary for the monastery to run efficiently.

There were five main monastic orders:

Benedictines	Carthusians	Cistercians	Augustinians	Cluniacs
Founded by St Benedict in AD 529. The largest order, the Benedictines, were noted for their learning. The four vows of these monks were to obedience, chastity, poverty, and manual labour for seven hours each day. St Dunstan, Archbishop of Canterbury from AD 960, was responsible for establishing a large number of Benedictine houses.	The Carthusians lived lives of isolation and silence, spending their days in their own individual cells. The monks wore hair shirts and gathered in church only three times a day, unlike other orders; they ate together only on Sundays and feast days. The main Carthusian monastery in Britain was at Charterhouse in London.	Begun in France under the influence of St Bernard of Clairvaux, the order chose isolated rural locations to build their monasteries, particularly in Wales and the north. They were not as scholarly as the Benedictines, but focused on agriculture and hard manual labour.	Founded in the 11th century, the so-called 'Black Canons' lived in communities but went out among the people to preach. As a consequence of this, and their propensity for giving alms and hospitality, the Augustinians were quite popular.	The Cluniacs were one of several orders which tried to return the Benedictine rule to its original simplicity. Their first house in England was at Lewes, founded in about 1078. The Cluniacs spent much of their time in devotion, and left the agricultural toil to paid servants. Most Cluniac establishments were small.

Activity

Research task

Use the internet to research how the work of religious orders affected the area in which you live. The English Heritage site is a very good starting point and uses a range of primary sources.

■ A closer look

A day in the life of a monk

2am	The monk would be woken by a bell. He would then go to the church for *Nocturns* which was the first service of the day, followed by *Matins*. After this he might go back to bed.
5am	At first light he would go into church for *Lauds*.
6am	At sunrise he would go into church again for *Prime*. After this service he would start work in the monastery.
8am	He would go into church for *Terce* and *Morrow Mass*.
9am	He would go to a meeting in the chapter house with the prior and other monks. At this meeting they would sort out any business. Then it was back to work or quiet study.
12.30pm	He would go into church for *Sext*, *Mass* and *None*.
2pm	He would go to the refectory (the dining hall) for the main meal of the day.
3pm	Now it would be back to work or study.
5pm	He would go into church again for *Vespers* before more quiet reading or study.
7pm	For the last time that day he would go back into church for *Compline* before going to bed.

■ Anti-clerical criticisms of the state of the Church and monasteries

For the majority of the population, the Catholic faith provided the structure of their everyday lives. They took part in religious ceremonies and attended church regularly. A number of the practices and beliefs on which Catholicism was based were being questioned, however, although it is difficult for historians to be precise about the extent of the challenges to the Church.

The problem was that few dared to criticise the practice and rituals of the Church openly. Outright dissent would be regarded as heretical and **heresy** was a crime punishable with death by fire.

Among the more educated and outspoken, however, there is evidence that a number of practices were under attack.

■ **Pluralism:** This was where one priest held the rights to more than one parish. He would take money from both and employ a sometimes partially educated cleric to take the services as his deputy. In extreme cases, such a man might only be able to recite the Latin services and not be able to read and write. These uneducated people did not live up to the ideals of the Church and the expectations of the people and, what is more, their wages could be less than those earned as an agricultural labourer.

■ Key term

Heresy: a belief which was not accepted or taught by the Church. It would be a heresy not to believe that the priest could turn wine into Christ's blood. Heresy was a sin and a heretic was condemned to hell.

- **Simony:** This was the sale of an ecclesiastical title. It occurred most frequently when a priest enjoying the income of a rich parish sold his position to the person willing to pay the most.
- **Mortuary fees:** When a person died his or her family would have to pay a fee in money or goods, to the priest. This was one of the main disputes in the Richard Hunne case.

Cross-reference

Heresy and the treatment of heretics are discussed in more detail on page 26.

A closer look

The case of Richard Hunne

The case of Richard Hunne has all the ingredients of new ideas and beliefs and the reactions of a conservative Church. It was also set in the City of London among the merchant class.

Richard Hunne was a merchant tailor in London and, some have argued, a Lollard. When his baby son died in March 1511 the parish priest asked for the baby's christening robe as a mortuary fee (this was a payment which churches routinely charged for burying the dead). Hunne refused. In November 1511 he was involved in a property dispute with the parish priest. The priest took Hunne to the archbishop's court. In October 1514 Hunne was arrested as a search of his house had discovered a Lollard Bible. On 4 December Hunne was found dead in his cell, having apparently hanged himself; however, his body showed signs of a struggle as if he had been murdered. During his trial for heresy it was said that he had not only questioned the authority of the Church to collect mortuary fees, but he had denied transubstantiation. On the authority of the Lord Chancellor his body was burned. The coroner's court declared that Hunne had indeed been murdered.

It was widely believed that the Church had killed a critic to protect clergy privileges; Hunne was regarded as a martyr and the Church's reputation suffered. The Hunne case was subsequently the subject of debate in the Reformation parliament in 1529.

Fig. 9 *An illustration produced in 1848 depicting the death of a Lollard leader charged with heresy*

Cross-reference

To recap on the **Lollards**, see page 29.

The **Reformation parliament** is discussed on pages 48–51.

- **Indulgences and the sale of 'holy relics':** Priests sold these 'pardons' to trusting people. It was believed that indulgences could lessen the time spent in purgatory, while relics could bring protection and good fortune. The counterfeit pardoner was one of the leading pilgrims of Chaucer's *Canterbury Tales*, which had been published in the 1470s by William Caxton.

The Pardoner describes his deceitful ways

With this trickery I have won a hundred marks, year by year, since I have been a pardoner. I stand like a cleric in my pulpit, and when the lay people are seated I preach as you have heard and tell a hundred more false stories. Then I take pains to stretch out my neck and bob my head east and west over the people, like a dove perched upon a barn. My hands and tongue move so briskly that it is a joy to see my movement. All my preaching is about avarice and such cursed things, to make them generous in giving their pence and especially to me. My aim is all for gain and not at all for the correction of sin.

3

Chaucer, G., The Pardoner's Tale

■ Activity

Research task

Read the Pardoner's, Monk's and Nun's tales. What picture do these present of the condition of the Church and its corruption?

■ A closer look

Chaucer's *Canterbury Tales*

The Canterbury Tales is a collection of stories written by Geoffrey Chaucer in the 14th century. The tales are told by a group of pilgrims on their way from London to the Shrine of Thomas à Becket at Canterbury Cathedral. The characters in the group sought to lessen their time in purgatory. They include people from all ranks in society and include some religious figures: a monk, a nun and a pardoner. While the tales can be read as an amusing account of life at the time showing contemporary views of courtly love, greed and treachery, they can also be read as a criticism of the abuses of the Church. Lollardy is mentioned in the text and the Pardoner is little more than a fraud selling forgiveness and promises to reduce time spent in purgatory to a gullible people.

The telling of the tales by the pilgrims was intended to be a competition as to who could tell the most engaging story. Chaucer ends the tales apologising for anything which might have been inappropriate. The original texts of *The Canterbury Tales* were handwritten and copied. By the end of the 15th century, as a result of the development of the printing press, *The Canterbury Tales* were reaching a much wider audience and illustrated with woodcuts. Very often the tales would be read aloud and acted out by the teller. Chaucer's English is quite difficult to read, but pronunciation in the 14th century was similar to that of the North-East today.

A description of 'holy relics' from before the Reformation

And here out of our records I shall mention some of the images and relics to which the pilgrimages of those times brought devotion and offerings such as the milk of our Lady (shown in eight places), the bell of St Guthlac and the belt of St Thomas of Lancaster, the ear of St Malchus and the blood of Jesus Christ brought from Jerusalem to Gloucestershire, being kept for many ages. This last has brought many great offerings to it from remote places, but was proved to be the blood of a duck, every week renewed by the priests. Besides which, it is possible to see an image of St John of Osulston (also called Mr John Shorne) who was said to have shut up the Devil in a boot.

4   *Lord Herbert,* **Life and Reign of King Henry VIII**, *1649*

■ Cross-reference

Pluralism, which led to the absence of priests, is outlined on page 18.

■ **Benefit of clergy:** If a priest was suspected of committing certain offences he could claim benefit of clergy and be tried in a Church court as opposed to one of the King's courts. If he was found guilty of a crime that would be punishable in the King's court by hanging, in the Church courts he would be able to escape the death penalty. The benefit of clergy was criticised as those brought in to undertake the work of absent priests could also access the Church courts if they were able to recite key Latin verses. These became known as 'neck verses' as they saved the man's neck. The right to 'benefit of clergy' could also be claimed by laymen who could read Latin.

■ **Tithes:** Each adult living in a parish had to pay a tenth of the goods produced from their land. Where a person worked rather than produced they would need to pay a portion of their income. This was paid to the clergy responsible for the parish, but in some cases the Church had sold the right to collect tithes to a member of the laity. Where parishioners refused or were unable to pay the tithes they would be taken to the Church court. Disputes over payments were common, but on the whole the system worked. Simon Fish, in his *A Supplication for the Beggars* in 1529, was to say of the demands of the clergy:

> These are not the shepherds, but ravenous wolves going about in sheep's clothing, devouring their flock. The goodliest lordships, manor, lands and territories are theirs. Besides this, they take a tenth part of everyone's wages, a tenth part of the wool, milk, honey, wax, cheese and butter that is produced, and even every tenth egg from poor widows. And what do these greedy, idle, holy thieves do with all these yearly exactions that they take from the people? Nothing, but suck all rule, power, authority and obedience from you (Henry VIII) to themselves!

5　　　*Fish, S., A Supplication for the Beggars, 1529*

Behaviour of the clergy: Priests and monks were expected to live to their vows of chastity and to be obedient to the laws of the Church. Not all were able to live to these high ideals. Gossip suggested that a number of priests had affairs and some were known to have children. It is difficult to know how widespread this actually was and how much was based on hearsay. William Melton, Chancellor of York Minster, was typical of the ranks of idealistic clergy who were often the fiercest critics of the failings of the Church, when he wrote in 1510:

> It is from stupidity and the darkness of ignorance that there arises a great and deplorable evil throughout the whole Church of God. Everywhere through town and countryside there exists a crop of oafish and boorish priests, some of whom are engaged on ignoble and servile tasks, while others abandon themselves to tavern haunting, swilling and drunkenness. Some cannot get along without their wenches; others pursue their amusement in dice and gambling all day long. There are some who waste their time in hunting and hawking, and so spend a life which is so utterly and wholly idle and irreligious even to advanced old age.

6　　　*William Melton (1510)*

The views of this modern historian, Eamon Duffy, are a reminder that it is easy to be unduly influenced by those who voiced criticism and to ignore the 'silent majority' who may well have been very content with matters as they were.

> The evidence for anti-clericalism is an optical illusion, there was no deep-seated dissatisfaction. Surviving evidence suggests very few complaints, and quarrels over tithes were rare. Levels of recruitment to the priesthood were at a record high in the first decades of the 16th century, something hard to explain if the laity was overwhelmingly anti-clerical.

7　　　*Duffy, E., The Stripping of the Altars: Traditional Religion in England, 1400–1580, 1992*

Exploring the detail
Sources 4–6

Although there was an increasing level of literacy in the 16th century, as demonstrated by the growing circulation of Books of Hours and stories such as *The Canterbury Tales*, the views of people about the Church were largely the result of hearsay and conversation. Source 4 includes information from the early 16th century but was not actually written down until the 17th century. Source 5 is taken from the time and was written by Simon Fish, who was sympathetic to the views of Luther. It was written from the Netherlands in the form of a plea to Henry VIII. Source 6 is taken from a sermon which was given to young priests. Melton was using this opportunity to attempt to raise the intellectual and moral standards of the parish clergy. The sermon, which was delivered in Latin, was published for a wider, but intellectual, audience in 1510.

Activity
Source analysis

Read Sources 4–6. How far were these sources criticisms of the beliefs of the Church or criticisms of the practices?

Popular Catholicism

Although some were beginning to criticise the Church, for most ordinary people it remained a powerful force in their everyday lives. Although it is not always easy to discover how ordinary people regarded their religion, preambles to wills, such as those below, can reveal something of the nature of popular Catholicism.

> I, Thomas Foldyngton of Barholm in Lincolnshire, will my body to be buried in the chapel of Our Blessed Lady within the parish church of St Martin in Barholm. I leave my best goods to my priest to pray for my soul and to provide a blue cloth to lay over the sacrament upon Corpus Christi day.
>
> Also I leave money so that my daughter may light candles before the image of Our Lady and repair the church bell, then give the bellringers a pennyworth of bread and a gallon of ale.

8 *Thomas Foldyngton, 22 June 1530*

> I John Mason, glover of the city of York … commend my soul to Almighty God, my creator and to the Blessed Virgin Mary, the mother of mercy, and to all the saints in Heaven, and my body to be buried beside my father and my mother in Saint Thomas' closet within my parish church of the Trinities in Micklegate.

9 *John Mason*

Pilgrimages and relics

Those who were able to would try to demonstrate their beliefs by going on a pilgrimage. This could be to visit the tomb of a saint, for example that of St Thomas à Becket at Canterbury, or to a shrine built where there had been a reported visitation of the Virgin Mary, such as at Walsingham in Norfolk. Pilgrims would wear a pilgrim badge to show that they had visited the shrine. Pilgrims to Santiago de Compostela in Spain would wear cockle shells. The very wealthy would wish to purchase relics of saints as well as

Fig. 10 *A fresco depicting the Canterbury pilgrims. What does this show about the type of people who went on pilgrimages?*

praying at the tombs. The pilgrimage to the relic of the saint would serve to reduce the time a person would spend in purgatory. Individuals would also make pilgrimages to certain shrines, such as that of Henry VI, in order to seek the saint's blessing and provide a cure for an illness or disease.

A closer look

The liturgical year

This shows how people's lives, the life of the agricultural community and the organisation of the Church all fitted together. The majority of feast days, or holy days, were days when the community would not work but would celebrate together.

The liturgical year began with **Advent**, which was the time of preparation for Christmas. This was when the harvest had been gathered and the seed sown for the next spring. December was the time to slaughter the pigs and turn them into a year's worth of ham, bacon, sausage, lard, pickled pig's feet, and innumerable other products. The days got shorter and people stayed close to home.

Christmastide began with Christmas Eve. The darkest day of the year, 21 December, also marked the beginning of longer days. Christmas Day, which celebrated the birth of Christ, was followed by a number of feast days. The celebration of the arrival of the wise men on 6 January brought to an end the Christmas celebration.

The three weeks of preparation before Lent was a time of cleansing. At **Candlemass** the community would process, carrying candles as a symbol of light. The cutting of willow branches for making fences and walls was one of the traditional activities in the community. Lambs were born around this time.

The last day before Lent was **Shrove Tuesday**, when the last good meal for a while was eaten. It was often marked by a celebration of misrule when fools and idiots rule. Customs varied from place to place, but the 'Abbeys of Misrule', which featured the election of a 'boy bishop' who would hand out pretend money and dispense false justice, appeared in many towns.

Lent began on Ash Wednesday, 40 days before Easter. The ashes made from burning the palms from the previous year were smeared on people's foreheads as a reminder of death. Lent was a season of fasting. No meat could be eaten. For the average poor peasant this was no different from usual, except that he couldn't throw a bit of lard into the pot. It was a time that coincided with declining food supplies in any case, when food needed to be conserved to get through until summer.

Lent culminated in **Holy Week**, which celebrated in great detail Christ's final days on earth. It began with Palm Sunday and Christ's entry into Jerusalem, which was celebrated with the blessing and distribution of palms. These were kept in houses as a blessing for the rest of the year. On Maundy Thursday the Last Supper was celebrated. Good Friday, the most solemn day of the year, commemorated the crucifixion. People would often march in processions, flogging themselves or carrying the cross in commemoration of Christ's suffering. They would often take part in a ceremony called 'creeping to the cross', when they crawled to a wooden cross. The vigil on Holy Saturday was a rich celebration, with the blessing of the huge Pascal candle (destined to burn continuously for 40 days). At daybreak on Easter Sunday morning, the bells erupted with joy.

Did you know?

The shrine of Henry VI

Henry VI had been a very different monarch from his father, Henry V, who had defeated the French at Agincourt. Henry VI had experienced periods of madness which had been interpreted as religious trances, in keeping with his reputation for piety. After his death a number of miracles were said to have occurred as a result of prayers said in his honour, and he was informally regarded as a saint. Large numbers of people visited his tomb in Westminster Abbey to seek cures for a range of disabilities.

Eastertide was the most joyous of Christian holidays, beginning with the resurrection of Christ on Easter Sunday. The lambs which had been born in February were eaten in the traditional Easter feast. In a number of towns, for example Coventry and York, plays showing the life of Christ, which were known as Mystery Plays, were performed in the streets.

March was a time to plough and sow the spring crops, like oats.

Rogation Sunday was a major event when the whole community 'beat the bounds'. A procession walked around the parish boundaries carrying banners and the parish cross; bells were rung and prayers said to ward off evil spirits and to establish the physical property of the parish.

Mayday fell during the Easter season. Officially the feast of Saints Philip and James the Apostle, it was celebrated by dancing around maypoles and going into the woods to gather greenery for garlands.

Pentecost (Whitsunday) occurred seven weeks after Easter and celebrated the descent of the Holy Spirit on his followers and the beginning of the Christian Church.

Following this was the 'ordinary time' of the church, which coincided with the ordinary business of rural life: sheep shearing, haymaking and the harvest. This was also the prime campaign season for making war.

There were a number of holidays of interest that occurred around this time. The Sunday after Pentecost was Trinity Sunday, and the Thursday after that was the Feast of Corpus Christi (the Body of Christ), a major community event: in the towns all the officials would take part in the procession throughout the town. People were expected to hang out decorations along the route, take off their hats, and kneel when it went by.

During the summer there were a number of holy days when people did not work and celebrations were held. These included:

- the birthday of St John the Baptist on 24 June – St John's Eve was a time for lighting bonfires and celebrating through the night
- the Transfiguration of Christ, celebrated on 6 August
- the Assumption of the Virgin Mary, a major holy day celebrated on 15 August
- St Bartholomew's day, on 24 August.

The summer activities were haymaking and sheep shearing in June, the harvest in July and threshing the grain in August. After the June shearing, sheep that were no longer productive might be slaughtered for mutton. Until the harvest was taken in and brought to market in July and August, food supplies could still be tight. The months of spring and early summer, encouraging because of the fine weather and long days, were also potential times of civic disturbance in the towns after years of poor harvest.

Fig. 11 *A hand-painted illustration from a Book of Hours showing a September scene. Why might this appeal to the family who commissioned the book?*

The last Sunday in October was the feast of Christ the King. This was followed by **All Saints' Day** (All Hallows' Day) on 1 November and **All Souls Day** on 2 November, when the dead were remembered. October was the time to sow the winter grain, and November saw the acorn harvest. Acorns naturally grew in the woods, and served to fatten the pigs just before slaughtering time in December.

 Activity

Research task

Use books and the internet to investigate the original meaning of the religious festivals and why certain symbols were chosen to represent events.

 Activity

Pairs task

In pairs use the drawing of the parish church on page 11 to show where people would undertake rituals and activities to demonstrate their beliefs.

The modern historian A. G. Dickens wrote of the medieval church in 1964:

> In the field of religion many weaknesses of the late medieval Church were apparent to contemporaries. The authority of priests had come to depend in too great a degree on its rituals and too little on the moral and intellectual importance of clergymen in society. Monasticism was uninspired; it shed little spiritual light into the world outside its own buildings. The popular cult-religion seemed to the sophisticated both childish and unduly directed to the raising of money.

10 *Dickens, A. G., in Elton, G. R. (ed.), **Renaissance and Reformation 1300–1648**, 1968*

According to the historian Eamon Duffy, writing in 1992:

> Late medieval Catholicism exerted an enormously strong hold over the imagination and the loyalty of the people up to the very moment of Reformation. Traditional religion had about it no particular marks of exhaustion or decay, and indeed in a whole host of ways, from the multiplication of vernacular religious books to adaptions within the national and regional cult of the saints, was showing itself well able to meet new needs and new conditions.

11 *Duffy, E., **The Stripping of the Altars: Traditional Religion in England, 1400–1580**, 1992*

 Activity

Source analysis

Using Sources 10 and 11 and your own knowledge:

Explain how far the views in Source 11 differ from those in Source 10 in relation to the condition of religion in the early 16th century.

 Summary question

How important was the Church to the daily lives of English people in the early 16th century?

2 Religious reformers and conservatives

Fig. 1 *A cartoon to illustrate the excesses of the papal court. What criticisms can be identified?*

In this chapter you will learn about:

- religious reformers including humanists, Lutherans and believers in royal supremacy

- religious conservatives and the Aragonese faction.

Activity

Use the material included in this chapter to identify what the people detailed in Source 1 had done to be executed as heretics.

- On September 24, 1518, John Stilincen was condemned as a heretic. He was chained to the stake in Smithfield amidst a vast crowd of spectators, and sealed his testimony to the truth with his blood. He declared that he was a Lollard, and that he had always believed the opinions of Wickliffe; and although he had been weak enough to recant his opinions, yet he was now willing to convince the world that he was ready to die for the truth.

- In the year 1519, Thomas Mann was burnt in London, as was one Robert Celin, a plain, honest man for speaking against image worship and pilgrimages.

- Much about this time, was executed in Smithfield, in London, James Brewster, a native of Colchester. His sentiments were the same as the rest of the Lollards; but notwithstanding the innocence of his life, and the regularity of his manners, he was obliged to submit to papal revenge.

- During this year, one Christopher, a shoemaker, was burnt alive at Newbury, in Berkshire, for denying those popish articles which we have already mentioned. This man had gotten some books in English, which were sufficient to render him obnoxious to the Romish clergy.

1

Foxe, J., **Book of (Protestant) Martyrs**, *1563*

Source 1 is taken from John Foxe's *Book of (Protestant) Martyrs*, produced in the reign of Mary I. In this he accounted for a number of executions of heretics in the reign of Henry VIII. The executions described took place in the years between 1511 and 1529.

These men were not just anti-clerical members of the laity who believed that the Church, and the clergy, were failing to be true to their Christian principles. Some were inspired by the thinkers illustrated in this chapter:

- **Humanists:** Humanists sought to revisit the original biblical texts to re-establish a purer religion.
- **Lollards:** There had been groups of dissenters known as 'Lollards' in England since the 14th century who challenged some of the core religious teachings of the Church. The majority of these were to be found in areas of the Midlands and the east of England; the majority of the supporters were from the literate artisan or merchant class.
- **Lutherans:** Similar to the Lollards, although often separate, were those who had taken up the teachings of Martin Luther, who had challenged the key beliefs of the Catholic Church and had put forward the view that it was more important for the individual to establish his or her relationship with God than through community action and the priest. Those who were discussing such views often had links with the continent through the cloth trade and were able to read the newly published books.
- **Believers in royal supremacy:** At the same time as people were reading teachings which had a different view of, or approach to, religion, and which challenged some of its practices, the new ideas were also being used to examine the relationship between the monarchy and God and the Catholic Church. It was this latter questioning which was to present the most immediate challenges to the status quo in England.

Religious reformers

Humanism

Humanism was a development of the Renaissance of the 14th century and affected not only religion but also politics and economics. It was based on a rediscovery of Latin and Greek texts, and leading humanists such as Thomas More spent considerable time learning Greek and translating key texts. Humanists believed in the basic principles of the Catholic faith, particularly in the notion of free will. What they sought to do was to purify the ideas of religion from errors which had developed through translations. They were not backward looking, not simply attempting to restore a lost world. They saw themselves as forward thinking and were rigorous in their search for knowledge. Their idea of progress depended on demystifying primary texts and restoring them to their original state. By the 16th century leading humanists such as Erasmus, Grocyn, Linacre, John Colet and More himself were moving around Europe and spending time in London and universities such as Cambridge, sharing ideas and commenting on each other's work.

Activity

As you read through this chapter, consider the profiles of Thomas More, Erasmus, John Wycliffe and Margaret Beaufort. What were their beliefs? What did they have in common? Where did they differ?

Fig. 2 *Holbein's portrait of Sir Thomas More. What characteristics of More are emphasised in this portrait?*

Thomas More

Thomas More (1478–1535) was a lawyer, author, adviser to Henry VIII and statesman. He was a close friend of Erasmus and he earned a reputation as a leading humanist scholar. More occupied many public offices, including that of Lord Chancellor from 1529 to 1532. Henry VIII had chosen him to take this position on the fall of Wolsey and because of his great knowledge of the law. More coined the word Utopia, the name he gave to an imaginary island nation whose political system he described in a book published in 1516. He became increasingly conservative in his defence of the Church. He resigned his position as Lord Chancellor due to his refusal to accept Henry VIII's claim to be Supreme Head of the Church of England, a decision which ended his political career. He was executed for treason due to his refusal to acknowledge Queen Anne Boleyn and her heirs.

It is critical that the development of humanist ideas was based on published texts rather than religious beliefs which were conveyed through an oral tradition and were accepted without question. Thinkers such as More were willing to offer criticisms of received wisdom. Thomas More's most controversial work was *Utopia*, which means 'no place' in Greek. In this he described a society which was very different from anywhere in Europe in the early 16th century. Although this society was seen to be ideal, some have seen it as prefiguring Karl Marx's theories of communism: it was a theory of society which was ultimately undermined by More as it was based on philosophy, rather than religious beliefs. Thomas More attempted to use the ideas which he had discussed and developed with fellow humanists in practical ways. He had spent time as a page in the household of Cardinal Morton, who had been Archbishop of Canterbury in the reign of Henry VII. From there he trained in the law, was sent on diplomatic missions by Henry VIII and became a member of Henry's Privy Council. Humanists such as Sir Thomas More did not challenge the beliefs of Catholicism but the practices. They sought to reform the Church from within.

The majority of those who went to Church could not read or write. One of the main developments of the late 15th century, however, was the growth in literacy among the merchants and the gentry. To some extent this was the result of the increase in grammar schools in the county towns. But it was also encouraged by the growth of the printing press and the availability of books. No longer did the wealthy have to sit and listen to a priest reading the Bible in

Fig. 3 *This is said to be the first illustration of a printing press. The woodcut was produced in 1521 and demonstrates the importance of women in the printing process*

church; they could have their own Bible or Book of Hours at home and spend time reading the word of God for themselves. This led in turn to support for the new learning, which was known as humanism, in which scholars sought to establish the true word of God by going back to the original Greek texts. Margaret Beaufort, the mother of Henry VII, was influenced by humanism. The key humanist in the reign of Henry VIII was Erasmus, and indeed both Henry himself and his first wife, Catherine of Aragon, considered themselves humanists.

Key profiles

Erasmus

Desiderius Erasmus (1469–1536) was a Dutch humanist and theologian. Using humanist techniques, he prepared important new Latin and Greek editions of the New Testament. He lived during a time when many learned people were critical of various Christian beliefs and practices. Like his friend Thomas More, who became Chancellor in 1529, Erasmus was critical of some Christian beliefs and practices but remained intellectually committed throughout his life to a Catholic notion of church and to papal authority.

Margaret Beaufort

Margaret Beaufort (1443–1509) was the mother of Henry VII of England. It was through her, rather than his father, that he could claim descent from John of Gaunt, on which he based his claim to the throne. Margaret married at the age of 12 and had Henry at the age of 13. She was a highly intelligent and well read woman and it was she who guided Henry in his claim to the throne. The Tudors used the Beaufort portcullis as much as the Tudor rose as their symbol as a result. She was politically very astute and married (as her fourth husband) Lord Stanley, whose intervention in the battle which secured the crown for Henry was crucial. The influence of humanism on Margaret Beaufort is clear. She was keen to promote learning: she founded schools and helped to refound two Cambridge colleges. It is significant that her portrait shows her at prayer.

Lollardy

Lollardy was originally a term of abuse used to describe the followers of John Wycliffe in the 14th century. It was meant to suggest that they were talking rubbish, as if their tongues were too big for their mouths. John Wycliffe had started the Lollard movement in the early 14th century and it was believed that his followers had been involved in the Peasants' Revolt of 1381. Those who shared Wycliffe's views, which questioned the role of priests as intermediaries between people and God, were seen as heretics. Lollardy became an underground movement: Lollards may have conformed outwardly by attending the parish church but they met secretly to share and discuss their own ideas. Because it went underground it is difficult to say how widespread the movement was by the reign of Henry VIII, or how many people shared its beliefs. However, some things can be established.

Activity

Thinking point

Why was the printing press important to the spread of ideas critical of the Church?

Fig. 4 *Erasmus, painted by Holbein*

Exploring the detail

The Peasants' Revolt of 1381

The Peasants' Revolt was a response to an attempt to enforce a poll tax to finance military activities. The rebels from Kent were led by Wat Tyler and marched with others from Essex on London. They were addressed by John Ball, a Lollard preacher who in his sermon asked 'When Adam delved and Eve span, who was then the gentleman?' The rebels attacked the Tower of London and executed a number of people sheltering there. They were met by Richard II, and although promises were made to them they were not honoured.

Fig. 5 *A 19th century engraving of John Wycliffe, leader of the Lollards*

Key profile

John Wycliffe

John Wycliffe (1320–84) was educated at Oxford and in many ways was influenced by Renaissance ideas; he pursued the study of natural sciences and mathematics before becoming interested in biblical studies. While he was vicar of Lutterworth in Leicestershire he developed his views on the role of the Church and also on the relationship between the Church and the State. His greatest work, *Summa Theologiae*, explored these issues and attacked both monasticism and the Pope. Wycliffe focused on the wealth of the Church and argued that it should be poor. He also undertook a translation of the Bible into English. Although he was called to account for his views on the Church he was not declared a heretic. Nevertheless, in 1428 the Pope ordered that his bones should be dug up from the churchyard where they were buried and thrown into the local river.

Lollards, like the later humanists, believed that Christianity should be based on the Bible. But they went much further than the humanists in suggesting that everyone should have a Bible of their own written in English, not Latin, and they should be allowed to interpret it for themselves. This emphasis on the individual and the individual's relationship with God was central to what the Lollards believed. They rejected the idea that a priest was needed to be a go-between with God. A man could confess his sins directly to God; he did not have to confess them to a priest. God would forgive him directly. Even more damagingly, the Lollards did not believe in transubstantiation – that the bread and wine became the body and blood of Jesus Christ when the priest prayed over them. This more than anything else was heresy. Lollards also believed in predestination. Where Catholics believed that a man could go to heaven if he did sufficient 'good works', Lollards believed that it had been decided before Adam and Eve had been banished from the Garden of Eden who would go to heaven and that these were 'the elect'. While Lollards continued to go to church and show outward obedience, they believed that only those who rejected the beliefs of the Catholic Church could be considered one of the elect and go to heaven.

Originally, Lollardy was seen as dangerous because it attracted followers from the nobility and gentry, including some members of the court. A significant number of these were frightened off when it was clear that their beliefs were classed as heresy. A law of 1401 which was concerned with defining heresy stated that those who possessed heretical writings or held heretical views and refused to recant would be burnt. When those who held views sympathetic to Wycliffe were banned from Oxford University, where he had first begun to preach, they went into the provincial towns and spread Lollard ideas to a wider audience. By the 16th century there were Lollard sympathisers in Leicester, Bristol, Coventry and London and in country areas in Kent and East Anglia.

The majority of those who could be considered Lollards at the time of Henry VIII's reign were craftsmen and merchants, rather than members of the nobility and gentry. Most were literate, but it is difficult, in the absence of firm evidence, to say exactly how many there were or precisely what they believed.

Lutherans

Protestantism was based on the ideas of Martin Luther and the beliefs which it promoted were to change European religion in a revolutionary way during the 16th century. The Church in England only became truly Protestant for a brief period during the reign of Edward VI. Henry VIII personally wrote a denial of Luther's views in 1521 but there were people in influential positions who made critical decisions during the years 1529–47 and who were sympathetic to the ideas of Martin Luther.

Fig. 6 *Martin Luther (1483–1546). Luther is attributed with the first serious challenge to papal authority*

Key profile

Martin Luther

Martin Luther (1483–1546) was an Augustinian monk, theologian and university professor. He also promoted the translation of the Bible into a language that people could understand. He challenged the papacy with his ideas by nailing them to the door of the cathedral at Wittenberg in 1517. His provocative stance resulted in his excommunication by the Pope, but his criticism of the corrupt practices of the church was welcomed by many, especially in areas of trade and manufacture.

Martin Luther wanted to take the Church back to its roots. His initial protest was against indulgences, which he argued were corrupt. However, it was not the actual protest against indulgences that was so shocking to the Church but the theological argument which he used to underpin his criticisms. Luther argued that Christianity was fundamentally a phenomenon of the inner world of human beings and had little to do with the outer world. This was stressed in his *Sermon on Good Works* in which he argued that good works do not benefit the soul – only faith could do that. Luther was to argue that faith was the gift of God to the individual;

Fig. 7 *The purchase of indulgences. Such a purchase would supposedly reduce the time spent in purgatory. It was rumoured that the sale of indulgences was to pay for the construction of St Peter's in Rome*

salvation could not be earned by doing good works approved by the Catholic Church. Luther had written his arguments in his *95 Theses*; Pope Leo X declared that 41 of these articles were heretical and Luther's books were burned in Rome. Luther responded by calling for the clergy to revolt openly against Rome, using military force if necessary. In 1521 the Holy Roman Emperor, Charles V, demanded that Luther appear before the imperial parliament (*Diet*) at Worms. Charles offered Luther an opportunity to change his views; when he refused to do this, Charles placed him under an imperial ban as an outlaw.

Later in 1521 Luther was also excommunicated from the Church. The Pope was prompted to take this action by Luther's publication of *The Freedom of a Christian*. This book was the basis of a new movement in which people first challenged belief and religion and went on to challenge political and economic beliefs and to assert a view of individualism which was very different from the community-based ideas of Catholicism.

Few in England were attracted to the ideas of Martin Luther; certainly none of the nobility were supporters. There were those who believed strongly in humanism in 1529, and who would later become influential when the Church in England broke with Rome in 1535. These included a key group of Cambridge scholars, for example Thomas Cranmer who, from about 1531, agreed with Lutheran ideas.

The earliest evidence we have for the arrival of Lutheran ideas in England relates to the circulation of books. An Oxford bookseller recorded the sale of twelve books by Luther in 1520 and at the end of that year a public burning of Lutheran books was held in Cambridge.

2   *Sheils, W. J., **The English Reformation 1530–1570**, 1989*

Fig. 8 *The burning of Martin Luther's books in 1521*

Cranmer was to become Archbishop of Canterbury and to secure the break from Rome. In 1540 Henry VIII denounced Thomas Cromwell, who had become his first minister and who had guided parliament through the break with Rome, as a dangerous religious radical: a man influenced by Martin Luther.

Believers in royal supremacy

In addition to questioning the beliefs of the Church in relation to the role of the priest, thinkers as early as John Wycliffe began to challenge the roles and relationships of the Church and the monarchy. Wycliffe had argued that it was a sin to oppose the power of the King. He also stated that those in the service of the Church should have a regard for the laws of the state. Earlier in the reign of Henry VIII, when the case of Richard Hunne was discussed in parliament, Dr Henry Standish attacked the immunity of the clergy and stated that the Pope and the clergy lacked the power to enforce the laws made in the Church unless they had also received royal assent. Luther and Tyndale also began to question the relationship between the Church and the monarch. These ideas were taken up by a group of theologians who met at the White Horse in Cambridge in the 1520s. They were keen to explore how religious change might come about.

■ **Cross-reference**

Thomas Cranmer is profiled on page 54.

Thomas Cromwell is profiled on page 49.

The **break with Rome** is the subject of Chapter 4.

■ **Cross-reference**

To recap on the **case of Richard Hunne**, see page 19.

■ A closer look

William Tyndale

The opportunity for English people to read the Bible and to come to their own conclusions about Christian teachings was provided by William Tyndale (c.1494–1536), who translated the Bible into English and arranged for its printing, using Gutenberg's moveable-type press, in 1526. To own a Bible in English was itself heretical but Tyndale's views went much further than challenging the laws against ownership of a vernacular Bible. Tyndale was a tutor in the house of a family in Gloucestershire where he came into contact with many Catholic dignitaries. In one dispute with a clergyman he stated: 'I defy the Pope and all his laws. If God spare my life ere many years, I will cause the boy that drives the plough to know more of the scriptures than you.'

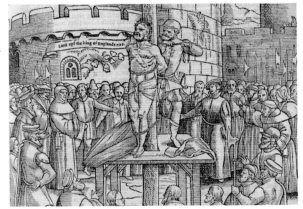

Fig. 9 *The martyrdom of William Tyndale. Why might Tyndale be calling out 'Lord open the king of England's eyes'?*

Tyndale fled to the Netherlands to continue with his work on the Bible and to publish other religious works that challenged Catholic ideas. He was pursued by agents of Sir Thomas More and was finally burned as a heretic in 1536. Ironically, in 1539 the Bible was published in English and placed in all parish churches.

Luther had sought a monarch who would serve true religion. He wanted a Christian community which would select its own religious leader. He argued that power would come from below, and although the people might do the wishes of the King they would not accept religious power coming from above. In contrast, William Tyndale was optimistic that religious change would come through a godly prince to whom subjects owed allegiance both in body and soul. Writing in 1528 in his book *Obedience of a Christian Man* Tyndale argued, based on the laws of Moses, that God required people to obey their ruler. The alternative to this, Tyndale stated, was damnation.

Adding to this, the lawyer Christopher St Germain (1460–1540) provided Henry VIII with the legal basis for extending his authority by arguing that the real authority over the Church in England came not from the Pope, but from the King.

Cross-reference

Thomas More's *Utopia* is outlined on page 28.

> ### Activity
>
> **Research task**
>
> Use the internet to find some extracts from Tyndale's *Obedience of a Christian Man*. What were his views about the powers of the monarch?

Religious conservatives

It would be wrong to suggest that the views of Luther and Tyndale were ignored by the established Church. One of those keen to protect Catholic beliefs and practices from Protestant ideas was Thomas More. More had been a close friend of Erasmus and had supported a return to original texts to find religious truths, but he became increasingly conservative in the defence of the Church against the challenges of Protestantism. In *Utopia* he stressed the importance of a strict hierarchy. All challenges to the existing hierarchy were perceived as dangers, and in practical terms the greatest danger, as he saw it, was the challenge that heretics, such as Luther and Tyndale, posed to the established beliefs and the Catholic faith. The most important thing of all for More was to maintain the unity of Christendom. The ideas of Luther and the actions of those who supported him, with all of the prospects of fragmentation and discord, were to his mind a dreadful thing.

More helped Henry VIII with the writing of the *Defence of the Seven Sacraments*, a response to Luther's *On the Babylonian Captivity of the Church*. When Luther replied with his 'Against Henry, King of the English', More was given the task of constructing a response, which he did in his 'Reply to Luther'. This exchange was criticised for being a series of personal attacks, but it strengthened More's commitment to the forms of order and discipline which he had outlined in *Utopia*.

Thomas More did not only produce arguments against the ideas of Luther and Tyndale; he actively worked to bring heretics to punishment. More was himself an extremely religious man who wore a hair shirt and regularly spent time with the monks at the London Charterhouse. He believed that those who preached and published ideas which were against those of the Catholic Church should be forced either to renounce their views or to die. Accounts produced after his death claimed that More had instruments of torture installed in the basement of his home to force those brought before him either to provide information or to change their views and be saved.

Support for the existing system of beliefs came from the scholarship of two austere monastic orders, the Observant Franciscan Friars and the Carthusians. While the main monastic orders could be criticised for their engagement with society and the economy, these two orders stressed a life of solitude and devotion with limited contact with the world. Their influence was significant, because the Observant Franciscans acted as confessors and preachers to Henry VIII as they had done to his father. Henry VIII defended the Catholic Church against the challenges of Martin Luther, he was the friend of More, who was determined to defend the Catholic faith, he was advised in spiritual matters by the conservative Observant Friars, and he was married to Queen Catherine of Aragon, who was increasingly absorbed by the teachings of the Catholic Church.

The Aragonese faction

Faction is a term used to describe informal groups within the Tudor court which had a single focus or cause. Generally, such factions represented interest groups. These were often based on a particular belief or person, and had as their members people who either believed that their positions could be bettered through promotion of that person or idea, or defended a person or belief that was being challenged. Some historians have identified an Aragonese faction grouped around Catherine of Aragon, which sought to protect the Catholic faith and the position of those who were loyal to the Catholic Church.

As Catherine suffered a succession of miscarriages and stillbirths, she became more and more pious. She sought the blessing of a successful pregnancy by going on pilgrimages and through religious devotion. In this she was supported by her spiritual adviser, whose loyalty was firmly to the Church. Chapuys, the imperial ambassador, played a significant role not only in advising Catherine and in maintaining links with her nephew Charles V, but also in court politics. What became known as the Aragonese faction had actually begun to develop in opposition to the power and influence exercised by Cardinal Wolsey. Thomas More and Bishop Fisher were loosely connected to the faction, but the strength of the faction lay in its supporters within the court. Two members of the King's household spoke out in support of Catherine: these were Sir Nicholas Carew, a gentleman of the Privy Chamber, and Sir Henry Guilford, who was controller of the Household. Two other key players were Lords Darcy and Hussey. As the strength of the opposing Boleyn faction grew, and as Henry tussled with the idea of annulling his marriage to Catherine, the Aragonese faction leapt to her defence.

■ Key profile

John Fisher

John Fisher (1469–1535) was chaplain and adviser to Margaret Beaufort, mother of Henry VII. He helped her in the refounding of Christ's and St John's colleges in Cambridge. Fisher was a humanist and a staunch opponent of Lutheranism. He was a close adviser of Catherine of Aragon and was against the royal supremacy. He was executed in 1535 as he refused to take the Oath of Supremacy.

The faction was later silenced by the execution of its key supporters such as More and Fisher, and the effective exile from court of Darcy and Hussey. Lord Darcy was in charge of Pontefract Castle, which, while being central to the security of the northern counties, meant that he was not present at court. Lord Hussey, who was in charge of Princess Mary's household, was removed from effective influence when Mary was sent from court. The political and religious 'exiles' were to play a significant role in the rising against many of the actions taken by the King and his chief minister, Cromwell, in 1536.

■ Cross-reference

The **rising of 1536** is discussed in Chapter 6.

For a profile of **Thomas Cromwell**, see page 49.

■ A closer look

How far the Church was under threat by 1529: historiography

The debate about the state of the Church in England in 1529 is still a very live one. The traditional view was that the Church was essentially decayed, corrupt and ripe for reform. This was the view that A. G. Dickens provided evidence and argument for in the 1960s and 1970s, although the belief that a reformation was inevitable went back to the historians of the 19th century. In the later 20th century historians looked again at a range of sources relating to the Church in England to assess the state of the Church and the beliefs of the people. A much wider range of material was used which included episcopal court records, churchwardens' accounts, wills, private correspondence and artefacts such as devotional literature. This research also failed to produce any consensus. The research of Diarmaid MacCulloch has shown the existence of groups who supported changes in religious beliefs through will-based evidence. He has shown that the introductions to people's wills changed from a Catholic-based approach to one which reflected Protestant views. He has also shown that in East Anglia, where there had been great investment in churches in the first two decades of the 15th century, there was very little opposition to religious change when it occurred in later years. This would suggest that people could support the Church but not necessarily support its beliefs.

By contrast, Eamon Duffy has demonstrated in his work, particularly *The Stripping of the Altars*, that there was great support for the beliefs and practices of the Catholic Church in the first two decades of the 15th century. He has demonstrated that the rituals of the Church were firmly embedded in town and village life and that there was real acceptance of such practices as transubstantiation and prayers for the dead.

■ Activity

Thinking point

Why might Thomas More support the work of humanist writers such as Erasmus who challenged religious writings but be committed to punishing heretics who challenged religious beliefs?

■ Activity

Revision and analysis

In pairs, use the material which you have covered in Chapter 2 to make a list of the changes that people were seeking. Use the material in Chapter 1 to list other criticisms of the concerns of those who criticised the Church. Identify areas of similarity and difference.

Learning outcomes

Through your study of this section you have gained an understanding of the structure of the Catholic Church at every level and its significance in people's lives. You should have developed an insight into the relationship between the Church and government as it existed in 1529. You should be able to explain why there was criticism of the Church and what arguments were presented against those who criticised belief and practices.

Practice questions

Read Sources 3–5 below.

Anticlericalism was very strong by the early years of the 16th century. Monasticism was inward looking and there was little support for it outside the monastery itself. Altogether, the English Church during the period 1500–1530 was poorly equipped to meet the challenges of the new age.

3

Adapted from Dickens, A. G. in Hurstfield, J. (ed.),
***The Reformation Crisis**, 1965*

Improvements were being made in the English Church in the early 16th century. More graduates went into the church; the learning of the parish clergy in most respects seems to have been adequate; more clergy appear to have lived in their parishes; more bishops paid attention to their duties. Too frequently historians have overlooked these real gains in the Church through their overriding need to discover explanation for the acceptance of Protestant ideas. Even so these changes were too little and came too late. Lollards did not remain satisfied with Humanism, they went to the new translation of the Bible which they could read in English for themselves.

4

*Cross, C., **Church and People: England,**
1450–1660, 1976*

Late medieval Catholicism exerted an enormously strong, diverse, and vigorous hold over the imagination and the loyalty of the people up to the very moment of Reformation. Traditional religion had about it no particular marks of exhaustion or decay and indeed in a whole host of ways, from the multiplication of vernacular religious books to adaptations within the national and regional cult of the saints, was showing itself well able to meet new needs and new conditions.

5

*Duffy, E., **The Stripping of the Altars:**
Traditional Religion in England, 1400–1580, 1992*

(a) Explain how far the views in Source 4 differ from those in Source 3 in relation to criticism of the Catholic Church in the early 16th century.

(12 marks)

Study tip

For part (a)
- Read the sources carefully and note down any points of disagreement.
- Decide how far they agree/disagree.
- Write your answer, referring to the sources throughout and with supporting own knowledge.

(b)   Use Sources 3, 4 and 5 and your own knowledge. How important was the spread of new religious ideas in the criticism of the Catholic Church in 1529?   *(24 marks)*

For part (b)

■ Write a brief plan – with an introduction, argument and conclusion.

New religious ideas may include

■ Humanism
■ Lutheranism
■ also longer established Lollardy.

Anti-clericalism may include

■ criticisms of the behaviour of monks and clergy
■ the taxation paid to the Church in England and to Rome
■ the political power of the Church.

Other factors to consider may include

■ the growth of literacy
■ economic changes.

In this chapter you will learn about:

- why Henry's lack of a male heir posed a major problem to the monarchy

- how his attempt to achieve a divorce led him into conflict with the Catholic Church

- the importance of Henry VIII's involvement with Anne Boleyn

- the ways in which Henry prepared for a divorce between 1529 and 1532.

Catherine's status as queen was at risk. For Henry had decided on a radical solution to the succession. He would no longer tinker with the symptoms and swing between his bastard and his daughter; instead he would go to the root of the matter and tackle his marriage and his wife.

1

Starkey, D., **Six Wives: The Queens of Henry VIII,** *2004*

The King's need for a divorce from Catherine of Aragon

The King's Great Matter

The King's Great Matter, which dominated the late 1520s and early 1530s, is the subject of much debate among historians. Most agree that the major issue was to protect the succession; this view has most recently been put forward by David Loades. The prompt for Henry to seek an annulment has variously been linked to the questioning of Mary's legitimacy by the French, or, as David Starkey has suggested, his courtship of Anne Boleyn.

Henry VIII had married Catherine of Aragon in 1509 shortly after the death of his father. The marriage was controversial; Catherine had previously been married to Henry's elder brother, Arthur, Prince of Wales, who had died in 1502, after less than six months of marriage. Catherine, who was nine years older than Henry, had languished in England while Henry VII had argued about payment of the dowry and sought a more advantageous marriage for his younger son. The marriage had required a papal dispensation as a marriage between a man and the widow of his brother was forbidden by canon law. However, it eventually took place on 11 June 1509 and on 24 June Henry and Catherine were crowned King and Queen of England at Westminster Abbey.

Although much disputed at a later date, there is evidence from contemporary sources that Henry and Catherine were blissfully happy in the early stages of marriage.

Fig. 1 *An early portrait of Catherine of Aragon*

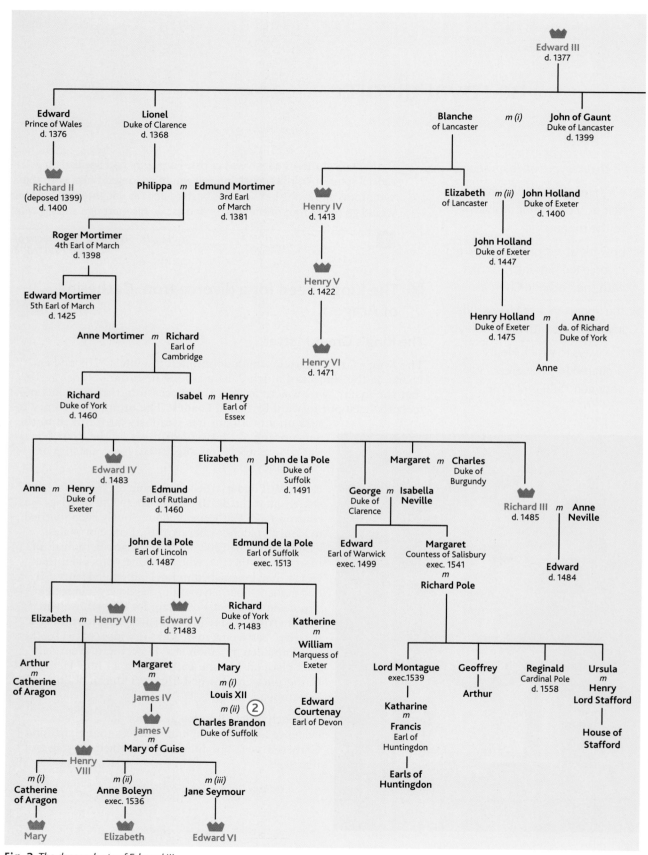

Fig. 2 *The descendants of Edward III*

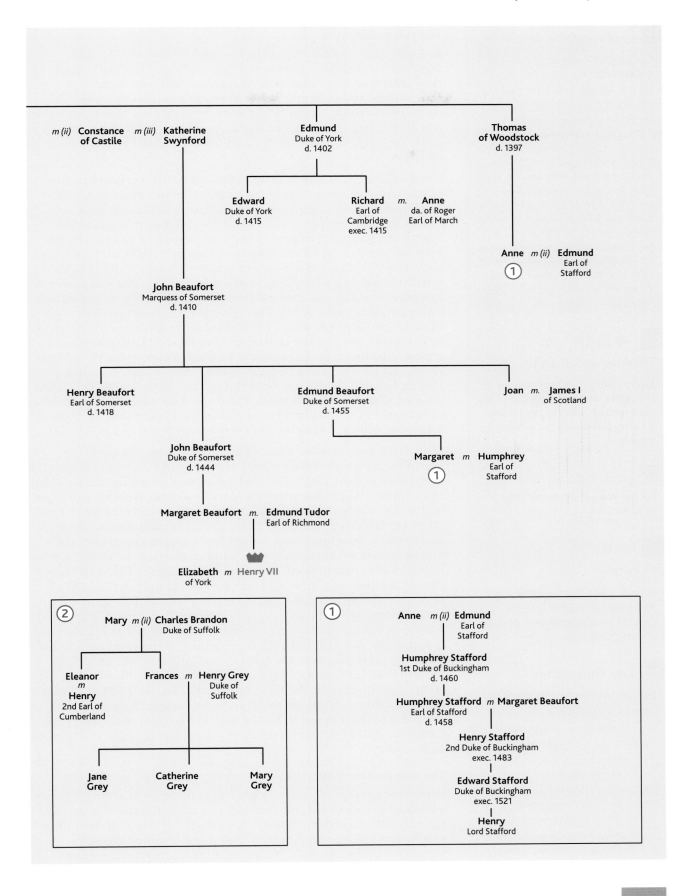

Exploring the detail

Canon law and papal dispensation

The Church had its own legal system, which had power over not only the clergy but also religious matters relating to the sacraments, including marriage. Under the law of the Church it was forbidden that a man should marry either his sister or his sister-in-law. A man who wished to marry his sister-in-law needed special permission from the Pope, who would allow the law to be dispensed with. Pope Julius II had given a dispensation for Henry to marry Catherine in 1503. By 1527 the current pope, Clement VI, was in the control of Charles V, the Holy Roman Emperor.

Activity

Thinking and analysis

Study Henry VIII's family tree. List the males who had royal blood and their relative claim to the throne if Henry VIII should die without a male heir.

Cross-reference

For the **Wars of the Roses**, refer back to page 4.

Activity

Pairs task

In pairs, make a list of what steps Henry would need to take to ensure that the succession of the Tudors continued.

Key chronology

Events leading to the divorce

c.1524 Henry ended marital relations with Catherine

1525 Rumours spread that the French were questioning Mary's legitimacy

1526 Henry decided to seek an end to his marriage. He became interested in Anne Boleyn

Proceedings began in secret for the annulment of Henry and Catherine's marriage

The succession issue

By 1527, after 18 years of marriage, Catherine was 42. Her last pregnancy had been in 1518 and it was likely that she had entered the menopause by the age of 40. Catherine had had a number of miscarriages and stillbirths but only two pregnancies in which the child had survived: a male heir, Henry, born on New Year's day 1511, who died tragically seven weeks later; and Mary, a daughter, born in 1516. By 1527, it was unlikely that Catherine would bear any more children.

Her daughter, Mary, had been well educated by her parents in matters of state but this was seen as preparation for her role as a future wife of a European prince, rather than as a monarch in her own right. Mary's hand in marriage was a marketable commodity and marriage agreements were used frequently to cement alliances. In 1518 she had been betrothed to the infant dauphin of France; in 1523, at the age of six, a new betrothal was arranged to Emperor Charles V; by 1524 this agreement was being abandoned and a marriage to James V of Scotland proposed. The idea that a woman should inherit the throne of England was regarded as unthinkable. The only previous queen had been Matilda, whose accession in 1135 had led to the seizure of the crown by her cousin Stephen and civil unrest. For those in England who still remembered the upheaval of the disputed succession of the Wars of the Roses, and for the second Tudor monarch, who was still surrounded by those who could claim royal blood through descent from Edward III, the prospect of civil war was horrific. The issue of the succession was further complicated by the fact that Henry had an illegitimate son, the Duke of Richmond, who had been born to his mistress, Bessie Blount, in 1519.

Henry VIII had therefore three options before him. He could legitimise the Duke of Richmond, which would be unpopular with the nobility and might prompt action by someone with a legitimate claim to the throne. He could marry off Mary as soon as possible and hope that she would bear a male heir in his lifetime who could inherit the crown on Henry's death; or he could get rid of Catherine and start again. When questions about Mary's legitimacy began to circulate during further negotiations for her hand in marriage in 1527 to either Francis I of France himself, or to his second son the Duc d'Orleans, the setting aside of Catherine seemed to be the only option. On 18 May 1527 the Spanish ambassador made a sensational report to Spain informing the Spanish king that Henry had secretly assembled a group of bishops and lawyers to sign a declaration that his marriage to Catherine was null and void. The Spanish ambassador stated that Henry was claiming that his marriage to Catherine was invalid, as she had been his brother's wife, and that Pope Julius II, who had granted permission for the marriage to take place in 1509, had been wrong. At this stage Henry told Catherine nothing: he needed to act with secrecy and speed. He did not take account of the fact that Catherine could find out from others – most significantly the Spanish ambassador.

The case for the divorce

Historians have questioned why after so many years of marriage Henry VIII came to believe that his marriage was invalid in the eyes of God. His reasoning has been regarded with a degree of cynicism, assuming that he was attempting to find any solution which would enable him to put Catherine aside. Yet in the 16th century, explanations for events were sought in religion, or in superstition, rather than in

Fig. 3 *A 19th century painting depicting 'Henry VIII and Anne Boleyn observed by Queen Catherine'. Anne has been playing the lute for the king, watched by a gathering of courtiers, while Wolsey looks on. Catherine, whose portrait is on the wall behind them, is in the doorway. The little dog, traditionally symbolising fidelity, is an ironic touch*

science. Henry had failed to produce a legitimate son with Catherine who had survived. Henry had, however, sired a son with his mistress. Therefore, he surmised, his marriage must be sinful in the eyes of God. Henry VIII required the Pope, Clement VI, to annul his marriage to Catherine. This would mean that effectively the marriage had never been valid. 'Divorce' and 'annulment' were used as interchangeable terms by people at the time. In normal circumstances Henry VIII would expect the Pope to respond favourably to his requests, but this demand was complicated by a number of different issues: first, the original granting of the dispensation; second, the biblical basis of the claim that the marriage was invalid; and third, that the Pope was virtually a prisoner of Catherine of Aragon's nephew, the Holy Roman Emperor Charles V.

Henry sought explanations in the Bible for his lack of a surviving son. The Old Testament offered two interpretations on a man marrying his brother's wife, from Leviticus and Deuteronomy (the third and fifth books of the Law of Moses).

Consider the following sources:

> If a man takes his brother's wife it is an impurity; he has uncovered his brother's nakedness, they shall be childless.

2
Leviticus 20:21

> If brothers dwell together and one of them dies and has no son, the wife of the dead shall not be married outside the family to a stranger; her husband's brother shall go in to her, and take her as his wife.

3
Deuteronomy 24:5

Exploring the detail

Royal mistresses

Most monarchs had mistresses. Elizabeth Blount was Henry's first identifiable mistress. His second was Mary Boleyn, who had ceased to interest him before he took up with her sister, Anne. Mistresses were married off; an advantageous marriage was seen as a reward. Despite recent dramatised accounts, Henry was not a great lover. He was a skilful and enthusiastic player of 'courtly love' in which courtiers pretended to be in love. Dramatic scenes of passion were acted out, gifts given and promises made, but all was supposed to be platonic.

Cross-reference

More information on the **position in Europe** and the **role of Charles V** can be found later in this chapter on pages 47–8.

Activity

Source analysis

Explain how far the views in Source 3 differ from those in Source 2 in relation to Henry's attitude to the validity of his marriage to Catherine by 1529.

God had spoken directly to his condition; Henry had no option as a devout Christian but to obey, to contract a legal marriage (indeed, this would be his first marriage and his reward from God would be a son). Post-Freudian scepticism may smile, but the vital historical point is that Henry believed.

*Ives, E., **Anne Boleyn**, 1986*

One reason why Henry VIII's approach has been questioned is that technically, he was not childless – he had a living daughter. However, in monarchical terms this was as good as being childless. The problem was further complicated by the condition of Catherine's marriage to Arthur. The explanation offered by Leviticus depended on Arthur and Catherine having 'dwelt' together; throughout the negotiations Catherine constantly asserted that the marriage had not been **consummated**. Although he later denied this, Henry had claimed in 1509 that Catherine was a virgin.

The solution found by those who argued for Henry was that the Old Testament contains a number of versions of the laws by which communities and nations were to govern themselves. Rather than being a divine law, the 'law' of Deuteronomy regarding marriage to a brother's wife could be seen only as a social custom of Jewish society; Christians were not bound to obey it. As the older of the two sections which give laws about marriage, Leviticus could be seen as binding on Christians. Here, it was possible to argue that the Hebrew word used in the Bible for 'childless' meant 'male childless' and not 'female childless', and that, as such, Henry's marriage must have infringed natural and divine law.

> By substituting the Hebrew for the Latin, Leviticus was thus cleverly made to fit Henry's situation exactly; he had married in contravention of Leviticus and as a result had incurred the punishment threatened there, as the loss of all his sons proved. This narrow understanding of Leviticus is important for it allowed Henry to reconcile Leviticus with his own circumstances. How deeply Henry believed [these] views … especially the rewording of Leviticus, is impossible to say, although it is probable that they reflected a genuine and strongly held conviction. Certainly the connection between the king's failure to have produced a surviving son and Leviticus would become a central theme of the treatises produced in his name.

> **5**
>
> *Murphy, V., in MacCulloch, D., (ed.) **The Reign of Henry VIII: Politics, Policy and Piety**, 1988*

Later in 1527 Henry confronted Catherine with the illegality of their marriage and claimed that his conscience was troubled. His intention was to seek an annulment from the Pope which, in turn, would allow him to marry as if for the first time and conceive an heir to secure the Tudor dynasty. The handling of the situation was disastrous. Henry had hoped that Catherine would withdraw quietly into a nunnery, accepting his interpretation of their situation. Unfortunately, Henry had already shown an interest in Anne Boleyn. This made Catherine's determination to protect her marriage all the more implacable and the task of Henry's Chancellor, Cardinal Wolsey, in persuading the Pope to grant the annulment, all the more difficult.

Key term

Consummated: for a marriage to be valid the husband and wife needed to have sexual intercourse.

Cross-reference

The position and role of **Thomas Wolsey** between 1514 and 1529 are detailed on pages 5–6.

Anne Boleyn

In around 1526, Henry appears to have become attracted to Anne Boleyn. He had tired of her sister Mary who seems to have given into his demands very rapidly. There is considerable dispute as to when an actual relationship with Henry began and whether it pre-dated Henry's decision to seek an annulment of his marriage to Catherine. Letters between Henry and Anne survive from about 1526–8. A further area of debate concerns the reason why Anne appears not to have become Henry's mistress. The general view is that she learnt from her sister Mary's relationship with Henry VIII and was determined to use her skills to ensure that she gained more from Henry's interest in her than a temporary affair.

Fig. 4 *Anne Boleyn*

Key profile

Anne Boleyn (1501–36)

Anne Boleyn was born in 1501, the daughter of Sir Thomas Boleyn, later 1st Earl of Wiltshire and 1st Earl of Ormonde, and his wife, Lady Elizabeth Boleyn (born Lady Elizabeth Howard), daughter of the Duke of Norfolk. As the daughter of a respected family, Anne spent a number of years at the French court, where she gained the most modern social skills, which reinforced her attractiveness to male courtiers who were taken by her striking, but unconventional, appearance and personal charisma. On her return to the English court in 1521 Anne became a Lady in Waiting to Catherine of Aragon and was initially courted by Henry Percy, Earl of Northumberland.

Cross-reference

For a profile of the **Duke of Norfolk**, see page 82.

Letters from Henry VIII to Anne Boleyn

1526

If it shall please you to do me the office of a true loyal mistress ... I promise you that not only shall the name be given you, but that also I will take you for my only mistress, rejecting from thought and affection all others save yourself, to serve you only.

6

Summer 1527

The proofs of your affection are such, the fine poesies of the letters so warmly couched, that they constrain me ever truly to honour, love and serve you, praying that you will continue in this same firm and constant purpose ...

Henceforth, my heart shall be dedicated to you alone, greatly desirous that so my body could be as well, as God can bring to pass if it pleaseth Him, whom I entreat once each day for the accomplishment thereof ...

Written with the hand of that secretary who in heart, body and will is

Your loyal and most ensured servant

Henry aultre A B ne cherse R

(Translation: Henry looks for no other)

7

Cross-reference

Reginald Pole is profiled on page 111.

Reginald Pole, who was to become Archbishop of Canterbury in the reign of Mary, argued that Anne Boleyn:

> ... has said that she will make herself available to you on one condition alone. You must reject your wife whose place she desires to hold. This lowly born woman does not want to be your concubine. She wants to be your wife. I believe that she learned from the example of her sister ... how quickly you can have your fill of concubines.

8 *Quoted in Bernard, G. W., **The King's Reformation**, 2005*

Alternatively, G. W. Bernard has argued that the reluctance to consummate the relationship was Henry's:

> It was Henry himself who came to the view that his first marriage was null and void, for nothing induces a man to question his marriage than falling in love with another woman ... In seeking an annulment Henry was staking a claim to the high moral ground. A visibly pregnant Anne would destroy his case. It would also affect public opinion in England which was suspicious of his motives.

9 *Bernard, G. W., **The King's Reformation**, 2005*

Activity

Source analysis

Using Sources 6–9 and your own knowledge, decide how far Henry VIII was determined to make Anne his wife by 1529.

Anne has often been portrayed as both feisty and uncompromising. Her unpleasantness to both Catherine and Mary is well documented. This should not obscure her interest in theology and in particular the new learning and religious ideas to which she had been exposed while in France. Anne was responsible for giving Henry a copy of Simon Fish's *A Supplication for the Beggars* which criticised greedy and overfed clerics. She was in regular contact with a number of clerics who were questioning the old orthodoxies of the Church.

Once Henry had decided in 1527 formally to seek an annulment of his marriage to Catherine of Aragon which would enable him to marry Anne Boleyn, he petitioned the Pope to reverse the permission which had been granted by his predecessor. In December of that year negotiations began in Rome. Most negotiations in the Vatican were protracted but this was even more so. As a result of the Pope's position as a virtual prisoner of Charles V, he was unable to decide in Henry's favour. To delay matters the Pope sent Cardinal Campeggio to hear Henry's case in England. The situation at court had changed in the interim. By the end of 1529 Anne was the King's constant companion and although Catherine was still queen, it was Anne who played the main role in court life. Frustrations built up, and Catherine continued to hold out for the decision of the papal court.

Measures taken to prepare for the divorce 1529–32

In March 1529 a court opened in Blackfriars in order to hear the case for the divorce with representations from Henry's lawyers. Although, behind the scenes, Wolsey sought to put pressure on Campeggio to find for the King, the biggest impact was made by Catherine of Aragon at her appearance at the hearing. Catherine appeared resolute in her position as Henry's legal wife. A marriage ceremony to her was a religious sacrament.

She made impassioned pleas to Campeggio and to Henry. Catherine was adamant that her marriage to Arthur had not been consummated and that the dispensation given to Henry by Julius II was valid. Henry endeavoured to prove that her marriage had been consummated. The whole unsavoury business, with very questionable evidence presented by Henry, dragged on without resolution. On 23 July, when a decision was expected, Campeggio announced that the court was part of the court in Rome and that the case was being adjourned there to meet in October. Catherine had already made it clear that she would, in any case, appeal to Rome should the commission's decision go against her. Wolsey could do nothing to stop this. The court did not meet in October and by the end of the year Henry had altered his tactics. In October 1529 Wolsey was replaced as Chancellor by Thomas More, and a month later Henry called parliament. This parliament would be used to put pressure on the Pope to force him to change his mind about the validity of the marriage.

Henry VIII had expected Cardinal Wolsey to achieve the annulment of his marriage to Catherine by using his position as Cardinal and *legatus a latere* to influence the Pope. Unfortunately for Henry, Pope Clement VII was the virtual prisoner of the Holy Roman Emperor, Charles V, in Castel Sant'Angelo in Rome, and the influence of Catherine of Aragon's nephew was far greater than any that Wolsey could bring to bear. Had Henry had the financial or diplomatic power to come to his aid, Clement might have been more receptive to his demands. As it was, the pressure of Catherine's nephew was much more immediate.

It is clear that Henry did have a case. Much was made of the 'word of God' as written in the Bible. If the prohibition of Leviticus was divine law, then the previous Pope, Julius II, had not had the right to dispense with it, and as a result the marriage between Henry VIII and Catherine of Aragon had not been valid. Catherine had backed herself into a corner based on morality and a belief in the ultimate power of the Pope. Henry, who needed to protect the best interests of the country by providing a male heir to prevent the slide into civil war, was forced to seek an alternative policy.

A closer look

Foreign affairs

Henry VIII wanted to reassert England's position as a significant power in the affairs of Europe, lost during the years of fighting and bankruptcy in the Wars of the Roses. Initially that aim was demonstrated in military prestige in regaining the French territory lost by Henry VI. Limited territorial success and spiralling costs resulted in England using Wolsey's diplomatic skills to reinforce England's influence. While it is tempting to portray England as holding the balance of power in Europe it is much more accurate to see Wolsey's foreign policy as being reactive to events rather than proactive in shaping them. The main players in Europe in the 1520s were France and the Holy Roman Empire. Francis I and Charles V vied for supremacy and specifically for territorial gains in the Italian states. Traditionally England was closer to the Habsburgs, whose military support was deemed necessary if a successful invasion of France was to be mounted. The success of the Habsburg forces in 1525 against the French at the battle of Pavia encouraged Henry to believe that a joint invasion of France would be possible; however, Charles V's subsequent lack of interest and the difficulty of raising

Exploring the detail

The role of Cardinal Wolsey – differing views

There are other views which consider the role of Wolsey in Henry VIII's government and in his role in the failure to achieve the annulment. Some historians have viewed Wolsey as the main architect of government policy. Peter Gwyn, in *The King's Cardinal*, argues that Henry ruled and Wolsey served. Gwyn argues that Wolsey was not embarrassed by his position as *legatus a latere*, or concerned about challenging the Pope; rather, Wolsey worked tirelessly to achieve the annulment, but believed that a technical approach rather than an attempt to challenge the Pope on biblical grounds would have a greater chance of success.

Activity

Research task

The annulment is one of the most controversial topics in Tudor history. Undertake your own research using the books on the booklist. G. W. Bernard and David Loades have detailed discussions.

Research task

Choose one or two of the events referred to in the section on foreign affairs and find out more about them. Explain their significance in the relationship between England and Charles V and Francis I. How far might these two monarchs be expected to support Henry's claim for an annulment as a result of the situation in Europe?

■ **Key term**

Act of parliament: when parliament proposed a law it had to be agreed by both houses of parliament and then signed by the King. The law would then come into force and a person who went against the law would be tried in the King's court. An act of parliament was known as a statute and the law was statute law.

taxation led Wolsey to a foreign policy which supported the French with the construction of the League of Cognac, which comprised France, the papacy, Venice and Florence. It was Wolsey's intention not to join the League but to act as peacemaker of Europe. The Treaty of Westminster in 1527, which achieved peace between France and England, moved this a step closer. However, the action of the imperial army, which ignored its commanders, sacked Rome and captured the Pope, undermined not only England's position in Europe but also Henry and Wolsey's attempts to secure a divorce.

The Reformation parliament – the early years, 1529–32

The parliament that met between 1529 and 1536 was called the 'Reformation parliament' by historians in the 19th century. Such a title is somewhat misleading. The members of the Houses of Commons and Lords who met in 1529 did not have an agenda for religious reform, and although the **acts of parliament** which were passed between then and 1533 fundamentally changed the relationship between England and the Catholic Church, the significant changes to religious beliefs and practices were achieved by parliaments that met in the reigns of Edward VI and Elizabeth I. However, the parliament that met in 1529 did agree on one key issue from the outset: that Cardinal Wolsey should be challenged.

There is a great deal of uncertainty as to why Henry VIII called parliament in 1529. Parliaments were usually called when the King needed money to provide forces either for invasion of a foreign country or to defend England from the attacks of enemies, which could either be foreign powers such as France and Scotland, or internal challenges. Monarchs were generally reluctant to ask parliament to grant taxation as it could lead to discontent and even rebellion. Additionally, to be persuaded to grant money, members of parliament expected to gain something in return. Usually this involved the passing of acts of parliament relating to the localities and private concerns.

Henry had called four parliaments before 1529. The first, which sat for five weeks in 1510, had been called primarily to ensure that Henry VIII was granted the right to collect customs duties for life. The second parliament, which met for a total of 36 weeks between 1512 and 1514, passed little legislation apart from an attempt to prevent further enclosures and granting relatively modest amounts of money towards the cost of Henry's foreign policy. The real significance of the second parliament was that it offered an opportunity for members to air concerns about what were matters for the King's court and matters for the Church courts which had been raised by the case of Richard Hunne. The parliament which was assembled in April 1523 and sat for 15 weeks was mainly noted for the passing of private acts and one act for the raising of taxation to enable Henry VIII to engage in European affairs; that act, however, like its

Fig. 5 *In what ways does this 16th century woodcut stress the relationship between the King and his parliament?*

predecessors, was insufficient for Henry VIII to play the strong military role he wanted to in European affairs.

Thomas Cromwell first experienced parliament in 1523 and wrote to a friend complaining of the difference between what was discussed in parliament and what was actually achieved:

> I amongst others have endured a Parliament where we discussed war, peace, strife, riches, poverty, truth, falsehood, justice, fairness, deceit, oppression, activity, force, treason, murder and how a commonwealth might be improved. However, in conclusion we have done as our predecessors have done before; that is to say, we left things where we began.

10   *Thomas Cromwell (1523)*

Cross-reference

For more on **enclosure**, see page 84.

The **case of Richard Hunne** is outlined on page 19.

Activity

Thinking point

Why might MPs use the House of Commons to raise their concerns about actions taken by the Church?

Key profile

Thomas Cromwell (his early career)

Thomas Cromwell was born in Putney, London. Like Thomas Wolsey he was a commoner and was also highly intelligent. Before 1512 he found employment with a powerful Florentine merchant banker family in the Netherlands. It has been suggested that while in the Netherlands he was exposed to, and became sympathetic towards, new religious ideas.

Evidence in the archives of the Vatican City shows that Cromwell was an agent for Cardinal Reginald Bainbridge and dealt with English ecclesiastical work. Cromwell was not only fluent in Latin, which was the language of official documents and religion, but also Italian and French. Following Bainbridge's death in 1514 Cromwell returned to England and found employment with Wolsey: despite being a layman, he was put in charge of important ecclesiastical business. He became a member of parliament in 1523. After the dissolution of that parliament, Cromwell wrote a letter to a friend joking about its unproductiveness (Source 10).

In 1524, using the legal knowledge he had acquired following his return to England, Cromwell was appointed at Gray's Inn. He helped Wolsey dissolve 30 monasteries in the late 1520s. The money from this was used to fund the building of Wolsey's grammar school in Ipswich (now known as Ipswich School) and the Cardinal's College, now Christ Church, Oxford.

Fig. 6 *Thomas Cromwell, painted by Holbein. How does this compare with the other portraits which he painted of key figures in the early 16th century?*

Preparing for the divorce

When parliament was called in 1529 the most important concern of Henry VIII was the failure of the papal court to grant an annulment of his marriage to Catherine of Aragon; the issues which concerned some members of parliament were Wolsey's fall from Henry's favour and their desire to pass an **Act of Attainder** against him. Nevertheless, when parliament first met, as with the previous parliament witnessed by Cromwell, little was formally decided. Significantly, however, as with the second parliament of Henry's reign, a small group of London MPs

Key term

Act of Attainder: could be passed by parliament which would ensure that the property of a traitor would revert to the crown. Such acts were used frequently by Tudor monarchs. Acts of Attainder for nobles were reversed if the noble family proved its loyalty. Reversal of monastic attainders did not happen.

Key term

Praemunire: to commit praemunire was to appeal to a power outside the realm for resolution of a situation within England that was under jurisdiction of the crown. It was established as a crime in England by a law passed by parliament in 1351 during the reign of Richard II.

who were merchants and lawyers began an attack on the abuses of the Church. Four separate acts were passed which focused on limiting the power of the clergy.

At this point three separate options of pressing the Pope to annul the marriage were being considered by Henry:

- weakening the will of the Church to resist what Henry wanted, by taking action against either the Church in general or leading churchmen in particular, based on **praemunire**
- forcing the Church to grant the crown a large sum of money
- taking legal control of the Church.

By using the attack of the London MPs on the Church, Henry VIII pursued a policy through parliament which combined all three elements.

Submission of the Clergy, 1532

In late 1530 Henry VIII took the decision that 15 churchmen of England and Wales should be charged with praemunire. Ironically, this charge related specifically to the action which the churchmen had taken in recognising the power that Wolsey had held as a papal legate. This was ironic, as Henry VIII had clearly hoped that Wolsey would be able to use his legatine powers to achieve the annulment. When the Convocation of the archdiocese of Canterbury met in early 1531 it was made clear to them that Henry would withdraw the charge of praemunire if the Church would provide £100,000 and agree to his title being changed to 'Supreme Head of the Church in England and Wales (as far as the word of God allows)'. In addition this would be enshrined in an act of parliament, which would give the action legal powers and a constitutional significance.

While Convocation, weakened by Wolsey's fall, recognised that they had little alternative but to accept their guilt, pay the fine and recognise Henry as Supreme Head of the Church in England (with the get-out clause relating to the word of God), it is not clear where Henry thought this action was leading. Certainly there was little positive response from the Pope.

Activity

Thinking point

Read Source 11. Why would the composition of the group that was to advise Henry be important to the members in the House of Commons and in the House of Lords?

> We your humble subjects do promise unto your majesty that we will never henceforth enact any new canons unless your Highness give your royal assent and authority. Secondly laws which have been enacted shall be committed to the examination and judgement of your Grace and thirty two persons. Of whom sixteen shall be of the Houses of Lords and Commons and sixteen of the clergy, all to be chosen and appointed by your most noble Grace.

11 _____

From The Submission of the Clergy, 1532

Supplication of the Ordinaries

In 1532, following this successful action by the House of Commons against the Church, MPs petitioned Henry to take action against the way in which churchmen abused their powers. This petition was known as the Supplication of the Ordinaries. Even before it had been debated, Henry presented Convocation with a series of specific demands which, taken together, meant that the Church lost its legal independence:

- they should surrender the right to pass new canon law
- all future changes in canon law would require the consent of the King.

Existing canon law was to be scrutinised by a committee which would be made up of 16 laymen and 16 clergy. Only those laws of which they approved would remain in force.

Act to remove annates, 1532

The actions taken up to this point had put pressure on the role of the Church in England and had pressurised the clergy themselves. Now Henry sought a direct attack on Rome itself. The charges against the clergy and the Supplication of the Ordinaries could, at a stretch, be seen as an extension of the independence of the Church in England from Rome which had been established over centuries. The bill to remove the payment of **annates** was a direct challenge to the Pope, as it removed the chief source of revenue that the Church in Rome received from England. Although not in itself a large sum, the payment had been the subject of much criticism, particularly in parliament. That it was a diplomatic bargaining tool was clear when Cromwell drafted a clause which held up the act until the King should confirm it. Unlike the previous steps taken by parliament to restrict the Church, the act to remove annates did not receive full support from the House of Commons. When the House of Commons divided to vote on the act, Henry VIII himself was present to ensure that it received support. While the original criticisms had been raised by members of parliament, the initiative for change was increasingly in the control of Thomas Cromwell and Henry VIII.

The situation by 1532

By 1532 Henry had been unable to persuade the Pope to annul his marriage to Catherine of Aragon. The treatment of Cardinal Wolsey which had hastened his death in 1530 had done nothing to persuade the Pope. The Submission of the Clergy and the Supplication of the Ordinaries were insufficient challenges to the powers of the Church to force the Pope to go against the greater power of Charles V. The Pope appears to have assumed that Henry would regard these as only temporary measures, and that as soon as his infatuation with Anne was over he would return to the pre-existing situation. It seems that neither Henry nor Anne was prepared to accept the Pope's procrastination. Anne's frustration continued, and the situation was complicated by the attitude of the Archbishop of Canterbury, William Warham, to Henry's need to annul his marriage. Warham's death in August 1532 appears to have opened possibilities to Henry. In the autumn of 1532 Henry VIII and Anne travelled to Calais to gain support from Francis I. Although Anne had been created Marchioness of Pembroke for the occasion to enable her to accompany Henry, Francis I refused to receive her formally. The welcome given to Henry himself, however, was sufficient recognition of the relationship to enable the pair to sleep together for the first time. Anne conceived almost immediately and a secret marriage was prepared. It was imperative that the marriage between Catherine of Aragon and Henry VIII be declared null and void. Key to the resolution of Anne's problems was Thomas Cranmer.

Key term

Annates: monetary payments made by English bishops to the Church in Rome from their first year's income from their diocese.

Exploring the detail
Bills and acts

An act of parliament was the outcome of a bill introduced into either of the houses of parliament. The details of the bill would be discussed and amended. The agreement as to the final form was needed from both houses. The final agreed form then needed to be signed by the King: this was known as the royal assent. The act of parliament would become law and had to be upheld in the King's law courts, so his agreement was not negotiable.

Fig. 7 *William Warham, Archbishop of Canterbury, whose death in 1532 enabled Thomas Cranmer to take over this key role and marry Henry to Anne*

Key profile

William Warham

William Warham (1450–1532) had been significant in the negotiation of the marriage between Catherine of Aragon and Prince Arthur. He rose swiftly to become Archbishop of Canterbury in 1504 and Lord Chancellor in 1509. He lost influence when Wolsey, whom Henry favoured, became the principal adviser to Henry. Warham did not agree with any of the legislation passed by parliament to limit the powers of the Church but he failed to defend the Church against the will of the King.

Activity

Research task

Research in pairs and present to the class one of the following perspectives:

1 The main reason for Henry wanting a divorce was his belief that he had gone against God's will.

2 The main reason was his love for Anne Boleyn.

3 The main reason was Catherine's inability to have any more children.

Summary question

How far was the Pope responsible for the failure to secure the divorce?

4 The establishment of royal supremacy

In this chapter you will learn about:

- why the belief that Henry VIII had supreme power over the Church in England developed

- how Henry's attempts to put pressure on the Pope increased his power

- the importance of the Act of Supremacy and other acts to 1534

- the ways in which the royal supremacy was opposed.

The monks of the London Charterhouse had been spiritual advisers both to Henry VII and to Henry VIII. These Carthusians were the strictest of all the monastic orders and were regarded as the most holy. When five Carthusian monks refused to swear an oath recognising the right of Anne's children to succeed, their loyalty to the Catholic Church was sorely tested. They refused to speak, even when subjected to the most extreme torture. The five monks were duly executed in a most barbaric way. They were dragged through the streets of London, hung with the thickest ropes which could be found and while still alive had their insides cut out of them. Their private parts were cut off and placed in their mouths, and when dead their bodies were cut into four. Finally their heads were cut off and boiled, ready to be coated in tar and placed on London Bridge.

Such treatment shows something of Henry's determination to get his own way and have his marriage to Anne Boleyn, and the legitimacy of their offspring, recognised, even if it meant forcing the reluctant into acceptance.

Fig. 1 *A graphic series of woodcuts illustrating the stages of the Carthusian monks' punishment for refusing to take the Oath of Supremacy. This was produced by those sympathetic to the Carthusians. What might they hope to achieve by its distribution?*

Fig. 2 *Thomas Cranmer, Archbishop of Canterbury. How does this portrait differ from that of William Warham on p. 52?*

The acts of the Reformation, 1533–4

Key profile

Thomas Cranmer

Thomas Cranmer (1489–1556) had been educated at Cambridge and was influenced by new ideas from the continent. In 1529 he had produced a document which defended the argument for the royal divorce. Although he had held a position no higher than Archdeacon of Taunton, surprisingly he was promoted to be Archbishop of Canterbury in 1532, having been recalled to England following the death of William Warham. His promotion was the work of Henry VIII, to whom he offered important technical support in the construction of arguments in support of the divorce. He established his own position and continued in his post through the reign of Edward VI. He was executed by Mary I.

In order to convince people that Henry had the powers which he claimed, and ultimately the power to divorce Catherine of Aragon, it was important that there should be an argument based on evidence to support his claims and actions. Key to promoting the arguments in support of the annulment of Henry and Catherine's marriage were evangelicals, most notably Thomas Cranmer, who was elected to succeed William Warham as Archbishop of Canterbury in October 1532. Cranmer was fortunate in receiving the patronage of the Boleyns, and Anne in particular. His real skill was in promoting intellectual justifications for the divorce campaign while recognising Henry's resistance to religious change and hatred of heretical ideas. Henry had previously shown himself unimpressed by the arguments put forward by the lawyer Christopher St Germain in his treatise *Doctor and Student*, which attacked the Church's canon laws and stated that its legislative independence should be swept away and that all people should be under English common law.

Opinions were also sought not only from English universities but also from France, Italy, Spain, Germany, Poland and Scotland. Debates took place on the interpretation of biblical law in the context of consummation or non-consummation, and on the technicalities of the original papal dispensation, but there was a lack of clarity in the responses received. What the evangelicals in general, and Cranmer in particular, were able to offer was a challenge to the power of the Pope in England. The *Collectanea Statis Capiosa* was produced by Cranmer, in which he sought to prove that English bishops had the right to pronounce on Henry's divorce without reference to Rome. A wide range of sources was used to 'demonstrate' that King Lucius, the first Christian ruler of England, had secured certain powers in AD 187, which had been 'lent' to Rome. A response to an enquiry by Edward the Confessor, the last king of Anglo-Saxon England (reigned 1042–66), was quoted in explanation:

> For you are vicar of God in your kingdom. … A king is named by virtue of ruling not for having a realm. You shall be king while you rule well, but if you do otherwise the name of king shall not remain upon you, and you will lose it. The omnipotent God grant you so to rule the kingdom of Britain that you may reign with him eternally, whose vicar you are in the said realm.

1 *Pope Eleutherius (2nd century AD)*

The political implications of what Cranmer stated went beyond the right of Henry to grant his own divorce: it had major significance for the constitution. While papal approval of the annulment was still being anxiously sought, his thinking remained hypothetical; but with the Pope's failure to respond, Henry was encouraged to use this intellectual justification to assume powers that would make the granting of the annulment legal. To achieve his ends, legislation would need to be passed which established the right to hear matters of dispute in England rather than have them referred to Rome.

Act in Restraint of Appeals, 1533

The act to prevent appeals to Rome was carefully crafted by Cromwell, principally to block Catherine of Aragon's appeal, but was rooted in historical precedent and grievances dating back to the 14th century. Parliamentary support was gained for an act of parliament that would enable English courts to deal with cases that would otherwise go to Rome, which would achieve results in legal cases much more quickly and would keep money in English lawyers' hands. The Act in Restraint of Appeals, which was passed in March 1533, went much further than enabling Henry to grant his own annulment: it was a general statute which placed all ecclesiastical jurisdiction in Henry's control. It represented the most significant step towards Cromwell's goal of expelling the papacy from England. Yet in many respects Henry had already taken matters into his own hands. In January 1533 he and Anne had been married secretly by Thomas Cranmer, Archbishop of Canterbury, and a child was due in September.

Fig. 3 *The Act in Restraint of Appeals to Rome, 1533*

> This realm of England is an empire and is governed by one Supreme Head who has the entire power and authority to render justice to all manner of folk, or subjects within his realm in all cases, matters and debates without reference to any foreign power. From henceforth any person attempting to obtain from Rome or any other foreign court an appeal or judgement will incur penalties under the statute of Praemunire.

From Act in Restraint of Appeals, 1533

On 5 April 1533 the Convocation of the ecclesiastical province of Canterbury ruled that the marriage between Henry and Catherine could not be nullified by the Pope but only by that court. This decision, in addition to the Act in Restraint of Appeals, allowed Henry's marriage to Anne to become legal in English law, so making the child she was carrying, which Henry hoped would be the longed-for son, legitimate.

Activity

Thinking point

The Act in Restraint of Appeals was intended to stop Catherine appealing to Rome. Why do you think it was accompanied by a charge of praemunire?

Fig. 4 *A gold coin produced showing Henry as head of the Church of England*

Cross-reference

For the **act to remove annates**, refer back to page 51.

Legislation regarding the right to elect bishops and abbots and the granting of supreme legal authority to the secular courts is outlined on page 50.

Acts of 1534

There were two parliamentary sessions in 1534: the first from 15 January to 30 March and the second from 3 November to 18 December. Both of these were managed by Cromwell to achieve a clearer and more formal break with Rome, which the previous Acts had prefigured. Reinforcing earlier legislation, the first session:

- confirmed the prohibition of payments of annates to Rome
- granted the right to elect bishops and abbots to the King
- confirmed the supreme legal authority of the secular courts by stating that appeals from Church courts were to go to the King in Chancery.

The first session also established significant new legislation, including:

Act forbidding papal dispensation and payment of Peter's pence, 1534

This put all ecclesiastical powers in the hands of the King. It restricted an archbishop's right to allow departures from canon law which had allowed priests to hold more than one parish; this was a major objection of many lay people and was seen to reinforce the view that the clergy were greedy. This act also prevented payment of 'Peter's pence' – a slang term for taxation paid to Rome – to the Pope.

Act of Succession, 1534

This act made Henry and Catherine's marriage invalid, declared Mary to be illegitimate and secured the succession for the children of Henry and Anne. Even more important were the clause which made it an act of treason to deny the succession and the requirement that the whole nation should swear an oath to observe it.

The second parliamentary session, which sat from November to December 1534, established the Act of Supremacy.

Act of Supremacy, 1534

Fig. 5 *The Act of Supremacy of 1534*

This act did not make Henry the Supreme Head of the Church of England but stated that he 'justly and rightly is and ought to be the Supreme Head of the Church of England and that he should be taken, accepted and regarded as the Supreme Head'. To support this role the act included other provisions:

- it gave the King the right to collect first fruits and tenths, a tax which had previously been paid by the clergy to Rome
- it made it treasonable to call the King or Queen a heretic or a schismatic.

In January 1535 Henry added the claim 'Supreme Head of the Church of England' to his title. But this did not add anything to the King's powers; that had been achieved by the parliaments of 1534.

Be it enacted by the authority of this present Parliament, that the King, our Sovereign Lord his heirs and successors shall be taken and accepted as the only Supreme Head in earth of the Church of England and shall have and enjoy, united to the imperial Crown of this realm, all honours, jurisdictions, privileges, immunities and profits ... and shall correct all heresies ... and increase the virtue of Christ's religion for the conservation of the peace, unity and tranquillity of this realm.

3   *From The Act of Supremacy, 1534*

Fig. 6 *A painting commissioned by Henry VIII to illustrate his hatred for the actions of the Pope.*

The royal supremacy, which was proclaimed by the act of appeals, the act of succession and the act of supremacy, was founded on anti-papalism. The Act of Appeals dealt directly with the King's divorce. The Act of Succession dealt with the consequences of the king's divorce at his death. Other statutes were practical measures dealing with the consequences of the removal of papal authority. An act for the punishment of heresy declared that speaking against the Bishop of Rome was not to be regarded as a heresy. Arrangements were made for the election of bishops, no longer to be decided by the Pope, and Italian officials would no longer be acceptable as absentee bishops of English dioceses.

4   *Bernard, G. W., **The King's Reformation**, 2005*

Activity

Source analysis

Study sources 1, 2 and 3. How far do the sources agree about:

1 the source of Henry VIII's power

2 the limitations on Henry VIII's power?

Activity

Thinking point

Look at Fig. 6. Why do you think that the rocks being thrown on the Pope have the names of Matthew, Mark, Luke and John on them?

A closer look

The Chronicle of Edward Hall

Much of the evidence for the activities of the Reformation parliament comes from the Chronicle of Edward Hall. Hall was an MP in the Reformation parliament, a London lawyer of Gray's Inn and a close friend of Cromwell. A Protestant sympathiser, originally he had been influenced by humanism through the works of Erasmus. Hall was critical of the stance taken by Sir Thomas More and Bishop Fisher, the highest ranking of the critics of the royal supremacy. Of Thomas More he said, 'I cannot tell whether I should call him a foolish wise man or a wise foolish man, for undoubtedly he beside his learning had a great wit, but it was so mixed with taunting and mocking that it seemed to them that best knew him, that he thought nothing to be well spoken except he had given some mockery in what he said.' It is important to be aware of the limitations of Hall's evidence. His Chronicle begins in 1399 and presents Henry VIII's view of the unification of the houses of York and Lancaster. Shakespeare used this as his main source for his own history plays. At times Hall fails to record events that happened. It is likely that his account suggested that the House of Commons was determined to pass legislation against the Church from the outset because that reflected his own personal view, his sympathy with Protestantism, and could secure him further patronage from Cromwell and Henry VIII.

Cross-reference

For a profile of **Erasmus**, see page 29.

For a profile of **Sir Thomas More**, see page 28.

For a profile of **Bishop Fisher**, see page 35.

Activity

Revision task

Copy and complete the following table to record the legislation passed by the Reformation parliament. An additional act has been supplied to start you off.

Year	Legislation passed	What it did	Significance – High/ Medium /Low
1529	Act passed to control clerical fees to be charged for burial and probate (wills)	Limited the power of the Church to raise money	Low
1530			
1531			
1532			
1533			
1534			
1535			
1536			

A closer look

Anne Boleyn's coronation

Thomas Cranmer gave an account of Anne Boleyn's coronation. Full of symbolism and pageant, it was intended to impress the people of London as a new beginning for Henry VIII which would, he believed, lead to the continuation of the Tudor dynasty through the child which had already been conceived.

Anne travelled from Greenwich to the Tower of London by barge and was greeted by a full gun salute. The next day Anne and Henry entertained and created 18 knights of a new order. On Saturday Queen Anne processed through the City of London towards Westminster Palace, accompanied by most of the nobility; she was surrounded by four chariots and the whole procession was over half a mile long. A banquet awaited her at Westminster Palace and following this she travelled to York Place by barge to be met by the King.

On the Sunday, which was Pentecost – one of the most significant days in the Church's calendar, the day when the followers of Jesus Christ had received the Holy Spirit – Anne was crowned Queen in Westminster Abbey. Although the actual coronation was conducted by Cranmer, all the leading bishops and abbots of the country were in attendance at the abbey. Having won over the centres of commerce and politics, Anne now was accepted by the Church. To celebrate this, the Te Deum was sung in thanks to God and a High Mass was conducted in the Church, which Henry now controlled.

Activity

Thinking point

Henry was determined that people should believe in Anne's legitimacy as Queen. How did he use her coronation to stress her legitimacy and to gain acceptance for her from those with influence?

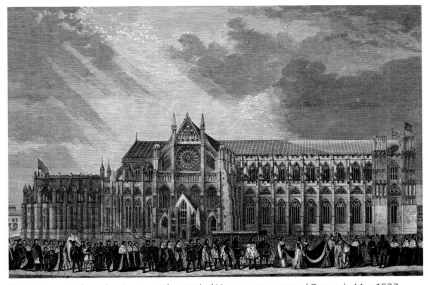

Fig. 7 *Anne Boleyn, having secretly married Henry, was crowned Queen in May 1533. Why was the coronation of Anne important to Henry?*

Opposition to the royal supremacy

Opposition to the work of the Reformation parliament, the break with Rome and the royal supremacy came from a number of different areas; it was motivated by different concerns and presented differing degrees of seriousness.

The main areas of concern were:

- **Economic**. Merchants and tradesmen were afraid that the Pope would pressure rulers to restrict trade with England. England depended on the export of wool and cloth. English agriculture was dominated by the profits that could be secured from sheep and many textile workers were employed in the production of cloth. This was exported, mainly from East Anglia to the principal port of Antwerp. The cloth was finished in Antwerp and exported throughout Europe. Charles V controlled the city of Antwerp and much of Europe.

- **Political**. Some members of the House of Commons opposed elements of the legislation. For example, the direct payment of Church taxes to the King rather than Rome suggested an undermining of parliament's power to control taxation. Up to this time a monarch either had to live 'of his own' (on the income of royal land and revenues) or seek specific permission from parliament to claim taxes. Parliament had, in the past, refused to grant the right to collect taxes if it did not feel the threat was sufficient to warrant the taxation.

- **Religious principle**. There were those who objected to the divorce and the break with Rome who were loyal to the Pope. Such people included not just the clergy, although they were at the forefront of this group, but also members of the laity. Humanists had wanted to purify the texts on which the Catholic Church based its views, not to destroy the Church itself.

Geoffrey Elton argued in *England under the Tudors* that 'the English Reformation under Henry VIII produced no victims and only martyrs'. This was to a large extent true. The main opposition had come from those who were true to the papacy. The most significant of these were Elizabeth Barton, who was known as the Maid of Kent, five Carthusian monks, Sir Thomas More, who had resigned as Chancellor, and Bishop Fisher. All were tried and found guilty on the charge of treason introduced by the Reformation parliament.

Cross-reference

For the fate of the **five Carthusian monks**, see page 53.

Activity

Thinking point

Historians sometimes change their minds and amend their arguments. At a later date G. R. Elton changed his mind to some extent about whether Henry created any victims. If you were to challenge the original view of G. R. Elton, who would you identify as victims?

A closer look

Elizabeth Barton

Elizabeth Barton was a servant girl who experienced miraculous 'visions'. In 1525 she had suffered an illness and claimed to have received revelations from God. Barton's visions suggested that people should pray to the Virgin Mary and follow the traditional teachings of the Church. Those who wished to pressure the King into renouncing Anne Boleyn and continuing with his marriage with Catherine saw an opportunity to make use of Barton's cult, and in 1528 she was invited to a private meeting with Cardinal Wolsey, followed by two with Henry VIII shortly afterwards. In 1532 she prophesied that if Henry were to divorce Catherine he would soon die. There followed a prolonged campaign to destroy her saintly reputation and provide the crown with an excuse to try her for treason. She allegedly confessed to having made the visions up and in 1534 she was hanged at Tyburn.

Exploring the detail

Tyburn

The gallows at Tyburn, the site today of Marble Arch in London, were sited at a crossroads of two major roads into London. The rotting corpses left there were intended to serve as a example and to deter others who might be planning crimes or undertaking treasonable behaviour.

Bishop Fisher and Sir Thomas More

John Fisher had been made Bishop of Rochester in 1504. He had been a protégé of Margaret Beaufort, and had been involved in the intellectual development of humanism, inviting Erasmus to Cambridge. He has been regarded by some as the real author of the attack on Martin Luther for which Henry VIII was rewarded by the Pope. Fisher became the chief supporter of Catherine of Aragon and stated that he would be prepared to die rather than see the marriage dissolved. In 1532 he spoke openly against the divorce, and shortly after the secret marriage of Henry VIII and Anne Boleyn in January 1533 Fisher was arrested. In 1534 a Bill of Attainder was lodged against Fisher for his support of Elizabeth Barton. It was, however, his refusal to swear the Oath of Succession which led to his arrest for treason. As a commoner, the result of the Act of Attainder, Fisher was ordered to be hung, drawn and quartered at Tyburn. Only a public outcry against the barbarity of treating a bishop so resulted in his being beheaded in June 1535.

When Thomas More was appointed Chancellor by Henry VIII, Henry had promised him that he would not involve him in the negotiations with the

Cross-reference

To recap on **Acts of Attainder** see page 49.

Pope. As the actions of the Reformation parliament became both more political and more clearly against the Church, More found himself compromised by his position. On the day after the Submission of the Clergy More resigned his position as Chancellor. He hoped that he would be able to continue his support for the Catholic Church, but not have to comment publicly on the divorce or the break with Rome. This was to prove impossible.

On 1 June 1533 More was invited to attend the coronation of Anne Boleyn: he declined. Henry VIII did not forgive More for his failure to attend the ceremony and Thomas Cromwell sought an opportunity to destroy him publicly. More narrowly escaped being attainted for treason by those who tried to implicate him in the case of Elizabeth Barton. The Act of Succession and the required oath presented More's enemies with an opportunity to attack him. He was called to take the oath, and when he refused he was imprisoned in the Tower of London. More was perhaps the best legal mind in the country and he argued that he had not strictly broken the law, as he refused either to swear the oath or to speak out against it. Nevertheless, on 1 July 1535 More was tried for treason at Westminster. Evidence against him was given by Richard Rich, Solicitor-General, who treacherously stated that when he had visited More in his cell, More had spoken against the oath, stating that 'Parliament could not make the King Supreme Head of the Church'; More denied this but it was one man's word against another's. He lost his case and on 6 July he was beheaded. However, before he was taken from court he did speak his mind.

More's speech at his trial summed up the beliefs of those who opposed the actions of Henry VIII and the Reformation parliament:

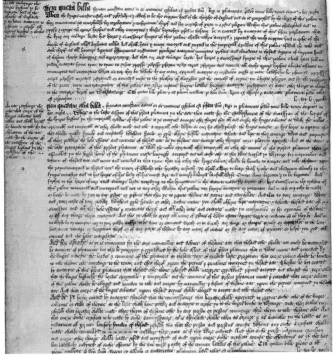

Fig. 8 *The Act of Attainder of Sir Thomas More, 1534*

> This Act of Parliament is directly against the laws of God and his Holy Church, the supreme government of which no prince, by any law, may take upon himself. These rights belong to the See of Rome, spiritual rights given by the mouth of our Saviour himself. These rights were given to St Peter and his successors, the Bishops of Rome. Christian men cannot be charged by a law which is against these rights.

5   *Thomas More (1535)*

> These honourable men stood in the way of a revolution; it is tragic but not surprising that they had to be removed, even if the law could only get to them by trickery. But no one need support the blood-lust displayed by the king, who resented opposition to his own will where Cromwell applied the dangerous but defensible principle of reason of state.

6   *Elton, G. R., **England under the Tudors**, 1956*

 Cross-reference

Richard Rich is profiled on page 129.

 Activity

Thinking and analysis

Use Source 5 and your own knowledge.

Why did Thomas More not oppose the earlier legislation but still refuse to take the oath?

Conclusion

The lack of direct opposition by the Church and the Pope to the acts of parliament which dismantled the historic relationship between England and Rome can be explained by a number of different factors. Although with hindsight it is clear that the break with Rome was to be permanent, at the time it was believed by many that the work of the Reformation Parliament would be reversed and that England would return to its previous relationship with Rome. Few people at the time thought that the legislation was irreversible. The initial intention had been to put pressure on the Pope to grant the annulment of the marriage to Catherine of Aragon. Once this had been achieved, many thought that reconciliation was still possible. The fact that Charles V had effective control of the Pope was a major stumbling block. The Pope had granted an annulment of the marriage of Francis I on more dubious grounds than that of Henry VIII and Catherine. Once the papacy was out of the control of Charles V it was believed that an agreement between England and Rome could be negotiated. Perhaps the main reason why the Pope was not able to put up effective opposition to what was happening in England was that the acts themselves, particularly the Act in Restraint of Appeals, removed any official means by which England could appeal to Rome and through which Rome could respond. It might be expected that the bishops in the House of Lords would state the case of Rome, but in the main they were the King's men, not the Pope's: they had been appointed by the King and were in the main loyal to him. The charge of praemunire against Wolsey would have further restricted their willingness to support the Pope.

> Henry was certainly a man who liked to keep his options open as long as possible. Even as late as 1534 he did not immediately give his royal assent to the Dispensations Act. This suggests that even at this late date he did not regard his break with the papacy as final and complete. The delay in activating the statute only makes sense if it was intended to be a means of applying pressure to Rome. There is no point in attempting to apply an authority which has been totally rejected.

7

*Smith, A. G. R., **The Emergence of a Nation State 1529–1660**, 1997*

(The Dispensations Act gave the Archbishop of Canterbury the authority to amend canon law.)

Learning outcomes

Through your study of this section you should have developed an understanding of why Henry VIII wanted to annul his marriage to Catherine of Aragon and how he went about this. You should also be able to explain why his failure to persuade the Pope led to parliamentary legislation creating a break with Rome and the creation of the Church of England. You should be aware of the change to the position of the King brought about by the Act of Supremacy and also the reasons why some opposed this. You will discover how Henry used these newly acquired powers after 1535 in the next section.

Cross-reference

The **charge of praemunire against Wolsey** is outlined on page 50.

Activity

Source analysis

Study Sources 6 and 7. How far do the views in Source 7 differ from those in Source 6 in relation to the intentions of Henry VIII with regard to royal supremacy?

Activity

Thinking point

The view of A. G. R. Smith given in Source 7 is not shared by all historians. For example, Professor Scarisbrick has argued that from an early stage of the annulment proceedings, perhaps as early as 1530, Henry had resolved on a fairly drastic redefinition of royal and papal authority. What evidence would you select to support the argument of each of the two historians' views?

Practice questions

(a)   Explain why so few people spoke out against the royal supremacy.   *(12 marks)*

In this answer you should supply a list of reasons and show the links between them.
Henry VIII was very clever in linking the oath to an act of treason. If people were openly hostile to
the royal supremacy they would have to forfeit their lives and livelihoods. Few people were prepared
to go that far.

- ▪ It is possible that some were silent because they believed that the steps taken by Henry and parliament
  would be short-lived and that once the immediate issue of an heir had been resolved England would
  return to papal obedience.
- ▪ Others were probably silent either because they were supporters of the new religious ideas, or because
  they would gain preferment through supporting what the King was doing.
- ▪ In your conclusion you may wish to point to the fact that there must have been large numbers of people
  who did not appreciate the wider significance of what was being suggested.

(b)   How far was the legislation that created the break with Rome motivated by
      a desire to reform the Church?   *(24 marks)*

In answering this question it is important to consider material supporting the premise – that is, the desire
for reform as the main motive, and other factors promoting the break with Rome.

- ▪ It could be suggested that there were those in parliament (and at court) who were influenced by the new
  learning and anxious to see the Church purified – and it was, of course, even better if power and money could
  remain in England.
- ▪ However, the legislation which created the break with Rome was motivated initially by the need to put
  pressure on the Pope and then to provide Henry with the means by which he had legitimate power to annul
  his marriage to Catherine of Aragon and marry Anne Boleyn. Without this legislation any children of this
  marriage would not be able to inherit.

The dissolution of the monasteries, 1535–41
The dissolution of the monasteries

Fig. 1 *The ruins of Fountains Abbey. Why might more of the church remain than the outlying buildings?*

In this chapter you will learn about:

- what the various motives were which inspired legislation against the monasteries

- the legislation to dissolve both the lesser and greater monasteries

- the way the dissolutions were carried out

- the part played by Thomas Cromwell in enforcing the dissolutions.

Consider the wealth and power of the great monastic houses:

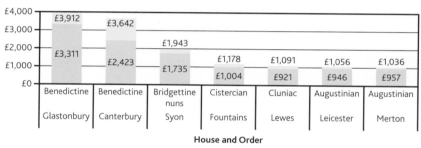

Fig. 2 *Relative wealth of some monastic orders at the time of the dissolution*

Between 1536 and 1541 much of this wealth was to find its way into the King's coffers. What had begun as a struggle to acquire a divorce was rapidly turning into a major overhaul of long-established institutions within the Church in England.

1

Knowles, D., **Bare Ruined Choirs,** *1959*

The motives behind the dissolutions

There are a variety of possible reasons why Henry chose to dissolve the monasteries – financial, religious, political and personal – and to some extent these are all interlinked. The most commonly held view is that it was the wealth of the monasteries that tempted Henry to act, for the revenue thus acquired would be sufficient to provide enough money to enable him never to need to raise taxes again. This leads to another, more political reason. If taxes were not needed, then parliament would not need to be called.

Activity

Thinking and analysis

As you read this section, try to decide which you believe was the main reason for Henry's decision to dissolve the monasteries. Was it for:

financial motives – for ordinary expenditure or extraordinary expenditure?

religious motives – including a desire to tackle corruption, attack superstition and idolatry, and instil new religious ideas?

political motives – confirming the break with Rome and establishing an independent nation state?

personal interests – not only on the part of the King but of other interested and influential individuals?

Financial motives

Ordinary expenditure

It is very clear that by the 1530s the crown was relatively poor. Henry VIII had spent the majority of his father's financial legacy on his attacks on France shortly after becoming king. In the 1520s his foreign policy had been mainly a peaceful and diplomatic one, particularly after the failure to secure the **Amicable Grant** in 1525.

By the 1530s Henry was finding it harder to meet the expenses of government. A monarch was expected to 'live of his own', that is to say he would need to find all the resources for government from his feudal dues. For Henry VIII this meant principally the revenue from crown lands. By the 1530s inflation was beginning to affect the revenue Henry was receiving from his own property. The Act for First Fruits and Tenths had been passed in 1534, bringing Henry £4,000 previously paid to Rome. This was made up of revenue from bishoprics and forced all the clergy to pay one-tenth of their income to the crown on an annual basis.

In 1534 the idea of confiscating all church lands was floated but abandoned. Cromwell did, however, suggest that a full valuation of church lands should take place in an attempt to place the taxation of the Church on a clear footing. This was one of the reasons behind the visitations organised by Cromwell: the visitors would assess the value of the monasteries and record the wealth of the property owned by the religious houses and their annual income. The *Valor Ecclesiasticus* was intended to list all the property owned by the Church in England and Wales, including the monasteries. It was completed in 1535 and showed that the annual income of the monasteries and convents was approximately £136,000 per year. This amount of money must have looked tempting to Henry VIII. It could make a significant difference to his ability to position himself as a European prince on a similar level to Francis I of France and the Holy Roman Emperor.

Extraordinary expenditure

While Henry VIII saw no conflict between the break with Rome and remaining a Catholic, such a view was not held by the two major

Key terms

Ordinary expenditure: money which was spent on the routine costs of government, personal items for the royal family, the upkeep of the royal household and the granting of gifts to supporters.

Extraordinary expenditure: money spent on waging war and defence.

Amicable Grant: in 1525 Henry VIII wanted to mount an invasion of France. For this he needed a large amount of money, which he did not have. There was no time to call parliament and a large grant had already been made the year before. A demand called the Amicable Grant was made based on a valuation of one-third of the goods of the clergy and one-sixth of the value of those of lay people. There was a massive demonstration in Suffolk and the tax was withdrawn.

Fig. 3 *Henry at the height of his power, depicted in the initial letter from the* Valor Ecclesiasticus, *the valuation of all monastic property in 1535*

Cross-reference

To recap on the **wealth of the monasteries**, see Chapter 1.

European powers and the Pope himself. Henry might see himself as being doctrinally Catholic, but his very actions in breaking with Rome made him clearly anti-papalist. It might be argued that Henry overestimated the threat from abroad, but there is no doubt that the Pope was keen to encourage both Charles V and Francis I to mount a military campaign against England. Such an attack might be delayed by the continuation of the disputes between the Habsburgs, headed by Charles V, and the house of Valois, headed by Francis I, over the control of Italian states. Nevertheless, the threat was there. Money acquired from an attack on the religious houses could be used by Henry VIII to construct the necessary defences to protect the south coast of England from a crusade instigated by the Pope to return England to the Catholic Church.

In the short term, while he was militarily weak, Henry was keen to maintain a state of isolated neutrality from what was happening in mainland Europe; his long-term ambitions, however, were to attack France, regain the French pension and re-establish the English claim to the territory lost in the reign of Henry VI. Henry VIII was, as had been demonstrated in his youth, committed to the idea that a monarch proved his worth on the battlefield. Money raised from the confiscation of monastic property could be used to finance an invasion of France.

Religious motives

Corruption of the monasteries

The attack on the monasteries can partly be seen as an attack on the doctrine of 'good works' as a means to salvation. Catholics believed that by doing good, or by giving money to the Church to do good works on their behalf, they would lessen their time in purgatory. Religious reformers did not believe in purgatory, so to them the attack on the monasteries could be seen as an attack on superstition. Injunctions drawn up by Cromwell in Henry's name in 1536 were intended to remove all superstition and forbade the monks to worship images, relics or miracles. Strict instructions were given against pilgrimages and praying to saints. People should not offer candles or money to images and

Cross-reference

Henry's foreign policy is outlined on page 107.

Activity

Research task

Work in groups. Each small group should use the English Heritage website to research the dissolution of an abbey. Consider the evidence for the abbey before the dissolution, the process of dissolution and what has happened since. Report back to the other groups, compare findings and identify similarities and differences.

Fig. 4 *A 13th century casket of elaborate metalwork which was made to contain relics of Thomas à Becket.*

relics of saints; only God, it was emphasised, could restore health and grant forgiveness. In 1538 the shrine of Thomas à Becket at Canterbury was destroyed by order of the government. This was one of the great pilgrimage centres of England. Similarly, the shrine of Our Lady of Doncaster was destroyed; in this case the statue of Mary was taken to London to be burned at Smithfield.

Consider the following sources:

Report on the Priory of Maiden Bradley

I send you a bag of relics, in which you will find: God's coat, Our Lady's smock. Part of God's supper and part of the stone manger in which was born Jesus of Bethlehem. The Prior is a holy father but has six children. He thanks God that he never meddled with married women, but all with maidens, the fairest that could be got, and always married them off right well.

2   *Dr Richard Layton, 24 August 1535*

Report on Godstow

I went to Godstow where I found all things well and in good order in the monastery and in the convent of the same, except that one sister 13 or 14 years ago, being then of another house, broke her chastity the which for correction and punishment afterwards was sent to Godstow, by the Bishop of Lincoln, where now and ever since that time she has lived virtuous.

3   *John Tregonwell, 27 September 1535*

Activity

Source analysis

What impression of the state of monasteries and convents in 1535 is conveyed by these two sources?

The public attack on the monasteries was an attack on the standards maintained by the monks and nuns. Elton argued that by the 16th century lay people had no respect for the monks because of their perceived behaviour and disrespect for their vows. The evidence provided by those who conducted the visitations, such as Richard Layton and John Tregonwell, was used to suggest that those living in religious houses were greedy, lazy, self-indulgent and, above anything else, engaged in a range of sexual relationships. Monks, it was stated, were in relationships with women and with other monks, and on numerous occasions had fathered children. Nuns were known, it was said, to have had children and not to have been punished for it. The monks and nuns were morally lax according to the visitations and were not fulfilling their vocations or their vows of chastity.

Key profile

Richard Layton

Layton was a relative of Robert Aske. He had studied at Cambridge and had been a colleague of Cromwell in Wolsey's service. By 1534 he was a clerk in the chancery courts and held a number of parishes which he staffed with ill-educated clerks. By 1539 he was Dean of York. He was known to be always keen to change his evidence to bring it into line with whatever Cromwell asked for. He used inquisitorial methods to get the evidence he wanted and was always telling bawdy stories.

More recent historians have challenged this dire picture of the religious houses. It has been argued that the visitations were flying visits, sometimes of only a few hours, and that much of the so-called evidence was fabricated. Nuns with children had not necessarily borne them after taking their vows, and it was common for widows to enter into a nunnery. This had certainly been the experience of Elizabeth Woodville, the grandmother of Henry VIII, who retired to an abbey after the death of her husband. Women such as Elizabeth Woodville had clearly already had children. Calculations have shown that there was one confession of homosexuality for every 30 monasteries visited, but even if all the accounts of sexual misconduct were actually true, it amounts to no more than a small proportion of all monks and nuns surveyed. Tudor monarchs had relied on the Observant Friars and influential members of the nobility had favoured the Carthusians. If these had been so corrupt, why had it only been discovered in a flying visit? Equally, the records suggest that in the stricter houses there were severe punishments for those who were unable to meet the high expectations of the order. At Mount Grace Priory there was a prison where Carthusians who rejected the discipline of the order were punished.

New religious ideas

Martin Luther, who was leading the development of religious ideas on the continent, had been a monk, and a number of those who argued against the continuation of the monastic orders had themselves been part of the system which they condemned. In 1521, Martin Luther had published *De votis monasticis* ('On the monastic vows'), a treatise which declared that the monastic life had no scriptural basis, was pointless and also actively immoral in that it was not compatible with the true spirit of Christianity. Such a view was a continuation of his attack on the clergy who believed that they were intermediaries between God and man. Luther also declared that monastic vows were meaningless and that no one should feel bound by them. These views had an immediate effect: a special meeting of German members of the Augustinian friars, of whom Luther was one, held during the same year, accepted them and voted that every member of the regular clergy should be free to renounce his vows, resign his offices and get married. Robert Barnes and William Tyndale were expressing the same views, but did not have such an impact on those who were members of religious orders.

Political motives

A key political reason for dissolving the monasteries must have been the need to break decisively from the power of Rome. The most forceful opposition to the break with Rome had been expressed through the religious houses. Those monks, and Elizabeth Barton, who had personally stated that Henry would not remain King if he married Anne Boleyn, had been brutally executed. While the majority of monks and nuns had not actively opposed the break with Rome, the presence of the abbots in the House of Lords offered an opportunity for resistance to further political changes. The religious houses had been asked to sign the oath of allegiance to both Henry and Anne and to recognise Henry as Supreme Head of the Church of England. They had been asked to deny the authority of the Pope and to agree not to pray for him, either publicly or privately. All the monasteries and the monks and nuns within them had been made to agree to this, which they did. However, it was uncertain how far they actually meant what they had agreed to. Anyone being asked to swear such allegiance knew what had happened to those who had refused to do so.

Cross-reference

To recap on **Martin Luther** and **William Tyndale**, see pages 31 and 33.

Cross-reference

To refresh your knowledge of **Elizabeth Barton** and the **Carthusian monks**, see pages 60 and 53.

N

North Sea

Holy Island
Alnwick
Newminster
Tynemouth
Carlisle
Jarrow • Wearmouth
Holme
Cultram
Durham
Bishop
Auckland
Shap
Mount Grace
Jervaulx • Rievaulx
Byland
Furness
Fountains • Ripon
Kirkham
Bridlington
Gisburn
York
Whalley
Beverley
Meaux
Kirkstall
Selby
Kingston-upon-Hull
Pontefract
Monk
Bretton
Epworth
Newsham
Manchester
Roche
Welbeck
Lincoln
Penmon
St Asaph • Basingwerk
Rufford
Bardney
Bangor
Maenon
Vale Royal
Southwell
Revesby
Chester
Dieulacres
Kirkstead
Valle Crucis
Beauvale
Tattershall
Combermere
Lenton
Swineshead
Tutbury
Garendon
Spalding
Walsingham
Cymmor
Shrewsbury
Burton-
on-Trent
Crowland
Castle
Acre
Horsham
Holme
St Benet
Strata
Marcella
Lichfield
Leicester
Thorney
Peterborough
Wymondham
Norwich
Wenlock
Merevale
Fotheringay
Thetford
Mettingham
Strata
Florida
Cwmhir
Bordesley
Coventry
Pipewell
Ramsey
Ely
Ixworth
Eye
Sibton
Stoneleigh
Combe
Higham
Leominster
Worcester
Warwick
Ferrers
St Neots
Bury St Edmunds
St Dogmells
Pershore
Northampton
Cambridge
Hereford
Gt.
Malvern
Evesham
Elstow
Warden
Stoke-by-Clare
St Davids
Brecknock
Tewkesbury
Hailes
Winchcombe
Woburn
Walden
Earls
Colne
Colchester
Caermarthen
Abergavenny
Gloucester
Notley
Tilty
Coggeshall
Neath
Tintern
Cirencester
Eynsham
Rewley
Thame
St Albans
Waltham
Prittlewell
Margam
Kingswood
Abingdon
Dorchester
Westminster
Barking
Langthorne
Llandaff
Malmesbury
Eton
Windsor
London
Stratford
Westbury
Bath
Stanley
Reading
Chertsey
Sheen
Rochester
Canterbury
Henton
Wells
Monkton Farleigh
Waverley
Malling
Baxley
Faversham
Cleeve
Witham
Wherwell
Maidstone
Glastonbury
Amesbury
Dover
Athelney
Muchelney
Wilton
Salisbury
Winchester
Robertsbridge
Dunkeswell
Montacute
Ramsey
Lewes
Battle
Crediton
Ford
Shaftesbury
Beaulieu
Chichester
Arundel
Ottery St Mary
Sherborne
Tarrant
Exeter
Cerne
Milton Abbas
Quarr
Polsloe
Newenham
Abbotsbury
Bodmin
Tavistock
Buckland
Buckfastleigh
Penryn

Key
■ Cathedral church
• Monastery

0   50 km

Fig. 5 *Distribution of monasteries*

Cross-reference

Cardinal Reginald Pole is profiled on page 111.

Key term

Royal minority: when the heir to the throne is not of an age to assume full powers of government. Eighteen was the age deemed appropriate, although Henry VIII was a few months short of this in 1509 when his father died.

Fig. 6 *Jane Seymour (1508–37). In what ways does the image of Jane differ from that of Anne Boleyn?*

Allied to breaking the power of the Roman Church was the importance of establishing an independent nation state. Henry VIII and Cromwell would be aware not only of the potential allegiance to the Pope, an external power, but also that the centres of the monastic orders, of which those in England were settlements, were located in mainland Europe: over these Henry had no control. The dissolution of the monasteries was therefore also motivated by the changes which led to the formal establishment of an English nation state. If the monasteries were dissolved, the separation of church and state which had begun with the confirmation of Henry VIII as Supreme Head of the Church would be complete.

Personal motives

Just as Henry was unable to finance his military ambitions, so he was also unable to underwrite an extensive system of patronage. Keeping the support of the nobility and preventing potential challenges to the authority of the monarchy were particularly critical. Henry VIII was in his forties, his only son was an infant and there were still descendants of Yorkist kings alive whose claims were as good as his. One such person was in fact a leading Catholic, Reginald Pole, who worked with the Vatican and was the grandson of Edward IV's younger brother, the Duke of Clarence. The spectre of a **royal minority**, should Henry die before his son Edward reached adulthood, was almost as serious as the threat of dying with only a female heir. It was important for Henry to tie members of the ruling classes to support for the continuation of the Tudor dynasty.

A closer look

Jane Seymour and Prince Edward

Jane Seymour (1508–37) was Henry VIII's third wife and the mother of his only son. Like Anne Boleyn she was the daughter of an English gentry family with connections to the nobility; in Jane's case her father was Sir John Seymour of Wiltshire. Also like Anne Boleyn she began her career at court as Lady in Waiting to the Queen. But unlike Anne, she was quiet and deferred to Henry; and unlike both Catherine and Anne, Jane was not well educated. She was not a supporter of new religious ideas, although she was very much aware that she should follow the King in everything including her religion. It is very likely that it was these qualities which attracted Henry VIII to Jane. Henry had begun courting Jane before Anne's death; the evidence suggests that this began in February 1536. On 20 May 1536, the day after Anne's execution, Henry was betrothed to Jane, and married her 10 days later. While she was not crowned, unlike the two previous queens, Jane did produce a male heir, Edward, who was born on 12 October 1537. Jane went to his christening on 15 October but died from puerperal fever nine days later. Henry VIII mourned the death of Jane Seymour, who was to him the ideal wife: not only was she subservient and beautiful, but unlike any of his other queens, she had borne him a son. While the Tudor dynasty was not fully secure he had, at last, a legitimate male heir.

The break with Rome had gained the support of members of the nobility in the House of Lords. The dissolution of the monasteries was even more attractive to this group, and would be still more acceptable if they could be convinced of the corruption of the monasteries. It is clear that members of the gentry and the nobility were keen to benefit from the crown's acquisition of monastic property which would follow from the dissolution. Cromwell did put into place systems to augment the crown's income, but it was not possible for the crown to administer all the property which it would acquire. Opportunities would exist for the nobility and gentry to gain more property and with it more power and influence in their localities. This patronage from the King would bring both economic and political benefits. There were clear reasons why the Act for the Dissolution of the Smaller Monasteries in 1536 gained the support of the members of the Commons and Lords.

 Activity

Group task

Having considered the various reasons for the dissolution of the monasteries, list them in order of importance. Present and justify your views to the rest of your group. You could design a class diagram to illustrate the reasons.

The enforcement of the dissolutions

A closer look

Roland Blyton, abbot of Rievaulx

Blyton had been a Cistercian monk and then abbot of Rufford, a monastery in Nottinghamshire which was a daughter settlement of the larger abbey of Rievaulx. The Cistercians had been founded in 1089 and had focused on a return to primitive monasticism. They intended to uphold the Rule of St Benedict with its emphasis on manual work and a strict order of prayer and praise. Blyton was elected to the abbacy of the mother house of Rievaulx in Yorkshire in 1533. The circumstances in which this took place were rather controversial. The former abbot had been investigated by royal commissioners on allegations of misconduct and had had to resign. As abbot, Blyton seems to have benefited from the relaxation which the Cistercians had experienced in diet and necessity of manual work. As the monasteries had grown in wealth, abbots and monks who had come from aristocratic families believed that they should share some of the comforts of this wealth. Blyton, more than many abbots, who had their own separate lodgings, enjoyed an aristocratic lifestyle. According to one contemporary the abbot and six or eight of his community would frequently arrive at manors which belonged to the abbey for hunting and hawking, both sports that were the preserve of wealthy landowners. Blyton surrendered Rievaulx Abbey to the royal commissioners in December 1538 and he, like all the community, was given dispensation to hold a living. He seemingly retired to land previously belonging to the abbey, and received a handsome pension.

The process that led to the dissolution of the monasteries began with the appointment of Thomas Cromwell as the King's vicegerent. He was the person responsible for the day-to-day control of the Church. Cromwell introduced a programme of visitations of the monasteries in 1535 which was similar to the method of checking religious houses which had been carried out under the Catholic Church. This was quickly followed up with the compilation of the *Valor Ecclesiasticus*, which endeavoured to list the property owned by the Church in England and Wales including the monasteries. While the *Valor Ecclesiasticus* may have been primarily intended to assess property for taxation purposes, the answers to the questions which the visitors secured provided the evidence which could be used against the religious houses and so enable the King to acquire their property.

In March 1536 an act was passed by parliament for the dissolution of the smaller monasteries.

> For as much as manifest sin, vicious, carnal and abominable living is daily used and committed among the little and small abbeys, priories and other religious houses of monks, canons and nuns, where the congregation of such religious persons is under the number of twelve persons ... spoil, destroy, consume and utterly waste their goods ... to the high displeasure of Almighty God and to the infamy of the King's Highness.

4　　　　　　　　　*From the Act for the Dissolution of the Lesser Monasteries, 1536*

Three hundred religious houses were deemed to have an income of less than £200 per year. The 1536 Act was not presented as an attack on monasticism, as the members of the religious houses to be dissolved were offered the opportunity to transfer to larger establishments. Significantly, the act gave the King the power to exempt houses as he saw fit. In fact 67 religious houses of the 300 were exempted, for reasons which are obscure. They may have had redeeming features, or possibly paid bribes for the privilege.

Once the act received royal assent it was important to stop the monasteries' movable wealth disappearing out of the country. Commissioners acted quickly: inmates were expelled and all valuable goods, especially gold, silver, jewels, lead from the roofs and bronze from the bells were sent to the Tower of London. In many places local people were quick to join in the plunder, particularly of dressed stone which could be used for building materials. In the north of England the behaviour of the commissioners sent to confiscate property was a key factor in triggering the Pilgrimage of Grace.

Cross-reference

The **Lincolnshire Rising** and the **Pilgrimage of Grace** are discussed in Chapter 6.

Acts of Attainder are explained on page 49.

The Lincolnshire Rising and the rebellion known as the Pilgrimage of Grace were a direct response to the decision to dissolve the smaller monasteries. Whalley Abbey in Lancashire was one that became directly involved. While the Pilgrimage of Grace continued, both Henry VIII and Cromwell were reluctant to take any further action. Indeed the demand for the restoration of the smaller houses by the rebels seemed to be sufficient to persuade Henry to restore some of those affected.

Once the Pilgrimage of Grace and its leaders had been defeated, however, the houses in the north of England were punished severely. The abbots of the houses involved were declared to be traitors and in some cases Acts of Attainder were brought. The Acts of Attainder allowed not only for the abbots to be executed, but for all the property of their monasteries to be confiscated by the King. Where individual monks were not punished for their involvement in the rebellion they were forced out.

It is debatable whether it was the relative success of the dissolution of the smaller monasteries, the wealth the King had been able to acquire, or the involvement of monasteries in the Pilgrimage of Grace, which encouraged the King and Cromwell to take the next step in ending monastic life in England permanently. Whatever the reason for bringing to an end the existence of all religious houses, large as well as small, by 1540 all had been dissolved. The final assault was achieved through a combination of persuasion (commissioners persuading abbots to 'surrender' their monasteries), bribery, bullying and an act of parliament.

> I, Robert, abbot of the monastery of Furness, knowing the misorder and evil life both unto God and our Prince, do freely and wholly surrender, give and grant unto the King's Highness ... all such interest and title as I have in the said monastery of Furness, and in the lands, rents, possessions, revenues, services and in all goods and chattels all other things belonging to the said monastery.
>
> Signed in the presence of The Earl of Sussex, the King's Lieutenant in this county of Lancaster, Sir Thomas Butler, Sir William Leyland, Sir John Beron and Sir Anthony Fitzherbert.

5   *From the surrender deed of Furness Abbey, 1537*

In 1539 an act of parliament was passed which legalised the voluntary surrender of monastic property to the King. In fact voluntary surrendering had begun the previous year, when commissioners visited the religious houses and offered abbots the incentives of large pensions on behalf of the King to those who signed over their possessions. The commissioners' persuasive powers, or threats, achieved a great deal, but not all abbots and their communities were prepared to do the King's bidding. Most notable were the abbots of Colchester, Reading and Glastonbury. In these cases evidence was planted against the abbots to suggest treasonable behaviour and theft.

By such behaviour, in the space of four years the 800 religious houses in England were closed. The abbots and monks may have been simply frightened into surrendering. Some were bought off with large pensions or rewarded in some other way, perhaps with the provision of positions, such as working as a chantry priest. Only the nuns were thrown back on their families, with small amounts of money and a requirement to uphold their vow of chastity, while the lay brothers were forced to find work where they could.

Activity

Pairs task

Both of you are abbots. One of you should list the reasons why you would be prepared to surrender your monastery, and the other the reasons why you would be prepared to defy the pressure of the commissioners.

Fig. 7 *A record of land held by Roche Abbey at nearby Conisbrough. This land was taken by the King at the dissolution of the abbey*

■ A closer look

The destruction of Roche Abbey

Michael Sherbrook was a priest in a parish close to Roche Abbey; as a child he witnessed the destruction of the abbey and was also able to speak to his father about the events.

An uncle of mine was present at the breaking up of the abbey. When the community was evicted from the abbey, one of the monks told him that each monk had been given his cell where he slept, wherein there was nothing of value save his bed and clothing, which was simple and of little worth. This monk urged my uncle to buy something from him; the monk asked him for two pennies for his cell door, which was worth over five shillings; my uncle refused, as he had no idea what he would do with a door. Others who came along later to buy the monks' corn or hay found that all the doors were open, and the locks plucked off, or the door itself removed; they entered and stole what they liked.

Some took the service-books that were in the church; some took windows from the hay barn and hid them in the hay, and did the same with other things – but did not buy them – when the yeomen and gentlemen of the country had bought the timber of the church.

For the church was the first thing that was spoiled; then the abbot's lodging, the dormitory and refectory, with the cloister and all the buildings around, within the abbey walls. For nothing was spared except the ox-houses and pig-styes and other such houses or offices that stood outside the walls. This was done on the instruction of Cromwell. It would have pitied any heart to see the tearing up of the lead, the plucking up of boards and throwing down of the rafters. And when the lead was torn off and cast down into the church and the tombs in the church were all broken and all things of value were spoiled, plucked away or utterly defaced, the seats in the choir where the monks sat when they said service were burned and the lead melted, although there was plenty of wood nearby, for the abbey stood among the woods. It seemed that every person was intent upon filching and spoiling what he could. Even those who had been content to permit the monks' worship and do great reverence at their services two days previously were no less happy to pilfer.

For the better proof of this, thirty years after the Suppression I asked my father, who had bought part of the timber of the church, I said, then how did it come to pass that you were so ready to destroy and spoil the thing that you thought so well of? What should I have done, he asked, might not I as well as the others have had some profit from the spoils of the abbey? For I saw that everything would disappear and therefore I did as the others did.

| 6 | *www.cistercians.shef.ac.uk/roche/history/spoilation/sherbrook.php* |

■ Activity

Challenging your thinking

Use the account of Michael Sherbrook. From what you have read, how would you explain popular reaction to the dissolution? Do you think that the action of both rich and poor suggests a rejection of Catholic beliefs?

As a result of the dissolution of the monasteries it was necessary to change the makeup of the House of Lords to reflect the disappearance of abbots and priors, some of whom had played a significant political role as members of the House of Lords. As the buildings and organisation of the Church were now under the control of the Church of England, of which Henry was head, representation needed to go to the leaders of the Church of England. The abbeys and abbots had played a significant role in the spiritual lives of the people. Following the break with Rome and the dissolution of the monasteries, Henry was responsible for the souls, as well as the lives and property, of his subjects. To ensure that this responsibility was carried out Henry created a number of new bishoprics, the majority of which were on the sites of former abbeys. The new bishops replaced the abbots in their political role and sat in the House of Lords. (Wolsey had already planned diocesan reform in 1528–9 and significant parts of his plans were revived in 1540.)

The role of Thomas Cromwell

Thomas Cromwell played a great part in the whole process of the dissolution of the monasteries; however, it is important to remember, as Cromwell did, that he was the servant of Henry VIII. Indeed, to begin with it seemed that Cromwell was following in the footsteps of Cardinal Wolsey as Henry VIII's chief minister. Yet there were significant differences: while Wolsey had been Henry's principal minister, he had been responsible for the dissolution of 29 small religious houses. All of those religious houses suppressed by Wolsey had been in decline and the money recovered from the sale of their property was used to fund his educational foundations in Ipswich and Oxford. Thomas Cromwell seems to have had very different objectives: to raise money, to gain the support of members of the nobility for the continued break with Rome and to pursue a religious policy intent on destroying superstition and what he regarded as unacceptable Catholic practices.

Cromwell, in his role as vicegerent, worked with Henry VIII to plan the organisation of the Church of England and its finances once the break with Rome had taken place. The position taken by Cromwell from early on seems to have been to challenge the existence of the monasteries. The choice of the people who conducted the visitations was Cromwell's, the questions asked at the visitations were Cromwell's and it is likely that the timescale of visitations was also his. Henry VIII trusted Thomas Cromwell; he believed that Cromwell was acting in his own best interests.

It is not clear whether either Henry VIII or Cromwell envisaged that the whole of the dissolution would happen at such a rapid pace. At the time it would have been difficult to justify what seemed to be the case – that only the religious houses which were small and worth less than £200 per year were corrupt. It is possible that Cromwell was testing the support for an attack on the monasteries with this first act: if this met with no opposition then the attack on the large monasteries would follow; but equally there are grounds for thinking that the dissolution never followed a master plan but was a haphazard response to events.

Real skill and talent were shown by Cromwell in establishing the structures to facilitate the transfer of the property of the Church to the King. His overall transformation of the bureaucracy of the state will be dealt with in a later chapter, but a number of departments were established principally to administer the property that had belonged to the monasteries. The Court of Augmentations (augmentation meaning 'adding to') was set up by act of parliament in 1536: this was specifically to deal with the growth of the King's revenue as a result of the transfer of property to the crown.

Key chronology

Membership of the House of Lords

1529 Summons to parliament were issued to:

51 lay peers

49 spiritual peers (20 bishops, 29 abbots and priors)

1540 Approximate membership (numbers of lay peers necessarily fluctuated a little because of deaths):

50 lay peers

20 bishops

1540–2 Henry created six new bishoprics (Bristol, Westminster, Oxford, Chester, Peterborough and Gloucester)

Cross-reference

For a profile for **Thomas Cromwell**, see page 49.

Cardinal Wolsey's actions are outlined in the Introduction.

Cross-reference

Cromwell's transformation of the government is detailed in Chapter 7.

Justices of the peace: these were members of the gentry and large landowners appointed by the King to be responsible for the justice system in the localities. The position was unpaid and they were frequently placed under pressure from those higher up the social ladder in their attempt to secure impartial trials and appropriate convictions.

Perhaps Cromwell's greatest skill in achieving the dissolution of the monasteries was in dealing with local opposition. Evidence from local archives has suggested that there was a great deal of grumbling even where people were unwilling to take direct action. Cromwell saw to it that **justices of the peace** and private informers kept him up to date with the activities of dissidents. Each of these cases was considered and where the actions of the objectors were deemed to have broken the law then these people were tried and punished. About 65 people were executed as a result of the general grumblings against religious change. This was a small number for what was such a momentous change.

> The dissolution destroyed the last possible refuge of Papalism, enriched the crown, and anchored the new order firmly in the self-interest of the land-owning classes who purchased the estates. It did all this with the thoroughness and amazing ease which characterised all Cromwell's achievements.

7   *Elton, G. R., **England under the Tudors**, 1956*

The dissolution of the monasteries, which took place between 1536 and 1540, irrevocably destroyed an established part of English life. The monasteries had provided a focus of spiritual, literary and educational activities; they were key to the economic and social life of the country and some had held political power too. In four years these functions were removed; in four years the wealth of the monasteries was redistributed; in four years the art and the cultural inheritance of these institutions and many of their magnificent buildings were ruined. Yet for some contemporaries and subsequent historians, this was regarded as progress. To these people the dissolution of the monasteries represented the removal of corruption, superstition and the interference of external powers in the concerns of England. However, the view that the dissolution was motivated by religious considerations is held by only a minority today. Richard Hoyle, for example, has argued that the dissolution was little more than a political move intended to consolidate the power of Henry VIII in England and to provide him with a war chest with which to attack France.

Summary question

Explain why Thomas Cromwell carried through the dissolution of the monasteries.

6

Popular reaction and the impact of the dissolutions

In this chapter you will learn about:

■ what happened in the Lincolnshire Rising and the Pilgrimage of Grace

■ why the disturbances occurred in 1536 and who was involved

■ how the government of Henry VIII responded to the events of 1536

■ how far the concerns of the Pilgrims were met by the end of Henry VIII's reign

■ the impact of the dissolutions on society, culture and the Church.

In 1536 it seemed as though the actions of the Henrician government had gone too far, as the dissolutions were met with an outburst of protest firstly in Lincolnshire and then in Yorkshire.

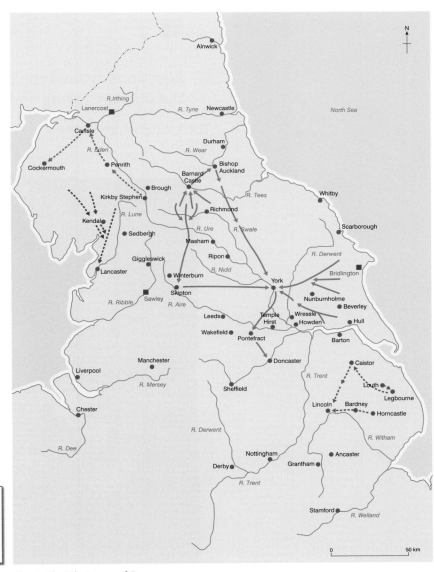

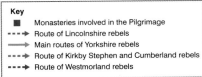

Key

■ Monasteries involved in the Pilgrimage
╌╌➤ Route of Lincolnshire rebels
──➤ Main routes of Yorkshire rebels
╌╌➤ Route of Kirkby Stephen and Cumberland rebels
╌╌➤ Route of Westmorland rebels

Fig. 1 *The Pilgrimage of Grace*

Geoffrey Moorhouse's book *The Pilgrimage of Grace* was published in 2002. It argued that the aims of the Pilgrims were more ambitious than had been suggested by other historians:

> There can be little doubt that if the 30,000 rebels had crossed the river Don they would have smashed their way through the King's men. And if the Pilgrims had succeeded in their enterprise, to the extent of toppling Henry VIII or obtaining his lasting compliance, the course of English history would certainly have been changed.

1

*Moorhouse, G., **The Pilgrimage of Grace**, 2002*

Reactions against the dissolutions: the Lincolnshire Rising and the Pilgrimage of Grace

The Lincolnshire Rising

Fig. 2 *The banner carried before the Pilgrimage of Grace. It displays the Badge of the Five Wounds of Christ – the four nail wounds and the spear wound in Christ's side, which were believed to have been inflicted when Christ was crucified. How do the symbols reinforce loyalty to the Church of Rome? (The banner is now the property of the Dukes of Norfolk)*

The Act for the Dissolution of the Lesser Monasteries, which was passed in 1536, required commissioners to visit each area of the country to enquire into the suitability of monks and to assess the value of the monastic holdings. Such visitations were going to be unpopular as they challenged institutions which were valued and revered both for their religious roles and also for their social and economic importance in the localities. In the absence of solid information, and in an atmosphere of panic and alarm, rumours as to what was to happen gained credence. While rumours circulated through much of the Midlands without any action being taken, they resulted in riots in Lincolnshire. Concerns were raised about the confiscation of church property and the disappearance of treasures such as processional crosses, and there were even reports of the pulling down of parish churches. In an age when news was spread by word of mouth, few people questioned the truth of all the allegations.

Nicholas Melton, a shoemaker nicknamed 'Captain Cobbler', led the rising. He encouraged a hard core of 20 men including five other shoemakers, two weavers, two sawyers, a blacksmith and three labourers to band together in order to seize the representative of the Bishop of Lincoln and the royal commissioners who were at work in the area – some collecting taxes and others dissolving monasteries. A reported crowd of 3,000 men advanced from Louth to Caistor on 3 October to capture the commissioners. Gathering support from Horncastle, 10,000 marched to Lincoln, the county town and, more significantly, the religious centre of the region. There, on 4 October, the crowd attacked a leading official of the Bishop of Lincoln and murdered him. In a symbolic gesture, his money and clothes were divided among the crowd.

The army of the King under the leadership of the Duke of Suffolk was dispatched to Lincoln with the King's response to the rebels' demands. Although Suffolk did not arrive until the rebellion was over, the message was unambiguous: there was to be no negotiation; the action that had been taken was **treasonable**. This was sufficient for the gentry, who decided to sue for pardon and encouraged the common people to disperse. There was great reluctance to follow this advice and there was serious unrest in the area for 12 days. Significantly, on their return to Horncastle the people who had been involved in the rising placed a banner in the parish church, which demonstrated that they had fought in Christ's name; it proclaimed the five wounds of Christ.

> ■ Key term
>
> **Treason:** a crime in which a challenge is made to the authority, or person, of the monarch, and which is punishable by death.

M. E. James has written that the gentry played a significant role in the organisation of the rising:

> It seems that the Lincolnshire movement originated less in tensions within the society than in fears of invasion from abroad. The common people were 'more easily roused by the prospect of plunder of parochial treasures than invasion by an alien religion' and, most contentiously, the gentry who rose together in opposition to royal policy.

2   *James, M. E., 'Obedience and Dissent in Henrician England: The Lincolnshire Rebellion 1536'*, **Past and Present**, *48, 1970*

The Pilgrimage of Grace

The activities of the rebels in Lincolnshire had escalated rapidly from the first expression of discontent by the people in Louth. Elsewhere in Yorkshire, Northumberland, Durham and Cumberland, concern about the policies of the King's government was also being expressed and acted upon. In common with those in Lincolnshire, men in the north voiced their concerns about the challenges to religion; like them they marched

The Lincoln Articles, 9th October 1536

1. An end to the suppression of so many religious houses ... the suppression is a great hurt to the commonwealth ...
2. That the act of uses may be suppressed because by this act we, your true subjects, are restricted in the declaration of our wills concerning our lands
3. The tax on sheep and cattle is an excessive charge on people considering the poverty that they be in already and the loss which they have sustained these two years past.
4. That your Grace takes of your counsel from persons as be of low birth and small reputation who have taken the profits for their own advantage, most notably the lord Cromwell and Sir Richard Riche ...
5. We are grieved that there are bishops in England who have been promoted that do not have ... the faith of Christ. These are the Bishop of Canterbury, the Bishop of Rochester, the Bishop of Worcester, the Bishop of Salisbury, the Bishop of Saint David, and the Bishop of Dublin, and especially the Bishop of Lincoln.

Cross-reference

Richard Rich is profiled on page 129.

The Pontefract Articles, December 1536

1. To end the heresies within this realm
2. To have the Pope as the Supreme Head of the Church of England
3. To have the Lady Mary made legitimate
4. To have the abbeys restored
5. To have the Observant friars restored
6. To have the heretics punished by fire
7. To have Lord Cromwell, the Lord Chancellor, receive punishment

Activity

Source analysis

Using Fig. 2, Source 2, the Lincoln Articles and your own knowledge, decide how far the Lincolnshire Rising was the result of the commons protesting against challenges to their religious beliefs.

Fig. 3 *The Lincoln and Pontefract Articles*

under the banner of the five wounds of Christ, and the separate risings, of which there were nine, were known as the hosts. The clear leader of what was to become 'The Pilgrimage of Grace for the Commonwealth' was Robert Aske, a successful lawyer who had received his legal training at the Inns of Court in London. He proved capable of organising companies of armed men and training them, and was sufficiently astute to organise the range of different concerns into a series of demands which everyone could agree with.

A number of key features set these disturbances apart from other riots of the time:

1 the scale of the rising
2 the attack on those carrying out the King's wishes in his role as Supreme Head of the Church
3 the list of demands raised by the rebels and sent to the King
4 the fact that the risings were led and/or organised by the very people on whom the King relied to ensure peace and law and order. The leadership of the commons was assumed by the gentry and in some cases the aristocracy.

Key profile

Robert Aske

Robert Aske (1500–37) was the younger son of a gentry family who lived in North Yorkshire. The family was well connected: one of his cousins was Henry Clifford, the Earl of Cumberland. Aske trained as a lawyer, and was a fellow at Gray's Inn. He was very devout and objected to Henry's religious reforms, particularly the dissolution of the monasteries. When rebellion broke out, Aske was returning to London from Yorkshire. He was not involved in the Lincolnshire Rising, but he took up the causes of people in his area and headed the Pilgrimage of Grace. He claimed to have been coerced but clearly sympathised with and articulated the grievances of the common people. By 10 October he had come to be regarded as their 'chief captain'. Aske was executed on a charge of treason in 1537.

Exploring the detail

The hosts

The hosts was the name given to the bands of people within the Pilgrimage of Grace, in a reference to the wafer given at Mass which became the body of Christ and was known as 'the Host'. There were nine hosts in the north of England: the host led by the lawyer William Stapaulton from Beverley; that led by Aske from Howden; the 5,000 men led by Sir Thomas Percy from Northumberland; that led by lawyer Robert Bowes from Richmond; the Hamerton host, raised to defend Sawley Abbey; the Tempest Host which besieged Skipton Castle; the Richmondshire host; the Atkinson host from Cumbria; and that led by minor gentlemen from Westmorland.

Fig. 4 *Pontefract Castle, painted in the mid-17th century. What does the painting suggest to confirm the importance of control of this castle?*

On 16 October 10,000 supporters of the Pilgrimage led by Aske entered York. The rebellion spread through the East Riding, Durham, Cumberland and Westmorland. At Penrith, four captains were chosen to lead the pilgrims, and took the names Charity, Faith, Poverty and Pity. Despite the emphasis placed by Aske on the peaceful intentions of those involved, the action taken challenged the established systems of law and order. Henry VIII was dependent on the authority and military might of the nobility locally. The Earl of Cumberland was held captive in Skipton Castle during a week-long siege; Barnard Castle yielded to the pilgrims; and, most significantly, Lord Darcy, who held Pontefract Castle, known as the key to the north, ceded it to the rebels. By late October, with the exception of a few isolated areas, the rebels, numbering 30,000, had control of the area north of central Lancashire and the river Don in Yorkshire. Most importantly, Aske had secured the support or at least the acknowledgement of key establishment figures; not only Lord Darcy, but the Archbishop of York and 40 knights and gentlemen. Together they were united in opposing the advice which the King had been given to dissolve the monasteries.

Key profile

Lord Darcy

Lord Darcy was born about 1467 and by the time of the Pilgrimage of Grace he was old and infirm. He had gained the attention of Henry VIII for his prowess on the battlefield, and had signed the collective petition to the Pope asking for the annulment of the King's marriage. He had long been in charge of Pontefract Castle, one of the most important fortresses in the north of England. Despite appeals for clemency on the grounds of his infirmity, he was convicted of high treason on the charge of delivering up Pontefract Castle to the rebels, and was beheaded on Tower Hill on 30 June 1537. Because he had been attainted, all his honours were forfeited.

The government of Henry VIII may have initially underestimated the scale of the challenge in the north of England. This may partially be explained by difficulties of communication, but for three weeks, while the Duke of Suffolk was occupied in Lincolnshire and the Earl of Shrewsbury awaited orders in Nottingham, the rising was able to proceed unimpeded. The Duke of Norfolk, who had the largest private army in the country, was sent by Henry to disperse the pilgrims massed at Doncaster. The 8,000 men commanded by Norfolk were fully trained. Norfolk had played a central role in the battle of Flodden against the Scots in 1513, when the ratio of English to Scottish troops had been similar to that which he now faced across the Don; but rather than attack the rebels, fearing defeat, he decided to negotiate with them.

Key profile

Thomas Howard, Duke of Norfolk

Thomas Howard (1473–1554), third Duke of Norfolk, fought for Henry VIII at the battle of Flodden in 1513 and became Lord Lieutenant of Ireland. He was instrumental in the defeat of the Pilgrimage of Grace and the downfall of Thomas Cromwell. He later fought for Henry in the war against the Scots in 1544. He was imprisoned on a charge of treason but escaped execution because of Henry's death.

The meeting, which took place on St Mary's Bridge at Doncaster on 27 October 1536, was not documented, but the agreement was clear. A truce would be called while the petition of the Pilgrims was taken to London. There is little doubt that Norfolk played for time. The Pilgrims, on the other hand, would have been very aware not only of Norfolk's military prowess, but also of his earlier success in achieving a negotiated settlement. On that occasion, in 1525, he had persuaded Henry of the rightness of the demands of those who had refused to pay the Amicable Grant, and had secured both significant concessions and a pardon for them. Norfolk's representatives returned from London carrying the King's request for greater clarification of the Pilgrims' demands. Aske and the key figures of the Pilgrimage reviewed the demands to present to Henry. On 6 December a bargain was struck at Doncaster. The rebels were assured that Norfolk would act as a suitor to the King to request that a parliament be held to discuss the demands, and that a free pardon would be granted to all those who had taken part in the rising. It was also agreed that until parliament met, abbeys would continue to stand and the dissolutions be suspended. While Aske had to convince the rebels of the sincerity of the promises, there is little doubt that he believed that they had won and that the forthcoming parliament would reverse much of what had been done in recent years. Robert Aske had been invited to court to discuss the petition further, and the Pilgrims could return home confident that their concerns would be discussed and resolved.

> Given the combination of protest from a wide geographical spectrum of northern society, it is easy to see why the Pilgrimage could have been fatal for Henry's government: it came perilously close to succeeding, and was the largest popular revolt in English History. If more leading noblemen in the north had backed it, all would have been lost for those attempting to reform religion around Cromwell in London.

3   *MacCulloch, D. and Fletcher, A.,* **Tudor Rebellions**, *2004*

Fig. 5 *A Victorian engraving of the Pilgrimage of Grace*

Cross-reference

The **Amicable Grant** is outlined on page 65.

Activity

Pairs task

Make a list of the reasons why a member of the commons would be prepared to leave his or her village and choose to go and camp outside Doncaster in support of the Pilgrimage.

Activity

Research task

Try to find a monastery near where you live which was dissolved in 1536 or after. What was the outcome of the dissolution in your area? Alternatively you could use the website of English Heritage to find out more.

Activity

Thinking point

Explain how far the demands of the Pontefract Articles differ from those put by the rebels at Lincoln. How might you account for the differences?

Motives behind the Pilgrimage of Grace

The reasons why people rose in both Lincolnshire and the north have caused much debate among historians. For example, Michael Bush argued that it was about taxation, whereas Geoffrey Elton viewed it as a religious rising and a revolt of the aristocracy associated with Catherine of Aragon. Richard Hoyle has focused far more on economic causes, namely that there were different interest groups and individual concerns in separate areas of the country which also changed over the period of the rebellion. As with many other risings, it is important to be aware not only of the individual concerns of different geographical and social groups, but also of what issues they had in common and those on which they were prepared to agree. In broad terms historians have considered religious, social and economic, and political causes. They have also examined long-term concerns and short-term trigger factors. Key to understanding the rebellions has also been the question as to whether they were spontaneous uprisings of the commons or planned by a small but influential faction of the nobility or gentry.

Religious motives

Both in the Lincoln Articles and in those which were agreed at Pontefract, the main issue, which formed the principal demands, concerned religion. This was clearly a response to the events since the recent break with Rome. The demands for the destruction of heresies, the return to papal authority and the restoration of the monasteries were paramount in the Lincolnshire Rising and the Pilgrimage of Grace. The risings were united behind religious symbolism. In the same way in which the social and economic causes affected different groups in society in different ways, it is possible to see this with support for Catholicism. Robert Aske argued for the economic importance of abbeys such as Fountains to the north, and of their gifts of food and hospitality to travellers in the Pennines. He might have thought that the King would be more easily persuaded by such arguments and so emphasised these aspects. The commons did not make a distinction between religious and economic usefulness. Religion held communities together in both rural and urban contexts. People came together as a community not only to worship, but to organise and pay for the rituals of the Church. Numerous ceremonies – the beating of the bounds, which established the extent of the community; the procession of civil leaders, which was led by the priest; the giving of the peace; and the prayers for the dead and the chantries which supported them – all unified the different social groups. For those who joined the Pilgrimage of Grace, these had to be defended: the break with Rome and the heresies of Tyndale, who challenged transubstantiation, and Christopher St Germain, who challenged the authority of the Pope, needed to be destroyed.

Social and economic factors

At a very basic level, people will take action against a government if their livelihoods are threatened, for example if they do not have enough to eat or the means with which to support their families. There is evidence that the commons of the north were affected to some degree in 1536: there had been poor harvests in both 1535 and 1536, which led to rising prices and food shortages. **Enclosure** of land was often seen as a reason why the poor took action, as their access to the benefits of the common land was denied. Indeed there had been enclosure riots around Settle in 1535. The 13th 'item' of the Pontefract Articles requested an end to enclosures. For those who rented the land on which they farmed, there is considerable evidence of increases in rents, and in the money (**entry fines**) which had

■ Cross-reference

The **rituals of the Catholic Church** are described on pages 22–5.

■ Key terms

Enclosure: the enclosing of fields with hedges or walls. In most cases this was done to change land from growing crops to keeping sheep.

Entry fines: The lump sum a tenant would have to pay up front if he took over a piece of land or if his tenancy was renewed.

to be paid when a **tenancy** was renewed. This featured in the Pontefract Articles as the ninth 'item'. There were concerns about the introduction of, and increase in, taxation paid by farmers. For those who were 'owners' of land there was a clear request for the repeal of the **Statute of Uses**. Henry VIII had attempted to reassert his feudal right to the ownership of all the land in the country by payment of taxation when land changed hands through wills.

Political motives

Although Henry VIII accused the Lincolnshire rebels of treason, neither they nor the Pilgrims believed that they were acting against the King. Rather, they believed that Henry had been badly advised by two councillors in particular: Thomas Cromwell and Richard Rich. These low-born councillors were responsible for advising on the break with Rome, the dissolution of the monasteries and all the legislation to which they objected. The wider political issue is the extent to which what happened in 1536 was organised by an aristocratic faction who had been supporters of the former Queen, Catherine of Aragon.

Who was responsible for leading and organising the Lincolnshire Rising and the Pilgrimage of Grace has been the subject of much debate. This has focused on 'low politics' represented by the yeomen and the 'high politics' of the nobility and the court. Traditionally, it was felt to be the duty of the nobility to restore the political balance when the monarch suffered from the consequences of bad advice. It was also the responsibility of the nobility and the gentry to prevent the lower orders getting out of control. While in 1536 the supporters of the King might wish to portray the yeomen as having beliefs that were against the interest of the country, they would see themselves as caring about honest government with a clear sense of right and wrong. Following the failure of the Pilgrimage, nobility, gentry and yeomen would all argue that they were acting in the King's interest. The gentry and nobility stated that when the commons rose spontaneously it was they who took control of the situation in order to protect Henry's interests.

■ A closer look

The Pilgrimage of Grace: historiography

Historians have developed different arguments to explain the Pilgrimage of Grace.

- Geoffrey Elton, writing in 1983, argued that the Pilgrimage of Grace represented the effort of the defeated Aragonese faction at court to create a power base in the country to bring down the faction which had removed Catherine of Aragon. Elton denied the possibility of a spontaneous popular uprising and pointed to the evidence of prior planning and the key roles played by the Lords Darcy and Hussey, who had been supporters of Catherine.

- Steven Gunn, writing in 1989, argued against Geoffrey Elton. His examination of the actions of the gentry in Lincolnshire undermined the idea of a planned, regional uprising, and he argued that Lord Hussey lacked the necessary political clout to have orchestrated such a rebellion. He concluded that the parish clergy played an important role, but more important were the leaders of society in the villages and small towns – the richer yeomen and substantial tradesmen, who had often acted as churchwardens, parish constables, and so on.

■ Key terms

Tenancy: landowners would rent out parts of their land to others in a tenancy agreement which would be for a fixed period of years.

Statute of Uses: an act of parliament passed in 1535 which prevented those who held the right to use land owned by the King from setting up trusts, so that the use of the land could be passed from father to son without the payment of an entry fine to the King when the existing occupier (user) of the land died.

■ Cross-reference

For a profile of **Richard Rich**, see page 129.

Information on the **Aragonese faction** can be found on page 35.

Thinking and analysis

Try to read some of the works of the historians who have written about the Pilgrimage of Grace. Richard Hoyle and George Bernard's writings, as well as those mentioned here, would be worth reading. Try to discover what these historians have said about the part played by the nobility in the Pilgrimage of Grace.

In 1996 Michael Bush argued that the Pilgrimage was primarily a protest of the people. However, he also argued that the ordinary people's belief in the hierarchy of society led them to insist on the gentry and nobility assuming leadership. He suggested that the rebels' aims were to protect the 'commonwealth' (by which they meant 'the commons' and 'the material good of the realm') from unfair and heavy taxation, from the Statute of Uses and from the government's attack on the wealth of the local churches.

The King's response and the events of 1537

Robert Aske spent Christmas at court in London, believing that he was negotiating the agenda for the parliament which would meet at York, attended by the King himself. But, despite promises from the King, nothing happened. The problem for the Pilgrims was that they had no way of compelling Henry VIII to keep the bargain they thought had been struck at Doncaster in December 1536 – and for his part, Henry seemed to have little intention of fulfilling their wishes.

In Yorkshire the commons and a number of the gentry came to realise that they had been duped. There was also considerable discussion of how far the royal supremacy over the Church should be accepted. The ground had shifted and a new leader emerged: Sir Francis Bigod. He decided to act and to seize Hull and Scarborough, but only Beverley was captured and held for a short period of time. Bigod fled to Cumberland and was captured. A small number of incidents of unrest were reported across the East Riding of Yorkshire. On 16 February there was a mustering of the commons in Eskdale, but the gentry swiftly turned on them.

More serious was the reaction of the King. Henry pursued a systematic policy of punishment, and sent Norfolk north. There were 144 executions; not only the key leaders such as Aske but members of the gentry and the nobility, including Sir Francis Bigod, Sir Thomas Percy, Lord Hussey and Lord Darcy. There were a number of vicious reprisals, such as the burning at the stake of the wife of a member of the gentry who had been on the very fringe of the rebellions. The clearest evidence of Henry's fear for his government was his execution of Thomas Miller, who had been instrumental in securing the negotiations with the Pilgrims in Doncaster. His crime: he had pointed out to the Pilgrims their military superiority over the King.

Key profile

Sir Francis Bigod

Sir Francis Bigod (1507–37) seemed a surprising rebel. He was a member of a gentry family and had written an attack on the wealth of the monasteries. He was a commissioner who had taken part in the valuation of monastic lands for Cromwell and was known as a supporter of the new religion. It would seem that his actions were partly motivated by a hatred of Cromwell and partly a result of his own headstrong, impetuous character. He was not recognised by the main leadership of the Pilgrimage as a key negotiator; his own rising seems to have been an individual response and a belief that he could achieve a breakthrough. He was executed at Tyburn in 1537.

The outcome of the Pilgrimage

The Pilgrimage of Grace had been rooted in political, religious and economic concerns; the longer-term policies of Henry VIII's government mirrored the same issues. Rather than hold a parliament at York, as the Pilgrims had demanded, Henry reorganised the Council of the North. He did, however, make a number of the erstwhile leaders of the Pilgrimage, such as Robert Bowes and Sir Ralph Ellerker (who claimed they had only joined the rebels under duress), members of this. Promises to restore the monasteries failed to materialise and even the largest had fallen by 1540. Yet when Henry dissolved a number of chantries in the 1540s in the south of England, he did not touch those in the north. Despite the belief that the break from Rome had been an aberration from which Henry would recover once a legitimate son had been born, Henry VIII was excommunicated by the Pope. Nevertheless, the main principles of Catholicism were restated in the Act of Six Articles – although it was a Catholicism without monasteries or pilgrimages. While the Pilgrimage failed to prevent the attempt by Henry VIII to recover feudal dues, the Statute of Wills passed in 1540 more firmly recognised the rights of landowners to dispose of property. In 1540 Cromwell was removed from power and in 1543 Mary was restored to the succession.

The view of G. R. Elton in *England Under the Tudors* (1956) presented a particular viewpoint which stressed his view that the commons were unable to organise an effective challenge and that the real architects of the Pilgrimage of Grace were a group of nobles who had lost influence at court when Catherine of Aragon had been banished:

> The Pilgrimage of Grace was never anything but a futile attempt to arrest the power of the revolution to which Henry had given his support since 1533. The Pilgrimage collapsed far too quickly to justify the common view of it as a genuine mass movement eager to overthrow a whole system and policy. The King and his Council knew what was happening – the executions in the North indicated that they did not think they were confronted by a peasants' war, or by a feudal conflict, or by a resistance movement involving a whole society.

 4   Elton, G. R., *England under the Tudors*, 1956

■ The impact of the dissolutions on society, culture and the Church

The impact of the dissolutions was profound. In the short term, it bred unease and, as we have already seen, some rebellion. The consequences that would be apparent to ordinary people were not obvious all at once. Some people may have been aware of former monks moving to their area; others would be aware of beggars who had previously been relieved by the monasteries moving into towns and asking for money in the streets. Richer people would need to look elsewhere if they wished to give money or do good works.

In the longer term, the consequences of the dissolution went much further than this. The disappearance of the monasteries marked a further shift from a society dominated by Church and state to one in which the state was supreme. Institutions and attitudes were forced to change in order to cope with the reality of life without monasteries.

 Cross-reference

For more detail on the events described here, see pages 85, 99 and 113.

 Activity

Source analysis

Read Sources 3 and 4.

Explain how far the view in Source 4 differs from that in Source 3 in relation to the Pilgrimage of Grace.

 Activity

Group task

Using the evidence in this chapter and Chapter 1, design a snakes and ladders game. Square one should be the decision to dissolve the smaller monasteries; square 100 should be the dissolution of all the monasteries. Draw ladders for things like the passing of legislation and the findings of the *Valor Ecclesiasticus*, and snakes for events such as the murder of the Bishop of Lincoln's official and the camping of the pilgrims outside Doncaster.

 Summary question

How far did the Pilgrimage of Grace succeed in achieving its aims?

Table 1. *Short-term and long-term impact of the dissolutions of the monasteries*

Area	Short-term	Longer-term
Society	Opposition from all levels of society	Significant social change
	Increased destitution of the poor	The development of local government responsibility for the poor
Culture	Destruction of monastic buildings and possessions	Development of a secular culture
	Loss of centres of learning	Education provided through grammar schools
Church	Dislocation of religious provision	Creation of new bishoprics
	Increase of number of priests in parishes	Replacement of political role of abbots by new bishops

Society

The abbeys of England and Wales had been among the greatest landowners and the largest institutions in the kingdom. Particularly in areas far from London, the abbeys, convents and priories were the principal centres and sources of charity and medical care. Monastic hospitals were lost, with devastating consequences for local people. Monasteries had also supplied free food and alms for the poor and destitute. Historians have debated how serious an impact the disappearance of these sources of relief actually had on the poor, but the problem of vagrancy and the presence of 'sturdy beggars', some of whom were the destitute lay brothers, in most urban centres, was a cause for concern. There were limited formal sources of relief for the poor and successive Tudor governments struggled to deal with the problem. A partial solution was later established through the Elizabethan Poor Law of 1601.

Fig. 6 *Before the dissolution of the monasteries the monks were key to the education of the sons and daughters of the nobility, gentry and merchants*

On the eve of the dissolution, the monasteries owned approximately 2,000,000 acres of land, over 16 per cent of England, with tens of thousands of tenant farmers working those lands. The monastic landlords were appreciated for their more lenient terms, and some of their tenant families had lived on monastery lands for many generations.

The sale of former monastic property meant that there was also a transfer of power into the hands of those who purchased the property. While a considerable amount was retained by the King, this was rented out to the nobility and gentry. A considerable amount of monastic property was also sold off either immediately or over the next ten years. The vast majority of those who purchased the lands were from established families, but the scale of the transfer of property also allowed lawyers and merchants to establish themselves with the landed classes. The passing of the **Statute of Wills** in 1540 also gave the purchaser a right of ownership of this property.

The disappearance of the monasteries also had an impact on charitable giving by members of the landed classes. Previously such people had given large amounts of money to the monasteries, either for Masses to be said for their souls, or as a fee when one of their children was accepted to train as either a monk or a nun. The dissolution brought this to an end, and with the later challenge to the belief in salvation by good works, there was a decline in giving to the Church as a whole.

■ **Key term**

Statute of Wills 1540: An act of parliament that restricted the amount of taxation which the king could claim when the right to use land was inherited. This effectively gave the users of land a part ownership in the property.

Culture

Along with the destruction of the monasteries, some many hundreds of years old, the related destruction of the monastic libraries was perhaps the greatest cultural loss caused by the English Reformation. Worcester Priory had 600 books at the time of the dissolution. Only six of them have survived intact to the present day. At the Augustinian friary in York, a library of 646 volumes was destroyed, leaving only three surviving books. Some books were destroyed for their precious bindings, while others were sold, including irreplaceable early English works. It is believed that many of the earliest Anglo-Saxon manuscripts were lost at this time. Some manuscripts and books were simply burned as people ransacked the monastic buildings. In addition to the loss of books, much of the silver and gold and many jewelled possessions were taken to the Court of Augmentations and given away or sold off. Much of this treasure was lost, as crucifixes and reliquaries were no longer needed, but new possessions could be created from the gold and silver.

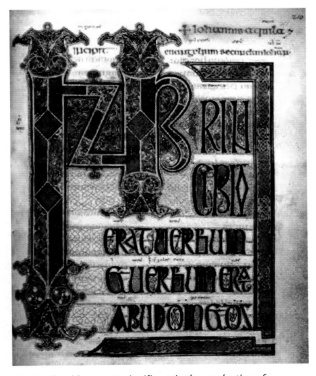

Nevertheless, Henry did invest some of the wealth he gained from the monasteries in education. New cathedral grammar schools were set up in Canterbury, Carlisle, Ely, Bristol and Chester. Christ Church, Oxford, developed from Cardinal College, which had been founded by Wolsey; and Trinity College, Cambridge was also established. In other towns and cities grammar schools were established by benefactors, many of them merchants. It is not totally clear how far this growth in urban education was the result of the dissolution of the monasteries, or reflected an increasing awareness of the importance of literacy in a growing commercial climate and with the availability of printed sources.

Fig. 7 *The abbeys were significant in the production of illuminated and illustrated holy texts. As the rate of literacy increased, so did the demand for books*

Exploring the detail

Purchases at Worcester Priory

The record of the purchases of the Prior of Worcester on one trip to London gives an indication of the cultural wealth of the monasteries. In 1520 the Prior had bought a ring, two chalices and four pieces of silver plate for £20, a cloth of gold for £87 and a new set of vestments which cost £90 18s. 4d. The purchase of books also featured in these shopping trips. Monasteries traditionally had many illuminated manuscripts which had been copied by monks over a long period of time. By the time of the dissolution the monastic libraries also contained a large number of printed books which covered the writings of the early Church fathers, books of canon law and scholastic books. The receipts of the Prior of Worcester show that he was also buying books for his own personal use.

A closer look

Grammar schools

In medieval times, the importance of Latin in government, international affairs and religion meant that there was a strong demand to learn the language. Schools were set up to teach the basis of Latin grammar, calling themselves 'grammar schools'. Latin was the language of all Church services and all Bibles were in Latin. The reason for this was twofold. First, it meant that all people prayed the same prayers in the same language and that there was no opportunity for translations to change the meaning of prayers. Secondly, it gave access to the written word of God only to an educated clergy. Grammar schools were often separate from the Church. Pupils were usually educated up to the age of 14, after which they would look to universities and the church. Six schools were founded or refounded with the proceeds of the dissolution of the monasteries by Henry VIII.

Teaching usually took place from dawn to dusk, and focused heavily upon the rote learning of Latin. In order to encourage fluency, some schoolmasters recommended punishing any pupil who spoke in English. It would be several years before pupils were able to construct a sentence in Latin, and they would be in their final years at the school when they began translating passages. By the end of their studies, they would be quite familiar with the great Latin authors, as well as the studies of drama and logic.

The Church

The dissolution of the monasteries represented the final break of formal links with continental religion and the Catholic Church. The organisation of the Church of England was immediately boosted by 8,000 priests, who as monks were well versed and able to conduct services. This went some way to addressing the issue of ill-educated clergy. Many of them found employment as chantry priests while prayers and Masses for the dead were still allowed.

Cardinal Wolsey had planned a reorganisation of the Church. The dissolution of the monasteries enabled this to be implemented. In 1540 six new bishoprics were created in Oxford, Chester, Gloucester, Bristol, Peterborough and Westminster. These eased the administration of Lincoln and Lichfield dioceses, which had been much too big. Most used the buildings of existing abbeys as their cathedrals, with some modification. The new bishops, who were sympathetic to the work undertaken by the King's servant, Thomas Cromwell, were happy to take the place of the dispossessed abbots in the House of Lords.

Fig. 8 *Market Harborough grammar school in Leicestershire was built to educate the sons of the merchants and gentry following the dissolution of the monasteries*

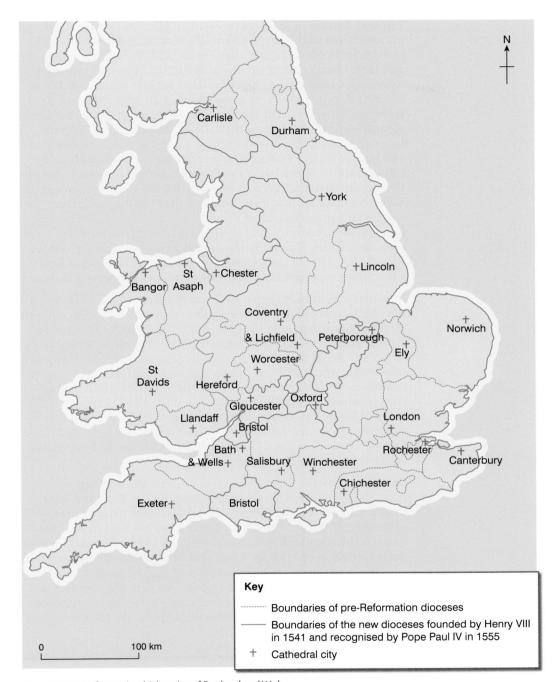

Fig. 9 *Post-Reformation bishoprics of England and Wales*

■ A closer look

The monks of Kirkstall after the dissolution

It has been calculated that the average age of the community at Kirkstall Abbey, near Leeds, was 43 years: most of the monks were aged between 40 and 49, three were over 70 and eight between 25 and 29. At least two members of the community lived on property formerly belonging to the monastery: Abbot John, 'a sober man who spoke little', was said to have spent the remainder of his days in the gatehouse of the abbey; and

Thomas Bartlett, a Leeds man, lived at Allerton Grange until his death in 1542. Two of Kirkstall's vicarages, Aldbrough and Hollym in Holderness, may have been held by Thomas Ellis and John Lister, former monks of the abbey. The community's names appended to the surrender deed suggest that a number of the monks originally came from within a 20-mile radius of the abbey, and it seems that the majority of them settled in the Leeds vicinity after the closure of their abbey. For example, Anthony Jackson, former bursar of the abbey, served as curate of Horsforth and later of Otley; Thomas Bartlett, Richard Ellis and Edward Heptonstall were priests in Leeds; and Gabriel Lofthouse, one of the monks who confessed to sodomy in 1535–6, was chaplain of Richmond and buried in the porch of the parish church there. In Cromwell's investigation of the monasteries, sexual intercourse between men, sodomy, had been considered to be the worst possible offence. Gabriel evidently led a rather frugal life, for his will of 1552 lists his possessions as simply his bedding, a long gown, a wooden spoon tipped with silver and just over a guinea.

In contrast, Thomas Pepper of Bramley seems to have enjoyed a life of relative comfort. Following the dissolution, Pepper, a junior monk of the abbey, was rector of Adel. Although he received an annual pension of only £5 from the abbey, Pepper inherited his father's lands at Bramley. His own purchases included Weetwood ironworks, which had belonged to Kirkstall and had been leased to Robert Neville 16 months before the surrender of the abbey; they remained in Neville's possession until 1542. Pepper's will of 1553 suggests that he had by this time accumulated a substantial fortune, for he left £86 and ten gold angels, and forgave his debtors the £20 owing to him; he also had two male servants and three female servants.

One former monk, Edward Sandall, angered the authorities. After the dissolution he was a chantry priest at York and later earned a living teaching boys, but did so without the licence of the Archbishop of York. He openly aired his hostility to the newly created Church of England and in 1568 was brought before the Archbishop of York as 'a misliker of established religion', who continued to pray to the saints and read romances instead of Scripture. Sandall denied all the charges save the last and was imprisoned in York Castle as a recusant – a person who refused to take communion in the Church of England. By 1568 this was no longer regarded as heretical.

Activity

Thinking and analysis

In the character of Thomas Cromwell, write a report to Henry VIII which outlines what you consider to be your achievements in dissolving the monasteries and how you have overcome the problems you have faced in dealing with this process.

To capture the full impact of the plunder we must remember that monks and parish churches were not the only ones to suffer. Bishops were forced to exchange their best estates by the Crown in response to pressure from courtiers and clients. Many humble folk joined in the scramble and by fair means or foul acquired furnishings and goods from religious houses and parish churches. There was a frenzy of getting, grabbing, buying, and begging without equal in English experience.

5

*Scarisbrick, J. J., **Henry VIII**, 1968*

Learning outcomes

Through your study of this section you should have developed an understanding of the various reasons why the monasteries were dissolved and how that dissolution was carried out. You should also be aware of the nature of the opposition to this action and understand the activities of the rebels both in Lincolnshire and in the Pilgrimage of Grace. You will have had the opportunity to reflect upon the implications of these risings and the short- and longer-term consequences of the dissolutions for the King and government, as well as society, culture and the Church. In the next section you will have the opportunity to look at other consequences of the English Reformation in the period 1535–41.

Practice questions

(a)   Explain why the people of Lincolnshire rose up in rebellion in 1536.   *(12 marks)*

Study tip   Take note of the date, 1536. You should comment on the short-term causes of the rebellion as well as the longer-term reasons.

You might include:
- ■ the action of the commissioners and the dissolution of the smaller monasteries
- ■ taxes and the Statute of Uses, which were indicated as issues in the Lincoln Articles
- ■ the importance of religion and the monasteries in people's lives
- ■ the importance of rumour in an age when news was passed by word of mouth.

(b)   'The most important consequence of the dissolution of the monasteries was its impact on society.' Explain why you agree or disagree with this view.   *(24 marks)*

Study tip   In answering such a question it is important that you structure your answer appropriately so that you:
- ■ decide whether you will agree/disagree, i.e. was this the most important consequence?
- ■ look at the premise of the quotation – what was the impact on society?
- ■ provide examples that challenge the premise of the quotation – what were the other consequences?

You might consider that:
- ■ for property owners there was greater wealth and power
- ■ for the poor the removal of the monasteries was the removal of their major support structure
- ■ society and its organisations were changed by the redistribution of wealth
- ■ culturally England was impoverished by the loss of centres of learning and the treasures contained in the monasteries
- ■ the organisation of the Church was transformed by the creation of the new bishoprics and their roles within the government of England.

In this chapter you will learn about:

- how Henry VIII increased his powers over his kingdom through further parliamentary legislation

- the ways in which the Church of England was changed in the years between 1535 and 1541

- how the relationship between King and parliament developed

- the ways in which the break with Rome altered the financial position of the state.

Fig. 1 *An illuminated manuscript showing Henry VIII as defender of the faith*

Fig. 2 *Henry VIII in about 1540 at the height of his powers, painted by Holbein*

The Henrician Reformation resulted in the creation of a system of government very different from that which had existed in the 1520s. By 1541 Henry VIII's powers were far greater than they had been in 1529. The independent position of the Church had been removed and the crown was significantly wealthier. So dramatic were the changes that the historian Geoffrey Elton, writing in 1953, described them collectively as a 'Tudor revolution in government'. Such a bold claim has been challenged by more recent historians. In 1986 David Starkey and Chris Coleman edited a book of essays entitled *Revolution Re-Assessed: Revisions in the History of Tudor Government and Administration*, in which it was suggested that the changes were much more limited than Elton had argued. Nevertheless, most agree that the person responsible for the significant changes was Henry VIII's chief minister – Thomas Cromwell.

▪ Parliamentary legislation and government actions to reform the Church, 1535–41

The years between 1535 and 1541 witnessed significant developments of religious beliefs and practices beyond the dissolution of the monasteries. There has been considerable debate as to why this was. It has been argued that Henry VIII and parliament were influenced by Cromwell, who was himself Lutheran. Alternatively, the developments have been seen as responses to domestic issues such as the Pilgrimage of Grace and what was happening on the continent, for example the relationship between Francis I and Charles V. Another explanation, which has been put forward by G. W. Bernard, is that the sole architect of the changes was Henry VIII himself.

Cross-reference

The **Pilgrimage of Grace** is covered in Chapter 6.

The **situation on the continent** is outlined on page 108.

A closer look

Execution of Anne Boleyn

In April 1536, a musician in Anne's service, Mark Smeaton, was arrested and possibly tortured too. Under torture he confessed he was the Queen's lover. Other courtiers – Henry Norris, Sir Francis Weston, William Brereton and Queen Anne's brother – were arrested on charges of having had a sexual relationship with Queen Anne.

On 2 May 1536, Anne was arrested and taken to the Tower of London. Four of the men were tried on 12 May 1536. Weston, Brereton and Norris maintained their innocence and only Smeaton supported the crown by pleading guilty. Three days later, Anne and George Boleyn were tried separately in the Tower of London. She was accused of adultery, incest and high treason. Although the evidence against them was unconvincing, the accused were found guilty and condemned to death by their peers. George Boleyn and the other accused men were executed on 17 May 1536, and Anne's execution followed two days later. The King commuted Anne's sentence from burning to beheading and employed a swordsman from France for the execution, rather than having a queen beheaded with the common axe. Anne refused to speak out against Henry on the scaffold. She spoke to the Constable of the Tower saying 'I have heard say the executioner is very good, and I have a little neck', and then put her hands about it laughing. The Constable wrote: 'I have seen many executed and they have been in great sorrow, and to my knowledge this lady has much joy in death.'

Key chronology

Changes to the liturgy and doctrine of the Church of England

1536 July	The Ten Articles	
August	Royal injunctions to the clergy	
Autumn	Pilgrimage of Grace	
1537 July	Bishops' Book published	
August	Matthew Bible published	
1538 July	Treaty of Nice signed by Charles V and Francis I	
September	Royal injunctions issued by Cromwell	
November	Trial and execution of John Lambert	
December	Henry VIII excommunicated by Paul III	
1539 April	Publication of the Great Bible	
June	Act of Six Articles	

Activity

Thinking point

How far did Thomas Cromwell extend his own power and influence in the changes which he made to Church and state?

Fig. 3 *A contemporary woodcut of the execution of Anne Boleyn. How can we tell that this was not the work of an eyewitness?*

The death of Catherine of Aragon in January 1536 and the execution of Anne Boleyn in May appeared to offer an opportunity to reconsider the position of the Church of England. While from a 21st century perspective the break with Rome seems unquestionable in its permanence, contemporaries believed that the steps taken by the King and parliament in the early 1530s were temporary and that England would return to the papal obedience. The decision to dissolve the smaller monasteries seemed to challenge that belief. The Act of Ten Articles, which was passed in July, was ambiguous and apparently rather conservative. The dissolution of the monasteries had been an attack on Catholicism. The Ten Articles were not an attack on Catholicism, nor were the articles a comprehensive statement of belief: instead they were intended to resolve certain disputed doctrinal and ceremonial questions. Essentially they established:

- the sacraments of baptism, penance and the Eucharist
- the nature of justification
- the use of images in churches
- the intercession of the saints
- rites and ceremonies
- the doctrine of purgatory.

A closer look

The beliefs of the Catholic faith – a recap

Key to the Catholic faith were (and still are) the seven sacraments of baptism, confirmation, penance, the Eucharist, marriage, ordination and the last rites. Each of these marked a stage in a person's life when they entered into a relationship with God. Baptism was when a child was made a member of the Church and was cleansed by holy water from the original sin that had been introduced by the fall of Adam and Eve in the Garden of Eden. Confirmation took place when a child was old enough to commit to the Church, usually around the age of seven. Members of the Church were expected to make a confession at least once a year to a priest who listened on behalf of God. The priest and the sinner would be separated so that the priest would not know who was confessing. To absolve the sin a penance would be given. The most important sacrament was the Eucharist, or Mass. When God joined a man and women in the sacrament of marriage, from that point on their union was regarded as permanent. Ordination – when a man became a priest – was the only sacrament not shared by the majority of the people. All people hoped to receive the last rites before they died which enabled them to die having prepared themselves to meet God.

Everyone, apart from saints, would expect to spend time in purgatory after death. How soon the soul passed to heaven would depend on how many good works a person had undertaken, how many indulgences he or she had acquired or how many prayers or Masses were said for his or her soul after death. Prayers were made to saints by people when they were alive and by relatives on their behalf when they were dead. In the same way masses for the souls of the dead would reduce the time a person spent in purgatory.

There was little in the Ten Articles which could be seen as overtly Lutheran and new. The paragraph on the Eucharist seemed to confirm the Catholic belief that the body and blood of Christ were present at the

Mass, although the term transubstantiation was not used. The section on rites and ceremonies explained the symbolism of various liturgical actions. Only in the article on purgatory was there any evidence of Protestant thinking, and even then there was a recognition of there being a 'state' after death.

In August 1536 Cromwell issued injunctions making the Ten Articles binding on the clergy. However, they did not resolve anxieties about the beliefs of the Church of England. Even before the Pilgrimage of Grace was over Cromwell had called together a number of bishops to resolve a range of doctrinal and liturgical issues and to determine canon law. The result of these sometimes heated debates was *The Institution of a Christian Man*, or the Bishops' Book as it was commonly called. As might be expected from bishops who were influenced by Lutheran ideas, the Bishops' Book was much more Lutheran in its views. Salvation by faith was emphasised, and there was no mention of transubstantiation. In 1536 one of Cromwell's injunctions had required each parish church to have an English Bible; shortly after the publication of the Bishops' Book a bible in English, the Matthew Bible, was published.

Cross-reference
To revise the doctrine of **salvation by faith**, refer back to pages 31–2.

> It is good that the Scripture should be read by all sorts and kinds of people in their own language, especially now that the King's Highness, being Supreme Head under this Church of England has approved with his royal assent the publication of the Bible.
>
> He that is ignorant shall find here what he should learn. He that is a sinner shall find his damnation to make him tremble for fear. He that works to serve God shall find here his glory, and the promise of eternal life.
>
> This book is the word of God. It is the most precious jewel and most holy relic which remains on earth. You should use your knowledge of it not for frivolous debate but to honour God and to become more virtuous.

1 *Cranmer's Preface to the Great Bible, 1539*

Activity

Thinking point

How similar were the lessons which Cranmer wanted people to learn from reading the Bible in English to the pictures which had been painted on church walls and illustrated in the stained glass of the doom windows?

In 1538 John Lambert, who had been in trouble for his religious views earlier in the 1530s, disputed the existence of the real presence of God in the Eucharist. Lambert's high profile campaign antagonised Henry, who became personally involved. Attacking traditional teaching on the Eucharist had always been considered a serious offence, and not only was Lambert burnt for heresy, but on the day of his execution Henry issued a royal proclamation. The royal proclamation upheld the 'real presence' at the Eucharist, upheld clerical celibacy and forbade heretical literature.

Fig. 4 *The frontispiece from the Great Bible, the first Bible in English authorised to be used in all churches*

■ Key profile

John Lambert

John Lambert was born John Nicholson in Norwich and educated at Queens' College, Cambridge. He was made a fellow there on the nomination of Catherine of Aragon. After theological disputes he changed his name and went to Antwerp. He became a friend of William Tyndale, and a member of the group of humanist theologians who met at the White Horse Tavern – a group that included the future Lutherans Edward Fox and Robert Barnes, and the arch-conservative Stephen Gardiner. In 1536 Lambert was accused of heresy by the Duke of Norfolk, but he escaped punishment until 1538, when he was put on trial for denying the real presence of Christ in the bread and wine of the Eucharist. Archbishop Thomas Cranmer condemned these views, even though he was later to adopt them himself. John Lambert was burnt to death on 22 November 1538. He is well known for his words spoken while the flames leapt from his raised hands: 'None but Christ, none but Christ!'

■ Cross-reference

For a profile of **Thomas Cranmer**, refer back to page 54.

At last the King himself did come as judge of that great controversy. He asked John Lambert 'Touching the sacrament of the altar, answer whether you say it is the body of Christ, or will you deny it?'

Lambert: I answer with St. Augustine, that it is the body of Christ after a certain manner.

King: Answer me neither out of St. Augustine, neither by the authority of any other, but tell me plainly whether you say it is the body of Christ or no?

Lambert: I deny it to be the body of Christ.

Henry rose up and turned to the sacrament and said 'this is the master of us all, the author of truth, that truth I will defend.' He added to Lambert 'You will be condemned.'

2
From the trial of John Lambert, 1538

The Lambert case showed Henry VIII how far doctrinal deviation among the laity had gone. This, with his excommunication and Pope Paul's call for him to be overthrown, led him to summon parliament in early 1539. The Act of Six Articles was the outcome of a committee set up to discuss religion. Like the Ten Articles, the Act of Six Articles was intended not as a comprehensive statement of beliefs but as a defence against heresy. The main points were that it:

- upheld the Catholic doctrine of transubstantiation
- defended communion in one kind (wafer not wine)
- upheld private Mass
- upheld auricular confession
- forbade the clergy to marry
- held that vows of chastity were binding under divine law.

The Act of Six Articles was not solely intended for domestic consumption but was intended to make a statement to foreign rulers that despite his break with Rome Henry was still essentially Catholic. The belief that the Church of England was 'Catholicism without the Pope, monasteries and pilgrimages' was further reinforced by the resignation of two reformist bishops. In 1540 parliament commissioned bishops and theologians of a predominantly conservative viewpoint to produce a replacement for the Bishops' Book. This was the King's Book, which was published in 1543.

Activity

Thinking and analysis

Compare the liturgy and doctrine of the Church of England in 1541 with what it had been in 1529. To what extent had the Church moved from Catholicism to Lutheranism?

The role of parliament

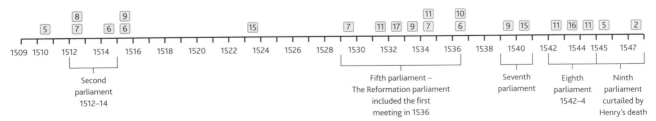

Numbers in squares = no. of weeks for which parliament met
In some years there were two sittings of parliament

Fig. 5 *Meetings of parliament in the reign of Henry VIII*

Key chronology

Sessions of the Reformation parliament

1 3 Nov 1529 – 17 Dec 1529

2 16 Jan 1531 – 31 Mar 1531

3 15 Jan 1532 – 14 May 1532

4 4 Feb 1533 – 7 Apr 1533

5 15 Jan 1534 – 30 Mar 1534

6 3 Nov 1534 – 18 Dec 1534

7 4 Feb 1536 – 14 Apr 1536

Acts of parliament, 1534–41

1534 Act of Succession

1539 Act of Six Articles

1539 Act of Proclamations

1539 Act 'for the precedence of the lords in the parliament chamber'

1540 Statute of Wills

Cross-reference

The acts passed by the **Reformation parliament** between 1529 and 1535 are outlined on pages 54–7.

The Reformation parliament which sat between 1529 and 1536 changed the fundamental nature of government in England. The increased importance of the role of parliament in giving legitimacy to the King's action was established through the legislation that confirmed the break with Rome, secured the King's supremacy and established the Church of England. The King's position was confirmed and reinforced by the actions of his parliament and, as a result, his power came to be seen as at its strongest when he was 'in parliament'. Statute law, namely laws made in parliament and given the King's consent, came to be accepted as having the greatest force of law in the land. As a result of the legislation of the Reformation parliament, any challenge to the Church of England and any challenge to the succession became punishable by law, and the supreme court of law was the House of Lords (part of parliament) itself. However, it must not be forgotten that while parliament emerged with new powers, it essentially provided a 'rubber stamp' to the legislation of Henry VIII's reign.

Fig. 6 *Henry VIII in parliament*

The Crown had become an integral part of Parliament and the important distinction now was between the limited power of *rex solus* (the king alone) and the sovereign authority of king-in-parliament. Henry himself acknowledged both of these points when, in 1542, he informed members of the Commons 'that we at no time stand so highly in our estate royal, as in the time of parliament, wherein we as head, and you as members, are conjoined and knit together into one politic'.

3
Graves, M. A. R, quoted in Dawson, I., The Tudor Century 1485–1603, 1993

Activity

Source analysis

How far had the relationship between King and parliament outlined by Henry VIII in Source 3 changed from when he had called the Reformation Parliament in 1529?

In the later sittings of the Reformation parliament and in the parliament which sat between 1539 and 1541 there were further changes to the role and functions of parliament which changed the relationship between the two houses and the King.

In 1536 parliament passed an act which, with amendments in 1539 and 1543, was to have significance throughout the remainder of the 16th century and further reinforced the importance of parliament. This was the second Act of Succession. Following the birth of the long-awaited male heir, the Tudor dynasty was a little more secure, but there were still concerns. Both Mary and Elizabeth were declared illegitimate by the act of 1536, that is to say their mothers' marriages were not recognised in law.

There were occasions when a swift response was necessary from the King, for example an economic crisis, or when action was needed and parliament was not in session. In these cases the King could resort to proclamation. In 1539 an act was passed by parliament which stated that proclamations should be obeyed as though they were made by act of parliament. This act was repealed in 1547 by a parliament which was nervous about the powers it would give those governing in the place of Edward VI, but in 1539 the intention was that proclamations would only be valid until they were ratified by parliament at its next sitting.

Additionally in 1539 another act 'for the precedence of the lords in the parliament chamber' marked an important step in the development of the House of Lords. Up to this point the great council of magnates had included professional councillors such as judges and officers of chancery. The 1539 act restricted the right to sit in the House of Lords to hereditary peers. Of the two houses the Lords was the most important: this was partially due to the now refined social status of its members, but it also carried the greater political weight. From 1539 Cromwell acknowledged this by being created baron. From this point all important legislation was introduced into the House of Lords; when Cromwell was a member of the House of Commons all important legislation had been introduced there.

A further development in the practices of parliament was seen in the Reformation Parliament. In parliaments before 1529 the bills to be debated generally came from members of parliament themselves and concerned local issues. The Reformation Parliament debated bills which originated in the Privy Council. Before 1529 most acts of parliament dealt with issues that mattered to members of parliament themselves, and were introduced in return for granting taxation to the King. From 1529 acts of parliament were introduced on behalf of the King by his ministers, most notably Thomas Cromwell. A further development was the crown's management of the House of Commons. While election to the House of Commons came from a very limited franchise both in the county seats and in the boroughs, there had been little attempt by the crown to manipulate this. At the calling of the seventh parliament in 1539 Cromwell used all his influence and resources to have MPs elected who would be the most willing to support the King's policies.

A closer look

The Statute of Wills, 1540

The Statute of Wills was of major significance in redefining the relationship between the King and those who held property. As by definition all members of both houses held property, the statute changed the balance of power between them and the King. Up to this point all land had been owned by the King and others had simply held the right to use the land. When this right was passed on at the death of the person who had the right to use the land, the person taking control of the property had to pay an entry fine to the King to have his right to use the property entered into the records. Over time those who had the right to use the property had become wise and had invested this right in a trust. This meant that the 'person' using the land apparently never died, and no money had to be paid to the King. Henry had tried to prevent this by the Statute of Uses, but this had caused discontent which had fuelled the Pilgrimage of Grace. The Statute of Wills passed by parliament was a compromise on the part of Henry: it undermined the feudal relationship by enabling those who used the property of the King to own two-thirds of the property, with only one-third remaining in the hands of the crown. It also encouraged people to purchase land from the crown following the dissolution of the monasteries.

Cross-reference

The custom of **entry fines**, the **Statute of Uses** and the **Pilgrimage of Grace** are discussed on pages 84–7.

The relationship between King and parliament

The changes to the government of England which took place between 1535 and 1541 affected not only the status of parliament but also the nature of **royal sovereignty** – essentially the King's powers. The Reformation of the Church increased both the King's personal power and also the areas over which his powers extended.

Key term

Royal sovereignty: the King's powers.

Activity

Revision exercise

List what powers and authority had been taken away from the Pope by 1535. Indicate which of these had been granted to Henry VIII and which had been given to the Church of England.

Royal sovereignty pre-1535

The traditional role of English monarchs had been rooted in the protection of property – principally their own, in terms of preventing invasion of the kingdom by foreign powers, but also that of their subjects, by maintaining law and order in England to ensure that an individual's life and his possessions remained secure. However, there were parts of what Henry VIII would describe as his kingdom where he had little effective power, which related to sanctuaries, liberties and franchises.

- **Sanctuaries** were areas in and around churches which could not be entered by the King's law officers. Whilst the sanctuary was essentially the railed area around the altar in a church, the recognised sanctuary could extend beyond the churchyard into the town around the actual church and churchyard. These areas were well known to criminals who could use them to escape the law. In some cases gangs of criminals used them as a base for their activities. At times they were also used by people who needed protection for political reasons.

■ **Franchises and liberties** were areas where the King had given the right to administer law to members of the nobility. In some cases in the past when the noble had died, the King at the time had used his feudal rights to reclaim the right to administer law in a given area, but many of these liberties and franchises continued into Henry VIII's reign.

Changes to sovereignty 1535–41

After the break with Rome, Henry VIII was fearful of possible opposition, and sought legislation to establish his control. Thomas Cromwell favoured making Henry's kingdom into a unified state in which the law of the King would be supreme and establish a national government. If this national state was established it was important that the whole of the kingdom should be represented in the House of Commons.

A range of legislation was passed to secure this:

■ **Sanctuaries**: In 1540 an act of parliament abolished the rights of most sanctuaries to provide a haven for petty criminals and completely abolished the right of sanctuary for serious crimes, for example murder, rape, arson and burglary.

■ **Franchises and liberties**: In 1536 an act of parliament was passed which restricted the rights of franchises and liberties and returned the power to run gaols, hold courts and appoint justices of the peace to the crown. The act identified the legal authority of the King's Highness and his heirs. Opposition to this act was one of the underlying causes of discontent which led to the Pilgrimage of Grace.

The largest area which Henry VIII regarded as part of his kingdom, but over which his actual power was limited, was Wales. Not only was real power in the hands of nobles known as the marcher lords, but Wales was not represented in parliament. Cromwell had begun the process of extending the power of the English monarch into Wales as early as 1534. He had appointed a close colleague as president of the Council in the Marches and an act of parliament had transferred the trial of serious crimes committed in the **Welsh marches** to English courts. From 1536, two acts together removed the semi-independence of Wales and increased the King's sovereignty.

1 the appointment of justices of the peace (JPs) for Wales as for England, which brought the systems of law and order into line

2 an act which formally incorporated Wales into England. This dissolved the marcher lordships; a subsequent act in 1543 incorporated some of the land into English counties and created a number of new counties. The creation of the Welsh counties allowed for their representation in the House of Commons through the election of members of parliament.

Together this legislation ended the separate identity and organisation of the principality of Wales. That it was successful and caused little disturbance was probably due to the Welsh ancestry of the Tudors and the loyalty they had shown to Henry VII.

■ **Exploring the detail**

Claiming sanctuary: Elizabeth Woodville

A good, earlier, example of someone claiming sanctuary for political reasons is Queen Elizabeth Woodville, consort of Edward IV. In 1470, when the Lancastrians briefly restored Henry VI to the throne, Elizabeth moved with her daughters into Westminster Abbey for sanctuary, living there in royal comfort until Edward was restored in 1471. She gave birth to their first son Edward while in sanctuary. She had all the comforts of home: she brought so much furniture and so many chests that the workmen had to knock holes in some of the walls to get everything in.

■ **Key term**

Welsh marches: the marches were those parts of Wales that were ruled as marcher lordships by marcher lords. These were Welsh kingdoms which had been conquered by Anglo-Norman barons, sometimes on the orders of the Kings of England, or at least with their approval. The marches amounted to about two-thirds of Wales. The remainder was the principality of Wales, which was part of the English crown's possessions.

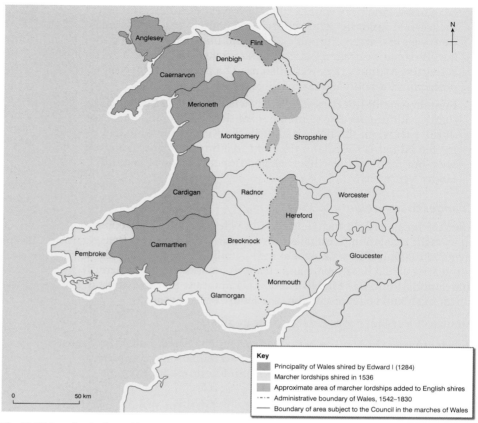

Fig. 7 *Wales after its formal incorporation into England*

The final area over which the King's sovereignty was extended and to which parliamentary participation was established was Calais. Virtually the same policy as had been introduced for Wales was used for Calais. Calais was England's last European possession and was important for trade. The act which was passed in 1536 made Calais part of the English system and allowed for the election of two MPs to the parliament at Westminster.

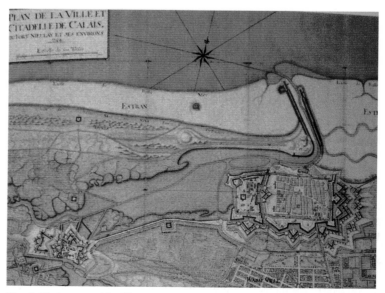

Fig. 8 *The town and fortifications of Calais. What does the illustration tell us about England's last French possession?*

The consequences of the Reformation for state finances

The Exchequer was the principal financial institution until 1530 and the income from crown lands went directly to it. Other income might be dealt with in the Privy Chamber, but accounting could be difficult there as the Chamber carried so many other responsibilities. The massive changes in the amount of money flowing to the crown as a result of the dissolution led to the establishment of four new departments of finance between 1536 and 1542.

Cross-reference

The **Privy Chamber** is described on page 2.

The **dissolution of the monasteries** is the subject of Section 3.

These were:

- the Court of Augmentations
- the Court of First Fruits and Tenths
- the Court of Wards and Liveries
- the Court of General Surveyors.

In addition there were two financial departments already in existence:

- the Exchequer
- the Duchy of Lancaster.

The four new courts were set up so that the crown could have more organised control over its lands and finances. The Court of Augmentations was formed to deal with the various property and financial problems brought on by the dissolution of the monasteries. The property had to be assessed and then disposed of by sale or rented out. Pensions had to be paid to the abbots, monks and nuns. In some cases debts owed by the religious houses had to be paid. As with the other courts established by Cromwell the Court of Augmentations had a chancellor and a treasurer as well as lawyers and auditors; in addition there were receivers who had charge of collecting rents from ex-monastic property in the various counties of England.

In 1542 the Court of General Surveyors was established out of the old household surveyors' department to administer crown lands, handle cases and register leases.

The remaining financial courts had very specific functions. The Court of First Fruits and Tenths was established in 1540 to collect from the churches the money which had previously been sent to Rome. The Court of Wards was also established in 1540 and became the Court of Wards and Liveries in 1542. This dealt with monies owed to the King in his position as feudal lord. It also enabled him to collect certain rights associated with marriage and wardship.

In Sources 4 and 5, P. Williams and B. W. Beckinsale respectively consider the changes which were made by Thomas Cromwell and their significance in altering the way in which government operated.

> Intervention by government in the social and economic life of the nation was seldom accompanied by the creation of new executive posts and enforcement was generally left to the existing officials, to local commissions, or to private enterprise. Nor was the bureaucracy well suited for the conduct of effective administration. Offices were held in plurality; meagre salaries tempted men to take gratuities and bribes; and payment by fees sparked off fierce demarcation disputes which often absorbed the energies of officials.

4   *Williams, P., quoted in Dawson, I.,*
The Tudor Century 1485–1603, 1993

Activity

Source analysis

How far does Source 5 agree with Source 4 about the reasons for the reorganisation of the administration?

Cromwell's treatment of the administration did not amount to a preparation for bureaucratic government. He did not reorganize the bureaucracy. He was an improver and exploiter of what existed. His new institutions, the Court of Augmentations and the Council of the West, were based on existing models and neither survived as institutions for long. It may be claimed that in the Secretary-ship and the Privy Council he produced what were virtually new institutions and that he altered the centre of gravity in the administration. Yet these changes appear to be more nearly related to the principal needs of his personal ascendancy and the position, allowed to him by the king, than to any plan for a national bureaucratic government. They were to the advantage of royal rather than bureaucratic rule.

5

Beckinsale, B. W., quoted in Dawson. I.,
The Tudor Century 1485–1603*, 1993*

Cross-reference

For the **wealth of the monasteries**, and of the Church in general, in 1529, refer back to Chapter 1.

The finances of Henry VIII

The break with Rome and the dissolution of the monasteries had a significant impact on the income which Henry VIII received. It has been estimated that the capital value of the monastic lands taken as a whole was £1,250,000. Prior to the dissolution of the monasteries the King received on average £25,000 per year from crown lands. Following the establishment of the Court of Augmentations and through the General Surveyors he was receiving approximately £86,000 per year from crown lands. This was made up of £48,000 through the Court of Augmentations and £38,000 from the General Surveyors. This money enabled Henry to endow the crown with a new livelihood even greater than that which he had inherited from his father and had subsequently spent on warfare in the first two decades of his reign. It also enabled him to reward those he favoured with outright gifts or favourable sales of church land. However, the monastic estates carried large financial burdens, such as the pensions paid to ex-monks, and this money had to be subtracted from the money brought in. The cost of these has been estimated at approximately 23 per cent of the value of the monastic lands, or roughly £19,780.

The Levy of First Fruits and Tenths, which before the break with Rome had been paid to the Vatican, also boosted the finances of the crown. The suspension of payments from the English Church to Rome brought in an average of £47,000 (£18,162,803) over the period from 1535.

Activity

Thinking and analysis

Geoffrey Elton argued that the work of Thomas Cromwell amounted to a revolution in government. Draw around your hands and identify and note *on the one hand* which of Cromwell's methods or policies were new and *on the other hand* those which used existing systems and methods.

Summary question

'The consequences of the Reformation for the improvement of state finances have been much exaggerated.' Assess the validity of this view.

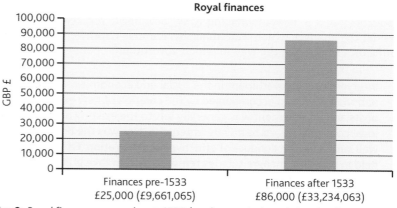

Fig. 9 *Royal finances pre- and post-1533 (modern equivalents in brackets)*

8 The impact of the Reformation abroad and at court

Fig. 1 *The cloth trade was very important to England. This early 15th century image shows women carrying out the various stages in the manufacture of cloth: washing and carding the wool, spinning the yarn, and finally weaving the cloth at the loom*

Cross-reference

For an explanation of the **Auld Alliance**, see page 133.

The break with Rome and the changes made to the government of England and the powers of the King over the Church of England distanced England from Europe. When Henry VIII sought another bride who would secure the dynasty he had to look beyond the traditional countries of France, Spain and Scotland. This decision was to have significant repercussions for Cromwell's domestic position.

> The unfortunate Cleves marriage did not cause the fall of Cromwell in April 1540. Nevertheless it affected Cromwell's fortunes. It made Henry lose confidence in his minister at a time when Cromwell's political position was being challenged by his rivals, Norfolk and Gardiner, and perhaps too it made Henry a prey to the charms of Catherine Howard, Norfolk's niece. Certainly Cromwell's reluctance to dissolve the Cleves marriage shook the king's faith in his minister and made possible his fall.

1   *Doran, S., **England and Europe 1485–1603**, 1996*

Neither Henry VIII nor his ministers could ignore what was happening in Europe. The Pope and the prominent Catholic powers of France and the Holy Roman Empire, led by Francis I and Charles V respectively, were keen to ensure the return of England to the Roman Catholic faith. England was very much in a minor league of powers, but had traditionally supported the Holy Roman Empire in the Habsburg–Valois conflict. The unsuitability of Anne of Cleves as a matrimonial partner for Henry resulted in a shift of power to the conservative faction – a shift reinforced by the Howard marriage. It culminated in Cromwell's fall and, paradoxically, a changed relationship with the countries of Europe. This was a time of diplomacy both in foreign policy and in domestic affairs. It was a period marked by false starts, failures and the start of Henry VIII's demise.

The impact of the Reformation on English foreign policy

Henry VIII's aims in foreign policy

During his reign (1509–47) Henry VIII had a number of foreign policy aims. The importance given to individual aims changed over the different phases depending on domestic circumstances and external threats.

1   To regain control of the former French territories. All English kings since Edward III had claimed to be King of France. Waging war against the French was also a means of gaining support from the nobility, who could use their military skills on the battlefield and gain property at the same time. Henry himself hoped to collect the French pension which had been paid to English kings every year in compensation for the lands lost by England in France. Attacking France had implications for relations with Scotland due to the Auld Alliance between the two countries.

2   To establish himself as an equal with Francis I and Charles V. Henry VIII was very concerned about his reputation. He wished to recreate

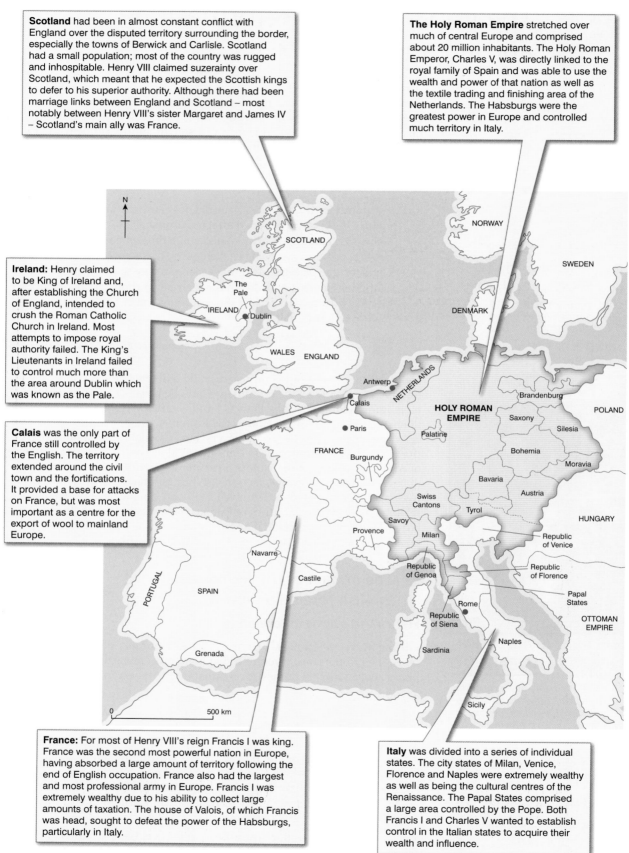

Scotland had been in almost constant conflict with England over the disputed territory surrounding the border, especially the towns of Berwick and Carlisle. Scotland had a small population; most of the country was rugged and inhospitable. Henry VIII claimed suzerainty over Scotland, which meant that he expected the Scottish kings to defer to his superior authority. Although there had been marriage links between England and Scotland – most notably between Henry VIII's sister Margaret and James IV – Scotland's main ally was France.

The Holy Roman Empire stretched over much of central Europe and comprised about 20 million inhabitants. The Holy Roman Emperor, Charles V, was directly linked to the royal family of Spain and was able to use the wealth and power of that nation as well as the textile trading and finishing area of the Netherlands. The Habsburgs were the greatest power in Europe and controlled much territory in Italy.

Ireland: Henry claimed to be King of Ireland and, after establishing the Church of England, intended to crush the Roman Catholic Church in Ireland. Most attempts to impose royal authority failed. The King's Lieutenants in Ireland failed to control much more than the area around Dublin which was known as the Pale.

Calais was the only part of France still controlled by the English. The territory extended around the civil town and the fortifications. It provided a base for attacks on France, but was most important as a centre for the export of wool to mainland Europe.

France: For most of Henry VIII's reign Francis I was king. France was the second most powerful nation in Europe, having absorbed a large amount of territory following the end of English occupation. France also had the largest and most professional army in Europe. Francis I was extremely wealthy due to his ability to collect large amounts of taxation. The house of Valois, of which Francis was head, sought to defeat the power of the Habsburgs, particularly in Italy.

Italy was divided into a series of individual states. The city states of Milan, Venice, Florence and Naples were extremely wealthy as well as being the cultural centres of the Renaissance. The Papal States comprised a large area controlled by the Pope. Both Francis I and Charles V wanted to establish control in the Italian states to acquire their wealth and influence.

Fig. 2 *Europe in the reign of Henry VIII*

the glory of Henry V, who had defeated the French at the battle of Agincourt in 1415. Henry V had been a warrior prince. Gaining honour and glory, particularly through war, was a major driving force for Henry VIII.

3 To maintain links with the Netherlands. This was important to Henry VIII because the English cloth trade was dependent on the Antwerp market. Additionally, the Netherlands was part of the territory which belonged to Charles V, who was in conflict with Francis I for much of this period.

4 To secure his family's inheritance. Henry's father had demonstrated the importance of linking the English royal line with that of other royal families in Europe through marriage alliances. Henry VIII's marriage to Catherine of Aragon had been part of an attempt to solidify the anti-French alliance.

The years after 1529 were marked by a foreign policy which was very different from that which Henry VIII and his chief minister Wolsey had pursued in the 1520s. The main cause of the shift was the increasingly fractious relationship with the Vatican. The pressure placed on the Pope by the Holy Roman Emperor to insist on the rightness of the marriage between Henry VIII and Catherine of Aragon left very little room for manoeuvre in foreign affairs and was itself costly in terms of energy and resources. Although trade links and the continuation of the Habsburg–Valois conflict had placed Charles V in a position where friendly relations with England might have been advantageous, this position was not particularly close, even in the years before the annulment.

When seeking recognition for the annulment of his first marriage and his subsequent marriage to Anne Boleyn, Henry had turned to Francis I. The overture to the French was not, however, turned into a formal alliance. The French did not need the support of England, as between 1529 and 1536 there was peace, albeit an uneasy one, between Charles V and Francis I.

In 1536 the situation between Charles V and Francis I changed again, when war broke out between the two major powers. Had the circumstances been different Henry might have sought to exploit the vulnerability of France. Catherine of Aragon had died, so removing the personal cause of conflict between Henry VIII and Charles V. Indeed, overtures were made by the imperial ambassador, Chapuys, although by the autumn Henry's attention was focused elsewhere as he was forced to turn to the crushing of the Pilgrimage of Grace.

In 1538 the situation deteriorated dramatically, as far as England was concerned, with the declaration of a 10-year truce between Francis I and Charles V. Cromwell saw the Treaty of Nice as posing a massive threat to England, and this led him to a search for allies in Germany. Cromwell's concern was further increased by the papal bull which excommunicated Henry. The excommunication was accompanied by the withdrawal of the French and imperial ambassadors from London. Cromwell believed that the Pope was encouraging Francis and Charles to support a crusade against England. Partly in response to this perceived threat, Cromwell held negotiations with several Protestant German princes who were organised in a group called the Schmalkaldic League. The Schmalkaldic League had been organised to defend Protestantism against the militant Catholicism of Charles V. Although Cleves was not in the Schmalkaldic League, the Duchy was hostile to the authority of the Holy Roman Emperor; it was to Anne of Cleves that Cromwell arranged a marriage for Henry VIII. This marriage was a failure from the outset.

 Activity

Thinking and analysis

As you read through this section, from the aims given here, select the factors which you think were important to Henry in shaping his relations with foreign powers in the years between 1535 and 1541. When you have finished, try to reorder your factors by their degree of importance.

 Cross-reference

To refresh your knowledge of the **Pilgrimage of Grace**, see Chapter 6.

 Exploring the detail

The Schmalkaldic League

The Schmalkaldic League was a defensive alliance of Lutheran princes within the Holy Roman Empire. The Schmalkaldic League had a substantial military force to defend its political and religious interests. It took its name from the town of Schmalkalden, in the German province of Thuringia.

The League was officially established on 27 February 1531 by Philip I, Landgrave of Hesse, and John Frederick I, Elector of Saxony, the two most powerful Protestant rulers at the time. It originated as a defensive religious alliance, with the members pledging to defend each other should their territories be attacked by the Holy Roman Empire.

Fig. 3 *Anne of Cleves, by Holbein. Why might Henry have trusted this miniature to be a true likeness of his prospective bride?*

■ **Key profile**

Anne of Cleves

Anne (1515–57) was the daughter of John III, Duke of Cleves. Her brother William, who succeeded his father in 1538, had rejected the authority of the Pope in religious matters, so the Duchy of Cleves was a suitable ally for King Henry VIII following his break with Rome.

When Anne was identified as a possible match for Henry, the artist Hans Holbein was sent to Cleves to paint portraits of Anne and her sister, Amelia, another possible wife for Henry.

Henry favoured educated, sophisticated and cultured women, but Anne had none of these qualities. She had not received any formal education as a child, and had learned to read and write only in her native German. Anne was similar to Jane Seymour in being considered gentle, virtuous and docile, qualities that made her a realistic, if unexciting candidate as a wife for Henry. However, he was unimpressed by his first night with Anne, as she was not the type he found physically attractive. After three months he ordered an annulment of the marriage on the grounds of non-consummation.

The King has heard that the Bishop of Rome and his supporters have taken counsel together how to utterly abolish the maintenance of Christ's word. They are of the opinion that the King, being one of the three principal princes who had most openly rejected the authority of the Bishop of Rome, might set an example to others. And, if they could overthrow him, the rest of the princes would yield to the Bishop of Rome's pleasure. The rumour is that the Emperor Charles V and the French king will attack England at the Bishop of Rome's request. The Papists malice against the King is grounded only on their envy of his religion.

2   *Letter from Thomas Cromwell to the King's representative in Germany, 1539*

Henry remained apprehensive and when Francis and Charles signed a peace treaty at Toledo on 12 January 1539 he became almost paranoid. One of the reasons for this was that he had too much information, most of it of dubious value. Thomas Cromwell, who had become his chief adviser in 1532, was a spymaster. His agents, both at home and abroad supplied him with vast amounts of intelligence, much of it completely undigested. Consequently he knew of every plot against England (real and imaginary), but had few means of assessing how dangerous they were.

3   *Loades, D.,* **Henery VIII: Church, Court and Conflict,** *2007*

■ **Activity**

Thinking point

Why did Henry VIII take the rumours of the threatened crusade against him so seriously?

While the suggestion of the threat from a joint crusade by Francis I and Charles V was provided by Cromwell's spies on the continent, there was one voice on mainland Europe speaking out openly against England's religious stance, and this was Cardinal Reginald Pole.

Margaret, Countess of Salisbury, Pole's mother, was the sister of the Earl of Warwick who had been executed by Henry VII because of his superior claim to the throne. Pole's family therefore had a strong claim, although, as a younger son, Reginald's personal position was less strong. To threaten Cardinal Pole and to prevent any further challenges to the Tudor dynasty, Cromwell appears to have 'exposed' a secret plot (although this may have been no more than criticisms of the royal policy) which enabled him to execute the Countess of Salisbury, Reginald's older brother, Henry, and two other apparent Catholic sympathisers with distant claims to the throne. Cardinal Pole remained at large, protesting against the action which he believed had been taken by Henry.

▪ Key profile

Reginald Pole

Reginald Pole (1500–58) was educated at Oxford where he was taught by the leading humanists. He was financially supported by Henry VIII. Pole also gained a position at Corpus Christi College and, as part of his research, spent time in Europe meeting many of the key Renaissance thinkers. In 1526 Henry offered Pole the Archbishopric of York when it came vacant, if he would publicly support an annulment of Henry's marriage to Catherine of Aragon. Pole refused and went into exile. His eventual response was to produce a treatise denouncing Henry's action against Catherine. In response to his loyalty to the Church Pole was made a cardinal in 1536.

At the same time as Cromwell had been making approaches to the Schmalkaldic League, Henry VIII sent the Duke of Norfolk to France. Sir Thomas Wyatt was also sent to the Imperial Court. Together Wyatt and Norfolk were able to exploit divisions based on plots being conjured by each side against the other. The 10-year truce was rapidly unravelling. By the winter of 1540–1 Stephen Gardiner (Bishop of Winchester) was sent to the imperial court to negotiate an alliance with Charles, which was agreed in the spring of 1541. The period of diplomacy and lack of military engagement was coming to an end.

▪ Conservative reactions against the Reformation

The Six Articles and the role of the conservative faction at court

The Act of Six Articles, passed in 1539, had shown Henry's personal conservatism in matters of doctrine. Formally titled 'An Act Abolishing Diversity in Opinions', the Act of Six Articles had asserted traditional Catholic doctrine as the basis of faith for the English Church. What is more, it had made disagreement with such doctrine heretical and punishable by death. The act was a political defeat for Cromwell, Archbishop Cranmer and the other reformist leaders at court and it had even led Hugh Latimer, Bishop of Worcester, and Nicholas Shaxton, Bishop of Salisbury, to resign their sees. By upholding points of Catholic doctrine that Protestants had begun to question, it marked the beginning of a period in which traditional beliefs were reaffirmed, which was to last until the end of Henry's reign.

Cross-reference

The **Act of Six Articles** is detailed on page 99.

Fig. 4 *Thomas Howard, third Duke of Norfolk, by Holbein*

■ Cross-reference

For a profile of the **Duke of Norfolk**, see page 82.

■ Cross-reference

For a profile of **Anthony Denny**, see page 138.

■ Activity

Research task

Not all historians share the view that the last years of Henry VIII's reign were shaped by faction. Some historians dispute whether factions actually existed. One point they use is that Henry Howard, Earl of Surrey, the son of the Duke of Norfolk, who is seen as part of the conservative faction, was reformist in his religious beliefs. Undertake some extra reading to identify evidence which challenges the idea of faction.

■ Cross-reference

For a profile of the **Earl of Surrey**, see page 139.

The Act of Six Articles gave hope to the conservatives at court that they might yet be able to assert their authority. Groups of courtiers seeking to advance their personal concerns were a feature of the reign of Henry VIII, and Cromwell's failure to provide a suitable wife for Henry in the fiasco of the Cleves marriage opened up opportunities for those who had not enjoyed the opportunity to influence Henry VIII since the late 1520s. This was a group which coalesced around the Duke of Norfolk and could loosely be called the conservative faction. The key people associated with this group were:

■ **Thomas Howard, third Duke of Norfolk:** Norfolk had served Henry VIII well, initially on the battlefield at Flodden in 1513. Norfolk had also been instrumental in his role as president of the Privy Council in bringing down Wolsey, and although he was the uncle of Anne Boleyn he had survived her disgrace and had helped to crush the Pilgrimage of Grace.

■ **the Duke of Suffolk:** Charles Brandon was a favourite of Henry VIII and had married his sister Mary. He supported the divorce of Henry and Catherine of Aragon; he himself had gained a papal dispensation to marry Mary.

■ **Bishop Stephen Gardiner:** Gardiner was Bishop of Winchester and the King's secretary. He has been described as a 'papist' at heart and was an outspoken defendant of the royal supremacy. The Act of Six Articles was mainly his work. Gardiner was in favour of building up relations with France as a counterpoint to Charles V, as opposed to seeking support among Protestant princes.

■ **Bishops Sampson, Stokesley and Tunstall:** Cuthbert Tunstall, Bishop of Durham, was the most significant of these three bishops. In 1537 he was made president of the Council of the North. He had remained Catholic by doctrine, although he had supported the royal supremacy.

■ **Sir Nicholas Carew:** Carew was executed alongside members of the Pole family with whom he was considered to be plotting. Despite being a cousin of Anne Boleyn he had turned against her and her reformist views.

■ **John Dudley, Lord Lisle:** Dudley was a fine soldier whose father had been a significant supporter of Henry VII. He was the King's Deputy at Calais.

By 1536 Thomas Cromwell appeared to have cemented his position. As Lord Privy Seal and Baron Cromwell he used his position to increase the presence of his supporters in the Privy Chamber. Two of his clients, Thomas Heneage and Anthony Denny, became Groom of the Stool and Chief Gentleman of the Privy Chamber respectively. Those such as the Duke of Norfolk, who felt that the dominance of the Cromwellian faction had gone too far, sought to topple him. The Duke of Norfolk's main power base was in the Privy Council.

There were reports of a furious argument between Cromwell and the Duke of Norfolk, possibly over a personal matter, in the spring of 1539. The failure of the Cleves marriage early in 1540 opened up opportunities for the Duke of Norfolk. Norfolk was able to present another niece, the teenage Catherine Howard, as a physically more appealing bride. Catherine was introduced to Henry at the house of Stephen Gardiner and immediately attracted him, as a result of both her looks and her lively personality. Yet despite Catherine's attractiveness and the slow process of ensuring the annulment of the Cleves marriage, Henry rewarded Cromwell further. In 1540 he was created Earl of Essex and Lord Great Chamberlain.

While the possibility of using Catherine to bring about the downfall of Cromwell was a potential strategy open to the conservatives, a far better strategy for the conservative faction lay in employing differences in religious belief. The fears of disunity in religion demonstrated by the John Lambert controversy provided an opportunity for the conservative faction. Above all Henry wished to establish his personal interpretation of religion. Reports of an investigation about a heretical group in Calais forwarded by Lord Lisle showed that although he himself had tried to remove the heretics, Cromwell, who did not think, at first, that they were heretical, had allowed them to stay. Cromwell tried to get his own back by suggesting that Lisle was involved with the supporters of Cardinal Pole. He also had Bishop Sampson arrested for treason. However, Cromwell had little ground on which to defend himself: his religious sympathies were too well known. On 10 June Cromwell was arrested on a charge of treason; he was taken to the Tower of London and executed on 28 July. He was not formally tried, but an Act of Attainder was passed against him.

The significance of the fall of Cromwell

The downfall of Thomas Cromwell was a personal tragedy for Henry VIII's chief minister but was consistent with the way in which the King had dealt with those who could no longer help him achieve his ambitions. In the Act of Six Articles Henry had placed his religious beliefs into law. It might be judged that these beliefs were very different from those of Thomas Cromwell, although the evidence on this is inconclusive. Thomas Cranmer, who also disagreed with the Six Articles, was able to hold on to his position as Archbishop of Canterbury because it was not as central to the overall government of the country and, whatever he thought, he was prepared to conform outwardly.

Fig. 5 *A contemporary painting of the Tower of London. What does it illustrate about the main functions of the tower?*

According to the historian G. W. Bernard:

> Henry wanted to have his religious cake and eat it; he wanted his royal supremacy, he wanted the destruction of the monasteries and the shrines; but he also wanted to maintain orthodoxy and unity. At times, the tensions between these aims were too great and Cromwell in 1540 paid the price. Henry was ruthless in his disposal of ministers (Wolsey) and wives (Catherine of Aragon, Anne Boleyn, Anne of Cleves) who for whatever reason no longer suited his purposes or who crossed his will. Henry from the start had been prepared to sacrifice the lives and happiness of people.

5   *Bernard, G. W.,* ***The King's Reformation****, 2005*

Cross-reference

The case of **John Lambert** is outlined on pages 97–9.

Activity

Thinking point

Using the material given and further research, what evidence can you find to support the following statements?

- The main issue linking the conservatives at court was religion.
- The main factor linking the conservatives was hatred of Thomas Cromwell.
- The main factor linking the conservatives was a desire to increase their own personal position and power.
- The main factor linking the conservatives was a desire to promote a pro-French foreign policy.

When you have completed your research, use your ideas to answer the following examination-style question.

- Explain why Thomas Cromwell was removed from office in 1540.

I beseech your Grace most humbly to pardon my rude writing and to consider that I am a most woeful prisoner, ready to take the death when it shall please God and your Majesty. Yet the frail flesh makes me constantly to call on your Grace for mercy and pardon for my offences. Written at the Tower with the heavy heart and trembling hand of your Highness' most heavy and most miserable prisoner and poor slave. Most gracious Prince, I cry for mercy, mercy, mercy.

4   *Letter from Cromwell to Henry VIII, June 1540*

Activity

Thinking point

What does Source 4 suggest that Cromwell thought about his fall?

Would the fall of Cromwell lead to further emphasis on the liturgy and doctrine of Catholicism?

Would the fall of Cromwell result in the emergence of another first minister, or would Henry govern through a group of advisers in the Privy Chamber or Privy Council?

Cromwell had been responsible for piloting through parliament the legislation that had achieved the break with Rome and established the Church of England. This legislation had been anti-Roman Catholicism, but Henry had resisted Cromwell's Lutheran leanings and the Six Articles had reinforced Catholic doctrine.

Cromwell had been the first minister for Henry and had effectively taken the place of Cardinal Wolsey as the minister who could get everything done. Cromwell had been brought down by a faction of conservative interests.

Cromwell had attempted to follow a foreign policy which established links with the Protestant princes in the Holy Roman Empire – the Schmalkaldic League. The marriage to Anne of Cleves was part of this policy. But the Cleves marriage had been a failure, and the truce between Charles V and Francis I had collapsed.

Cromwell had engineered the dissolution of the monasteries. This had resulted in a massive increase in the King's wealth. It had also enabled the nobility and gentry to acquire large amounts of property and had set up a new administration for the management of the new Crown lands and property.

Would the fall of Cromwell lead to a return to a foreign policy which was pro-Habsburg?

Would the fall of Cromwell enable Henry to make use of the money in an active foreign policy, and would Henry be able to maintain the financial systems and financial health established by Cromwell?

Fig. 6 *What was the impact of Cromwell's fall?*

Thomas Cromwell had been Henry VIII's first minister since the early 1530s. He had been responsible for almost all of Henry's policies. While there is considerable debate amongst historians as to whether Cromwell controlled Henry VIII or whether Cromwell put into practice the demands placed upon him by Henry VIII, there is little doubt that the removal of Cromwell led to change in a number of areas.

Cromwell's fall from power had both short-term and long-term consequences. The most significant is that it brought about the end of government by a single minister and a return to a form of government which was dependent on the interplay of faction. There has been much debate as to whether Henry manipulated the factions or whether the factions manipulated him. Until the last few days of his life, Henry remained very lucid and in control of his government. Nevertheless, he was increasingly ill from the long-term injuries sustained in tournaments: his legs were ulcerated, he had been seriously concussed and the immobility which had resulted from these meant that he was increasingly overweight. Henry VIII's dominating personality, which may have been screened from public view by Cromwell, was exposed by the latter's downfall. What came to the fore was not only his personality but his belief in his own honour. His sense of honour was based on military success, his view of religion, both personally and in terms of the Church of England, and what might be termed his sexual honour – ideally the King should have a clutch of legitimate and illegitimate children. After 1540 Henry was on his own, but his increasing ill-health meant that he had to establish the conditions in which his son Edward could succeed.

> The King liked to balance the factions, showing his ultimate power and control, rather than to lurch from one to the other like a frightened puppet. The king took charge and there was no conflict about who had most influence over him. In addition, there was little real trouble because the factions, reforming and conservative, were so well balanced. One could not destroy the other.

 6   *Pendrill, C., **The English Reformation 1485–1558**, 2000*

> The King had been stampeded by a faction bent on a coup d'etat and swept along by it, like the suggestible man that he was. For Henry was often this: a vulnerable and volatile thing. When the furore about Cromwell was over and it was too late to repair the damage, he began to see the dark truth about how he had been captured and exploited.

7   *Scarisbrick, J. J., **Henry VIII**, 1968*

The importance of the Howard marriage

Catherine Howard was little more than a pawn in the elaborate game being played by her family in their attempt to gain precedence at court following the removal of Thomas Cromwell. Although Catherine was a member of the Howard family, being the daughter of the younger son of the second Duke of Norfolk, and like Anne Boleyn the niece of the current Duke of Norfolk, her family's financially difficult situation meant that her upbringing had left her exposed to a range of experiences which were not suitable for a queen, and as such, would make her position vulnerable in the future.

Fig. 7 *The young Prince Edward. How does the artist emphasise that he is the son of Henry VIII?*

Fig. 8 *A miniature portrait of Catherine Howard. She was very attractive to the older Henry with her promise of youth*

Catherine Howard

Catherine was raised at Lambeth Palace, where she lived with her grandmother. She shared a dormitory with other girls of her age and her education was not intellectual. According to later accounts she enjoyed the company of a number of men who either exploited her, or with whom she sought excitement. It is clear that Catherine was flirtatious and that she was charming and sexually attractive.

The first man with whom she became involved was her music teacher, Henry Mannox. They first met in 1536, when Catherine was about 15. Hired to teach her the virginal and lute, Mannox soon began to seduce her. Catherine later swore the relationship was not consummated. 'At the flattering and fair persuasions of Mannox being but a young girl I suffered him at sundry times to handle and touch the secret parts of my body which neither became me with honesty to permit nor him to require,' she later told interrogators.

Catherine's attentions soon turned elsewhere. She fell in love with a gentleman-pensioner in her grandmother's household named Francis Dereham. This relationship was far more serious and undoubtedly was consummated. There is much evidence on this point, including Catherine's own confession: 'Francis Dereham by many persuasions procured me to his vicious purpose and obtained first to lie upon my bed with his doublet and hose and after within the bed and finally he lay with me naked and used me in such sort as a man doth his wife many and sundry times but how often I know not.'

Mannox, still with the household, was infuriated; his attraction to Catherine continued while she spurned his company for Dereham's. In revenge, he sent an anonymous note to the dowager duchess. She then discovered Catherine and Dereham together and there was a frightful scene.

In 1539, having moved closer to court and staying at her uncle's house, Catherine met Thomas Culpeper, a gentleman of the King's Privy Chamber, with whom she also fell in love. Shortly after meeting Culpeper, Catherine was taken to court to be a Lady in Waiting to Anne of Cleves. It was in this position that Henry VIII first came across her.

The overthrow of Thomas Cromwell and the marriage to Catherine Howard have been seen as victories for the conservative faction and it is clear that this group played the most significant role in advising Henry from 1540 to the end of 1541. There was, however, no real attempt to remove all Cromwell's placemen from the Privy Council or the Privy Chamber. Significantly, Cranmer remained as Archbishop of Canterbury. Rather, the fall of Cromwell enabled Henry to rule as he wished, to pursue his own religious policies and to marry whom he wanted, rather than being influenced by the political constraints which had been imposed by his previous ministers.

Henry VIII married Catherine Howard in August 1540; a little over a year later she was accused of adultery. During the year of their marriage Henry appears to have been deliriously happy and constantly gave presents and political favours to Catherine. The demands for political favours were fed through Lady Rochford, the widow of George Boleyn, Anne's brother, who was Catherine's minder at court. It was Lady Rochford who also facilitated secret assignations between Catherine and a number of men, including Thomas Culpeper. On one level this could be seen as outrageous behaviour, allowing a bored young woman some form of enjoyment. On the other hand it could be seen as a long-term strategy. If Catherine could produce a son, the Tudor dynasty and the Howard faction would be secure; producing a son would be difficult if Henry was unable to impregnate his wife. Henry desperately wanted another son.

As the stories about Catherine's behaviour became increasingly difficult to suppress, details were provided by a Lutheran sympathiser whose sister was part of Catherine's retinue. The Howards' political rivals decided to use the evidence to bring about the downfall of Catherine and her political backers. It was Thomas Cranmer who passed the details in a sealed envelope to Henry during Mass on All Souls' Day 1541. Initially Henry refused to believe the stories, but the evidence, especially that gained from torture, was overwhelming. The Queen and Lady Rochford were executed in February 1542; the two men with whom Catherine had committed adultery had been executed the previous December.

Although Lady Rochford and Catherine had been executed, Norfolk and his close associates were not punished; rather they were allowed to remain away from court in disgrace. Their triumph in the fall of Cromwell had ended not in disaster but in being eclipsed by others.

Learning outcomes

Through your study of this section, you will have gained an understanding of the means by which the powers of the King over the Church of England and his realm were strengthened in the years 1535–41 and the importance of the King in parliament. You should be able to explain what the consequences of the changes were, both for England and for Henry's relations with other European powers. You will also have gained an insight into the conservative reactions against the Reformation leading to the fall of Cromwell and Henry's marriage to Catherine Howard. The conservative stance adopted by 1541 was, as we shall see in the final section, to endure until Henry's death in 1547.

Practice questions

(a) Explain why a number of acts were passed in the years between 1535 and 1541
to increase the power of the King.

(12 marks)

You should be aware of the acts which were passed but do not fall into the trap of reciting details of those acts. This
question is focused on the reasons behind them.

The dates of the question, 1535–41, are clearly the period after the break with Rome, when Henry was trying to secure
the changes which he had made and address his newly defined position within Europe.

Your linking themes are likely to include Henry's desire to remove any remaining external religious influence, to extend
his laws throughout the country and to increase his personal wealth.

(b) 'The Church of England moved significantly away from the Catholic Church
in the years between 1535 and 1541.' Explain why you agree or disagree
with this statement.

(24 marks)

An important part of answering questions like this will be your introduction. This should be designed to indicate your
argument clearly and may well indicate the structure of your essay.

In agreement with the quotation you might want to stress that by 1535 the Church of England was separate from the wider
Catholic Church. However, you also need to consider the extent to which the Church had changed in terms of structure,
liturgy and doctrine and this may lead you to 'disagree'.

There was a further separation from the wider Church after 1535, with the dissolution of the monasteries and the creation
of new financial departments which absorbed the monies of the Church into the accounts of the King. In doctrine, however,
the Church of England remained very close to that of the Roman Catholic Church, as seen in both the Ten Articles and the
Act of Six Articles. Henry VIII's personal stand against John Lambert also indicated his position. In liturgy there was some
movement away from the Catholic Church in the placing of an English Bible in all parish churches and the encouragement
by Cranmer to the laity to read the Bible in their own language.

Decide which line you will take before you start to write and try to lead the reader to a clear and well-supported
conclusion showing your personal judgement.

In this chapter you will learn about:

■ how the conservative and reformist factions developed and influenced the King

■ the ways in which Catherine Parr influenced Henry VIII

■ how the position of Cranmer was affected by, and helped to change, policies

■ the significance of the King's Book, and debates and arguments on the Eucharist, liturgy and Bible and their impact by 1547.

Faction dominated the last six and a half years of Henry's reign. No single individual emerged to direct policy. The kingdom was controlled by an executive council that the King rarely attended. It was inevitable that the ambitions and personality clashes of the factions in the court and the council would be dominated by religion. In the final struggle the evangelicals emerged triumphant. In Henry's pain ridden last years fewer and fewer people had regular access to him; most of these such as his wife, archbishop Cranmer, and the gentlemen of his Privy Chamber were of the new persuasion in religion. That is why the conservatives mounted one last desperate attack on them in 1546.

1   Wilson, D., *In the Lion's Court: Power, Ambition and Sudden Death in the Reign of Henry VIII*, 2001

This argument has been put forward by D. Wilson, a historian who argues strongly for the existence of faction.

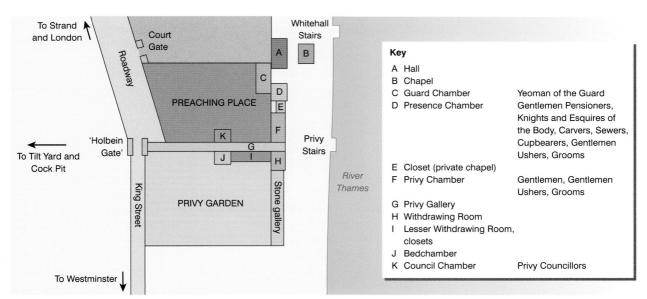

Fig. 1 *Layout of the court at the Palace of Whitehall*

The first and last years of the reign of Henry VIII were ones in which policies were not only enacted in the King's name, but also directed by him without day-to-day responsibility being entrusted to a single minister. Wolsey and Cromwell had directed the King's business from their own apartments and palaces. The focus in the last years was firmly back in the Privy Chamber, and those who were allowed into the inner sanctum were those who had the greatest influence on what happened.

The development of faction: Catherine Parr and Thomas Cranmer

The last period of Henry's reign was the longest in which he did not have a chief minister to direct his government. Wolsey and Cromwell had proved extremely valuable in advising Henry and putting his policies into action. They had been very useful in reconciling differences within the court and Privy Council, and in taking the blame when policies were unpopular or if the King wanted a sudden change of direction. The absence of a chief minister between 1540 and 1547 meant that the disputes between different interest groups were more exposed, to contemporaries as well as to modern historians. Faction had been present in the court of Henry VIII at key points: the Boleyns had worked with their relation, the Duke of Norfolk, to bring down Wolsey. The downfall of Thomas Cromwell owed much to the scheming of the Duke of Norfolk at the time of Henry's marriage to Anne of Cleves. Apart from a very brief period, after 1540, Henry was to remain in control of the direction of government until his death. It would be wrong to believe that he did not have a clear idea as to what he was aiming to achieve. At the same time there were undoubted attempts by the two sides to manipulate him and those who might have influence over him.

Table 1 *Conservative and reforming factions 1540–7*

	Conservatives	Reformers
Who?	The Duke of Norfolk Bishop Gardiner Sir Thomas Wriothesley The Earl of Surrey (although less so than the above)	Edward Seymour John Dudley Sir Anthony Denny Sir William Paget Archbishop Cranmer
What?	Catholicism Influence Personal gain	Protestantism Influence Personal gain
How?	Marriage to Catherine Howard Plots against Thomas Cranmer and Catherine Howard	Marriage to Catherine Parr Control of the Dry Stamp

The downfall of Cromwell and the marriage of Henry to Catherine Howard seemed to have placed the conservative faction at court, led by the Duke of Norfolk, in the ascendancy. The disgrace brought upon this grouping by Catherine's behaviour led to a shift in influence towards the reforming faction, whose nominal leader was Edward Seymour. This did not, however, lead to the disappearance of the Howards, who, after a short period of time in the country, returned to court. Each of the two factions was determined to pursue its own interests to the detriment of the other's. Two key people in the reforming influence at the court were a particular focus of the scheming of the conservatives to wrest the shaping of policy away from the reforming agenda. These were Catherine Parr, Henry's last wife, and Thomas Cranmer, Archbishop of Canterbury. Religious policy was the area of greatest contention.

Cross-reference

For a profile of **Thomas Cranmer**, see page 54.

■ **Key profile**

Edward Seymour

Edward Seymour (1506–52), Lord Hertford, was the eldest brother of Henry VIII's third wife, Jane Seymour. Edward had begun to gain influence at court whilst his sister was still Lady in Waiting to Anne Boleyn. Edward was able to demonstrate clear political thinking but it was his relationship to Jane, and then his position as the uncle of the heir to the throne, which gave Edward the greatest influence. Edward Seymour was a fine soldier and was able to use his military skills to good effect in the last years of Henry's reign. He became Lord Protector during the minority of Edward VI.

The influence of Catherine Parr

In his previous five marriages Henry's prime objective had been to continue his line. He had undoubtedly loved Catherine of Aragon and, while she was his mistress, Anne Boleyn. Jane Seymour had given him the much wanted son. It had been hoped that Anne of Cleves would provide more, but she had proved totally unattractive to the King. Henry had been very attracted to Catherine Howard, but he was unable to give her a child, or she him. His final choice in marrying Catherine Parr, who had already been widowed twice without having given birth to any children, does not seem to have been motivated by the belief that she would rapidly provide a number of male children. Catherine Parr appears to have been chosen for companionship in what was, increasingly, his old age.

Catherine Parr has often been portrayed as almost a saint by historians who have wanted to emphasise the triumph of the Protestant faith. In the following source Geoffrey Elton is very critical of this exaggerated view, but at the same time he recognises her other qualities and attraction for Henry VIII.

Fig. 2 *Catherine Parr, the last wife of Henry VIII*

> Catherine Parr proved capable of dealing with the ever viler temper of an egoist soured by ill-health and by what he conceived to be his unmerited tribulations. Henry's last queen, who apparently had Protestant sympathies, managed on the whole to keep out of politics, so that she survived her husband. She was a mild and moderately sensible woman much given to matrimony, but she scarcely merits the somewhat sanctimonious praise bestowed on her by the reformers and often echoed since.

 2   *Elton, G. R., **England under the Tudors**, 1956*

■ **Key profile**

Catherine Parr

Catherine Parr (1512–48) was the daughter of courtiers, Sir Thomas Parr and his wife, who was Lady in Waiting to Catherine of Aragon. Catherine Parr had already been married twice when she married Henry: first, at the age of 15, to Edward, second Baron Borough of Gainsborough, and after his death in 1533 to a major landowner in Yorkshire, Sir John Nevill. In 1536 Catherine and her stepchildren were held hostage by a group who were supporting the Pilgrimage of Grace. Following Nevill's death in 1543 Catherine joined the household of Henry's daughter Mary.

Fig. 3 *The Princess Mary, the daughter of Henry VIII and Catherine of Aragon*

■ Cross-reference

For a profile of **Erasmus**, see page 29.

The **case of Anne Askew** is detailed on pages 130–1.

■ Exploring the detail

Catherine Parr's beliefs

Source 3 is an extract from the preface of a book which Nicholas Udall dedicated to Catherine Parr, in which he praises her abilities. He illustrates some of the difficulties which we experience in explaining an individual's religious beliefs. Udall studied at Corpus Christi College, Oxford, and became headmaster of Eton. After the death of Henry VIII he is described as a 'Protestant'; during the reign of Mary Tudor he presented plays to the Catholic Queen. It is perhaps more accurate to describe both him and Catherine Parr as 'humanists'.

■ Key term

Regent: a person who takes the position of the rightful king until he is old enough to assume his full powers – or when he is absent, e.g. away fighting in wars.

There has been much debate about the religious sympathies of Catherine Parr and indeed there were several attempts to link her with known heretics such as Anne Askew. Like Henry VIII and Catherine of Aragon, she had been brought up a Catholic. Catherine's mother had been a Lady in Waiting in the household of Catherine of Aragon, after whom she was named; her father held influential posts at court and, as Lord Sheriff of Northamptonshire, he would not have held these posts in the early years of Henry VIII's reign if his household had been anything other than Catholic. Catherine Parr, in common with many literate women, such as Catherine of Aragon and Princess Mary, had been much influenced by the work of Erasmus. The conservative faction sought to demonstrate that she went beyond the humanist views of Erasmus and was sympathetic to the beliefs of Protestants. After the death of Henry she published two works, *The Lamentations of a Sinner* and a work she had commissioned which was a translation of a work of Erasmus.

> When I consider, most gracious Queen Katherine, the great number of noble women in this our time and country of England, not only given to the study of human sciences and of strange tongues, but also so thoroughly expert in holy scriptures, that they are able to compare with the best writers as well as editing and penning of godly and fruitful treatises to the instruction and edifying of whole realms in the knowledge of God, as also in translating good books out of Latin or Greek into English … I cannot but think and esteem the famous learned Antiquity … far behind these times.

 3   *Udall, N., quoted in Loades, D.,* **The Tudor Court**, *1986*

■ Activity

Source analysis

Read Sources 2 and 3.

How far does Source 3 differ from Source 2 in relation to Catherine Parr's abilities?

■ Activity

Talking point

In groups, discuss why Henry VIII might have chosen Catherine Parr for his wife. Was it a wise choice?

Henry's relationship with his wives in many ways reflected the relationship he had with his advisers. Increasingly, their viewpoints and actions needed to be sympathetic to his own; as was clear from the downfall of Cromwell, when their views were out of step with his, there was conflict. David Loades makes it very clear that Henry would not tolerate being lectured on any matter, but particularly on religion by Catherine Parr. His wives' views needed to be subservient to his own. At the same time he relied on their active participation in the government of the country. Catherine of Aragon had headed a successful military campaign against the Scots in 1513; and from July to September 1544 Catherine Parr was appointed queen **regent** by Henry as he went on his last, unsuccessful, campaign in France.

Catherine organised provisions, finances and musters for Henry's French campaign, signed five royal proclamations, and maintained constant contact with her lieutenant in the northern marches, the Earl of Shrewsbury, over the complex and unstable situation with Scotland.

■ A closer look

Catherine Parr and accusations of heresy

Although we cannot be sure of its veracity, a story by John Foxe, writing in 1583, told how Catherine dealt with attempts to implicate her by linking her with heretics and their ideas. A bill of articles was drawn up against her and signed by the King himself which would require her to state her views in public in front of Henry. Foxe argues that Catherine owned a number of religious books which were against the law and could have got her into very serious trouble had they been found. After hiding the books, Catherine took herself off to Henry's chamber where he was dining with a small group of his gentlemen. There she made a speech in which she argued that women were inferior to men and should do what their husbands directed and believe what they believed. Having then asked for Henry's direction, she said: 'I, a silly poor woman so much inferior in all respects of nature to you, how then it cometh to pass that your majesty will seem to require my judgement? Which when I have uttered and said what I can, yet must I and will I, refer my judgement to this and all other cases to your majesty's wisdom, as my only anchor, supreme head and governor here in earth next under God to lean unto.' She continued to state that she had perhaps been influenced by erroneous opinions but would refer all things to his majesty and be guided by him.

Catherine had, by using her intelligence, avoided being caught up as a victim in a major dispute between factions. She could have lost her head.

■ Activity

Thinking point

What role did Catherine play in promoting Protestant ideas?

The position of Archbishop Thomas Cranmer

The position and security of Thomas Cranmer as Archbishop of Canterbury were affected by the removal of Cromwell and the return to politics shaped by faction. If Catherine Parr could be targeted by the conservative faction in an attempt to pursue a more Catholic approach to religion, Thomas Cranmer was even more vulnerable. Archbishop Cranmer had not only been instrumental in securing the divorce for Henry VIII but had also carried out the plans for the Church of England developed by the King and Cromwell. Under Edward VI, Cranmer was to promote a very strongly Protestant theology. While Henry VIII was King, however, he was much more circumspect in his views. Nevertheless, the conservative faction under the Duke of Norfolk saw Cranmer as a major obstacle to returning the Church to a more conservative position and attempted to undermine Henry's confidence in Cranmer by linking him with heretical views.

An opportunity arose in 1543 when two reformers in Kent, Richard Turner and John Bland, were brought before the Privy Council. Just as the articles against these two men were to be presented to the Privy Council, additional articles were added by Stephen Gardiner's

■ Exploring the detail

The Prebendaries' Plot

The Prebendaries' Plot originated in a complaint made by conservatives in Kent against what they believed were heretical views which criticised, among other things, Masses for the dead. It was named after five canons of Canterbury Cathedral who made the original complaint, although linked to the plot were approximately 300 people, 240 of whom were priests and 60 local gentlemen. Among the gentlemen involved was Anthony St. Leger, who had been a supporter of Elizabeth Barton. Many involved had links to Oxford, which was seen very much as the university of the conservatives.

■ Key term

Prebendary canons: the clergy who were supported by a portion of the money owed to the cathedral.

■ Cross-reference

For more on **Elizabeth Barton**, see page 60.

Fig. 4 *Canterbury Cathedral, where the five canons linked with the Prebendaries' Plot were based*

■ Cross-reference

For details on the burning of Anne Askew, see pages 130–1.

nephew attacking Cranmer and linking him to what was known as the **Prebendaries**' Plot. The articles were delivered to the Council in London and were probably read on 22 April 1543. The King most probably saw the articles against Cranmer that night. The archbishop, however, appeared unaware until later that an attack had been made against him. His commissioners in Lambeth dealt specifically with Turner's case, where he was acquitted, much to the fury of the conservatives.

In Source 4 Jasper Ridley seeks to explain the complexity of the Prebendaries' Plot and the difficulties which historians face in presenting what happened. This plot is important in understanding the difficulties which Cranmer faced, but is also an example of the deeper complexities of a situation where two factions are seeking dominance over the other in terms of influencing the King.

> Several modern historians have challenged the theory that the Conservative Prebendaries conspired to ruin Cranmer by presenting a case based on lies. Rather, they put forward a different explanation in which the case was controlled by Cranmer. They believe that Cranmer was secretly furthering the Reformation in his diocese by protecting reformers who had broken the law and framing the conservatives on false charges. It is impossible to discover the truth from the accounts, for a consistent picture can be drawn on the basis of either interpretation; but if we consider Cranmer's career in its entirety, it becomes evident that the accusations of the orthodox Prebendaries were far more false than true.

4

*Ridley, J., **Thomas Cranmer**, 1962*

Henry did not inform Cranmer of the accusations being made against him until September 1543. Interestingly Cranmer was appointed by Henry to lead the investigations against him. To demonstrate his trust in his archbishop, Henry gave Cranmer his own personal ring. Such a gift was very symbolic: the wearing of the ring would demonstrate very visibly to Cranmer's opponents that he had the King's support. The ring could also be sent to the King should Cranmer find himself under threat. This demonstration of confidence in Cranmer was sufficient in the short term to enable Cranmer to ward off the challenge of the conservatives on this occasion, but the conservatives were prepared to try more than once more.

■ Activity

Thinking point

How important was Cranmer in the development of Henry's religious policy in the years 1540–7?

> Despite Cranmer's survival, the King's Book and the Prebendaries plot created an essentially conservative atmosphere. A number of former catholic fugitives returned to England at this time, while the number of Protestants seeking refuge abroad increased. Protestant polemic against the chief demon, Gardiner, became both strident and impotent. A series of notable recantations and the burning of Anne Askew in 1546 seemed to herald a new age for English Catholicism.

5

*Rex, R., **Henry VIII and the English Reformation**, 1993*

The King's Book and debates and arguments on the Eucharist, liturgy and Bible and their effect by 1547

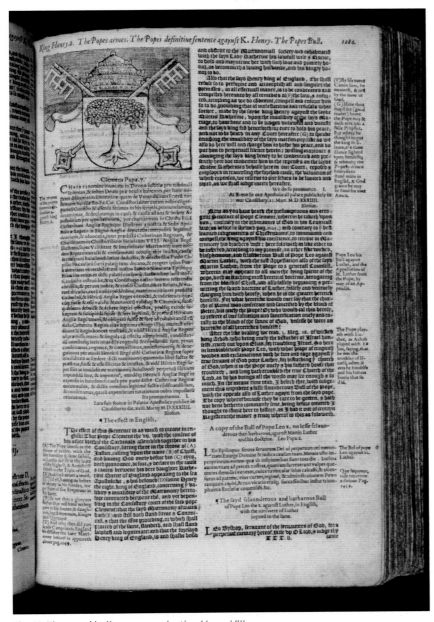

Fig. 5 *The papal bull excommunicating Henry VIII*

There seems to have been a lack of a clear line in the development of religion between 1543 and 1547, unless the view of G. W. Bernard put forward in *The King's Reformation* is accepted. Bernard argues that the religious policy was consistently that of Henry himself, rather than the product of the differing influences of conservative and reforming factions. On 5 May 1543 a new revision of the Bishops' Book, which had first been published in 1537, was issued. The revision, *A Necessary Doctrine and Erudition for any Christian Man*, was written by the bishops, but had a preface by the King and was known as the King's Book when it was released. According to the modern historian John Guy:

Cross-reference

The publication of the **Bishops' Book** is covered on page 97.

> In May 1543 a formulary to replace the Bishops' Book was read in the Council Chamber before the nobility of the Realm. Officially licensed by the supreme head, the King's Book revised its predecessor by expounding the Creed, seven sacraments, Ten Commandments, and Lord's Prayer according to the Act of Six Articles. The bishops were blamed by Protestants for the 'damnable doctrine' of the work, but the politics of the revision are clearly shown by the handwritten instruction on the inside cover of Henry's thickly annotated copy of the Bishops' Book 'not to be had out of the privy chamber'. Henry VIII penned the King's Book himself.

6   *Guy, J., Tudor England, 1988*

Doctrinally, the King's Book was far more openly conservative than the Bishops' Book. It reaffirmed traditional beliefs, such as the importance of Masses for the dead, and also explicitly rejected Lutheran views on justification by faith alone. On 10 May a further step away from the views of the reformers was taken when parliament passed the Act for the Advancement of True Religion, which abolished 'erroneous books' and restricted the reading of the Bible in English to those of noble status. From May to August, reformers were examined, forced to recant, or imprisoned.

■ A closer look

The English Bible

The English Bible, which had begun to be introduced to every parish church in England and Wales from 1538, had been commissioned from Miles Coverdale and was printed in Paris. The frontispiece appealed to Henry's sense of his own importance. It showed him as Supreme Head, flanked by Cranmer and Cromwell distributing the word of God. Although in the 1530s Henry had been pleased with what he saw as the parallels with the Kings of the Old Testament, by the early 1540s he was more circumspect. Coverdale's 1535 translation had been very dependent on translations made by Luther and Tyndale. When faced with a choice of translations from Greek and Latin to English, Tyndale had favoured those which reflected a Protestant rather than a Catholic flavour. This meant that the Bible was the focus of much contention: those who favoured a conservative, or Catholic approach to religion, argued that the translator was wilfully misrepresenting the text. Bishop Gardiner insisted that scripture had to be interpreted, and that to allow ill-educated people to have access to the Coverdale Bible would be to enable them to misconstrue Christian teaching. Henry VIII was increasingly sympathetic to this view. He argued that 'the most precious jewel, the Word of God is disputed, rhymed, sung and jangled in every ale house and tavern'. Henry recognised that the only way in which he could control the direction of religion was by restricting it to those who had a vested interest in maintaining his power.

Rather than these events marking the start of a return to even more conservative beliefs, however, they mark the end of backward-looking policies. Cranmer used his position to develop some reform of liturgy while leaving the doctrine as it was. In 1545 the King's Prymer was introduced to provide guidance for schoolmasters in religion. Cranmer was very astute both in realising that there needed to be an agreed presentation of religion in churches and in ensuring that he did not alienate the reformers too greatly. The attempt to remove him had demonstrated the need to try to keep the conservatives on his side and not to allow either side of the religious divide the opportunity to preach what they wanted. Cranmer produced a book of **homilies**, which could be used in churches. These homilies were short **sermons** written by him and other bishops, including the conservative Edward Bonner. Yet despite a number of experiments that Cranmer might have wanted to explore further, and which he presented in the reign of Edward VI, during the remainder of the reign of Henry VIII the Latin Mass remained central to the spiritual life of the Church of England.

Key term

Sermons and homilies: Protestant theology placed great emphasis on the preaching of the sermon. Sermons could be very lengthy. A homily was a short address to the congregation. It was a compromise between demands for preaching and the Catholic tradition, which placed the emphasis on the Mass.

Fig. 6 *A woodcut from Foxe's Book of Martyrs. What image of the Church after the break with Rome is suggested by this?*

A key feature of religious policy during much of Henry's reign is the seeming contradiction between his religious beliefs and his actions. A clear example of this in the later years of his reign is the attack on chantries.

Cross-reference

Chantry chapels are described on pages 12 and 15.

Activity

Research task

Undertake some personal research to locate and find out about any chantry chapels near your home.

The King's Book emphasised the importance of Masses for the dead to reduce the time spent by a soul in purgatory, and Henry's will stipulated that Masses should be said for his soul; yet the period 1540–7 saw a sustained attack on chantries, including the passing of an act of parliament in 1545. Chantry chapels were attached to the majority of churches and many of the monks from the dissolved houses had found employment as chantry priests. The chantry guilds were very wealthy institutions owning a great deal of property: to Henry VIII they offered a similar attraction to that which had been presented by the monasteries. Eighteen chantries were dissolved by royal initiative between 1540 and 1543, 10 in 1544 and 27 in 1545. The Abolition of Chantries Act of 1545 allowed for a further 19 chantries to be taken by the crown. The money from these was used to fund the wars against France and Scotland.

Fig. 7 *A chantry chapel at Wakefield. What might be the significance of having the chapel on the main bridge into the town?*

Activity

Thinking point

Why did Henry VIII torture and publicly execute those who shared the view of religious reformers?

A closer look

The English Litany of 1544

The English Litany of 1544 can be seen as both mildly evangelical and at the same time traditional. For the first time a service was conducted in English. However, it did not replace the existing form of service used in the church. The litany is a form of prayer which is said, or sung, as the clergy and the congregation process around the church. As the congregation went to ask for forgiveness for their sins they would process anticlockwise; the procession that went round the church clockwise was for celebratory occasions such as Christmas Day. The English Litany was detailed to be used on the three days before Ascension Day, St Mark's Day (25 April) and in times of emergency – plague, famine and foreign threats. It was also used as a response to drought and for relief from a wet summer.

The reason given for the service to be conducted in English was to deal with the perceived antipathy of the laity to such services. In addition to delivering the litany in English, the overall length of the service was reduced to 30 minutes from the previous two hours. During such crises the congregation had been used to offering prayers to saints, especially local ones. The new litany made it clear that no specific saints should be named, only 'the Virgin Mary and the blessed company of Heaven'. The use of the English Litany was extended from October 1545 to meet the threat of war.

The influence of Protestant ideas on those closest to the King, such as Queen Catherine and Archbishop Cranmer, was illustrated by the case of Anne Askew, who was executed for heresy in 1546. Strenuous efforts were made by the conservative faction to implicate both Catherine and Cranmer in the preachings of Anne Askew even to the point of torture.

The examination of Anne Askew

Master Rich sent me to the Tower. Then came Rich who asked me if I would tell them of others of my sect. They asked me about my Lady of Suffolk, my Lady of Sussex, my Lady of Hertford, my Lady Denny, and my Lady Fitzwilliams, I said that if I should pronounce anything against them, I were not able to prove it. Then they asked were there members of the Council who supported me. And I said no. Then they put me on the rack.

7

Quoted in Dickens, A. G., and Carr, D.,
The Reformation in England, 1967

Exploring the detail

Torture rack

The rack was the most painful form of torture in the 16th century. It was a wooden frame with two ropes fixed to the bottom and another two tied to a handle at the top. The torturer turned a handle causing the ropes to pull the victim's arms. Eventually, the victim's bones were dislocated with a loud crack. If the torturer kept turning the handles, some of the limbs were torn apart, usually the arms.

This method was mostly used to extract confessions.

Key profile

Richard Rich

Richard Rich (1496/7–1567) was knighted in 1533. As solicitor-general he was the main assistant to Thomas Cromwell in the dissolution of the monasteries. He helped to secure the convictions of Thomas More and Bishop John Fisher. Rich became the first Chancellor of the Court of Augmentations. His own share of the spoil, acquired either by grant or purchase, included about 100 manors in Essex. Rich also acquired – and destroyed – the priory of St Bartholomew the Great in London. In spite of the share he had taken in the suppression of the monasteries, his religious convictions remained Catholic.

Fig. 8 *The execution of Anne Askew in 1546. What does this suggest about the attitude of the crowd?*

Anne Askew

Anne Askew was born in 1521. She was from a gentry family in north-east Lincolnshire. She was forced into marriage at the early age of 15, and undoubtedly rebelled against this – for example, she refused to adopt her husband's surname. Anne came into contact with, and was influenced by, new religious ideas; the area of the country where she lived had established trading links with the ports of northern Europe where the new religion was taking hold. Anne believed it was more important to promote the gospel of Christ than to be a good wife and mother. She left both her husband and children to go to London, where she preached against the doctrine of transubstantiation. When she returned to Lincolnshire her husband refused to have her back in the house. In response she went back to London to ask for a divorce, on the grounds that her husband was not a believer; like Henry, she sought justification from the Bible, referring to 1 Corinthians 7:15. In London she gave sermons and distributed banned Protestant literature. Having so clearly broken the law, Anne was arrested: her husband was sent for and ordered to take her home. However, shortly afterwards she was preaching back in London, and was arrested again.

Some hoped that political use could be made of her: Anne was tortured on the rack in the hope that she would name Catherine Parr and Thomas Cranmer. However, Anthony Kingston,

Constable of the Tower of London, refused to carry on torturing her on the grounds that it was illegal to torture women; distressed, he asked Henry VIII to pardon him for not continuing with the torture. But while the King pardoned him, he refused to put an end to the torture. Instead the Lord Chancellor, Thomas Wriothesley, and Richard Rich took over, and continued to apply pressure on Anne.

Anne Askew did not break under the months of torture and refused to name either Catherine Parr or Thomas Cranmer, although, as a result, she was too badly crippled to walk to the stake. She was burnt at Smithfield, London on 16 July 1546. Smithfield was the main meat market for London, not far from St Paul's Cathedral, and was traditionally the site used for executing heretics and dissidents. Before the dissolution there had been two abbeys around the area used for selling and slaughtering sheep and cattle. That these abbeys had been destroyed by those who now criticised Anne Askew for challenging the Catholic belief in transubstantiation may have seemed ironic to people at the time. Smithfield also had other memories: Anne Askew may have been aware that it had been a meeting place for those involved in the Peasants' Revolt of 1381, when the views of another monarch had been challenged. It was also the place where St Bartholemew's Fair was held each year.

Activity

Constructing a timeline

Draw a timeline between 1537 and 1547. Detail above the line events which suggest a move away from Catholicism and below the line moves back towards Catholicism. This can be developed by placing the event closer or further away from the line depending on its significance.

Activity

Revision exercise

Copy and complete the following table showing the actions of Henry in support of:

Conservative faction	Reforming faction

Summary questions

1. Explain why Anne Askew as a heretic was burned at the stake.

2. How important was the doctrine of the Church of England in determining Henry's policies in the last years of his reign?

The final years of Henry VIII

In this chapter you will learn about:

- how Henry VIII's foreign policy became more aggressive in the later years

- the ways in which the influence of the Seymour faction grew and the influence of the Howards was destroyed

- the extent to which there were signs of change by 1547.

Key chronology

The final years of Henry VIII

1542 Execution of Catherine Howard

Defeat of Scots at Solway Moss

Death of James V

1543 Marriage of Henry to Catherine Parr

Conservative faction plot against Cranmer

1544 First debasement of the coinage

1545 Chantries Act passed

1546 Execution of Anne Askew

Anthony Denny becomes Chief Gentleman of the Privy Chamber

Henry's last will written

1547 Execution of the Earl of Surrey

Death of Henry VIII

Henry in 1544

By now he was becoming a man of huge girth, eating and drinking prodigiously. His great weight must have exacerbated his condition no less than did his dauntless zeal for riding. In March 1544 – just as he was about to set out on his last campaign – the ulcer flared up once more and the fever returned. But in July of that year he crossed to Calais and rode a great battle horse to the siege of Boulogne. Though he was carried about indoors in a chair and hauled upstairs by machinery, he would still heave his vast pain racked body into the saddle to indulge his love of riding and to show himself to his people, driven by an incurable will to cling to his ebbing life.

1   *Scarisbrick, J. J., **Henry VIII**, 1968*

Fig. 1 *A bloated King Henry VIII in the last years of his reign*

The foreign policy of later years

The desire which Henry VIII had demonstrated in the first years of his reign to stake his claim to France had not gone away. The work which Cromwell had undertaken to consolidate Henry's power in England and Wales still left a belt of land around the border with Scotland which was constantly disputed; Henry VIII wanted to force the Scots to recognise his superior authority.

According to the historian John Morrill:

> Henry did not claim sovereignty over Scotland; he did claim suzerainty: that is, he did claim that Scotland had been for centuries a feudal dependency of England. As a feudal lord, he could claim the right to supervise the arrangements for government during the minority of Mary Queen of Scots. In effect, whoever married Mary would bring Scotland into the control of his own family. Henry wanted both to acquire Scotland by a dynastic marriage between Mary and the Prince Edward, and perhaps even more to prevent her falling into the clutches of the royal house of France.

2   *Morrill, J., **The British Problem, 1534–1707**, 1996*

The dissolution of the monasteries and the subsequent sale of crown property had enabled Henry VIII to consider what might be achieved by a more aggressive foreign policy. There is little doubt about the fact that Henry believed that he could afford to embark on a war. There is much greater debate about what he was actually trying to achieve. A. F. Pollard believed that Henry was attempting to defeat Scotland and absorb the territory into England, as had happened with the Welsh Marches. The argument of J. Scarisbrick seems much more convincing in arguing that Henry's main aim was to acquire territory and prestige in France, but because of the 'Auld Alliance' between Scotland and France he was forced to defeat the Scots to prevent them attacking England while the army was active in France.

Scotland

Cross-reference

To recap on **foreign affairs in the 1530s**, see Chapter 8.

Exploring the detail

The Auld Alliance

The Auld Alliance was a series of agreements signed by Scotland and France specifically against England: the first was signed in 1295. Over the centuries it brought benefit to Scotland by preventing diplomatic isolation. It gave more practical help to the French: military support was given by the Scots in the defeat of the English in France during the Hundred Years War. Louis XII asked the Scots to invade England in 1513 to divert Henry's troops from attacking France. The attack ended with the defeat of the Scots at Flodden. By 1540 James V was married to a French princess.

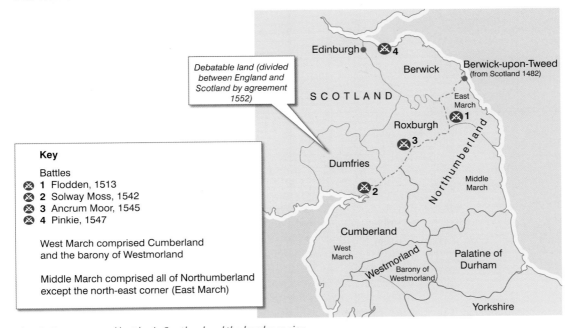

Key

Battles
⊗ **1** Flodden, 1513
⊗ **2** Solway Moss, 1542
⊗ **3** Ancrum Moor, 1545
⊗ **4** Pinkie, 1547

West March comprised Cumberland and the barony of Westmorland

Middle March comprised all of Northumberland except the north-east corner (East March)

Fig. 2 *Key towns and battles in Scotland and the border region*

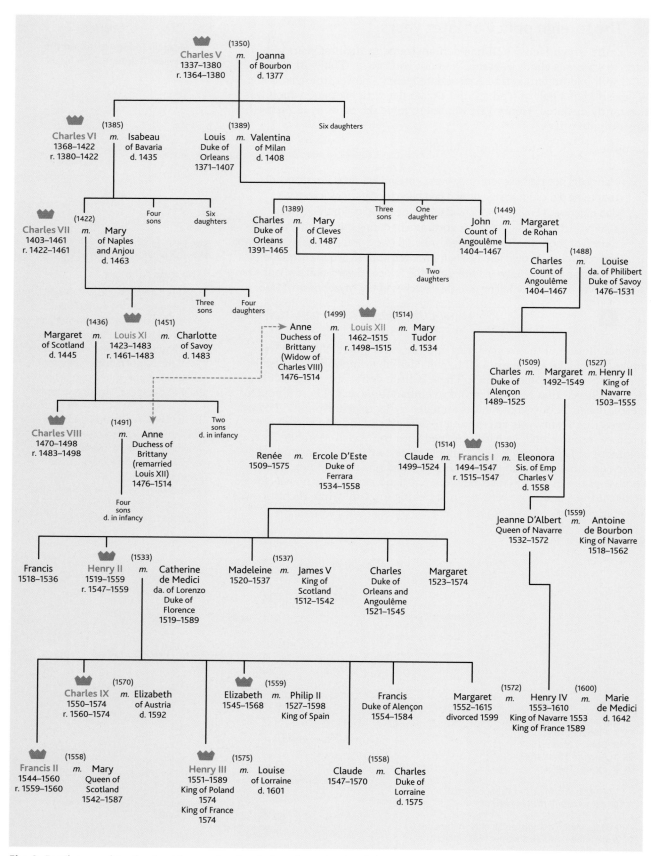

Fig. 3 *Family trees of Scotland and France, showing the interdependencies of the Auld Alliance*

The relationship between Henry VIII and James V was somewhat more complex. James had demonstrated close links with France through both his marriages which had been to French princesses. More significantly, although James was the nephew of Henry VIII, he failed to offer him the deference and support which Henry expected as the senior monarch. Also, James had provided sanctuary for some of the rebels who had participated in the Pilgrimage of Grace and in 1541 he failed to attend a meeting in York which Henry had arranged. While it was most likely that James's council would not have allowed him to attend, because of concerns about being kidnapped when passing through the unstable northern marches, Henry had marched to York with the majority of the court in great pomp, keen to impress his power on a region which had so recently supported the Pilgrimage of Grace. The fact that James did not turn up was a great and public insult to Henry.

In October 1542 Henry's army under the leadership of the Duke of Norfolk launched an attack on Scotland. This was not a carefully planned and executed attack, but rather an attempt to demonstrate English superiority through burning property, attacking people and stealing anything which could be taken. Following this frenzied attack, which lasted approximately six days, the English troops returned to the disputed border town of Berwick-upon-Tweed. A month later the Scots led an army of 20,000 men to fight the English at Solway Moss. The battle which followed might be more accurately described as a skirmish, but it was a decisive defeat of the Scots by a smaller English army. Henry was able to claim both victory and a significant number of Scottish prisoners. James V died shortly after, it was said through shame. While this rather extreme diagnosis is difficult to prove, the situation which Henry faced was more complex: James's heir was a two-week-old baby girl whose mother was a French princess; the Scottish regent was superficially pro-English; and there was a possibility that Henry's son Edward might be married to the baby Mary Queen of Scots and that Scotland could be brought under English control.

Despite the signing of the Treaty of Greenwich in July 1543, which seemed to secure the marriage of Edward to Mary, Henry's influence in Scotland was rapidly curtailed. By 1544 the Auld Alliance had been re-established, the Treaty of Greenwich had been repudiated and a pro-French regent was in power. All Henry could do was to try to force the Scots to submit through the tactics which had been so successful two years earlier for the Duke of Norfolk. The **rough wooing** conducted by Edward Seymour, Earl of Hertford and uncle of Prince Edward, drove the Scots even further into the French camp.

France

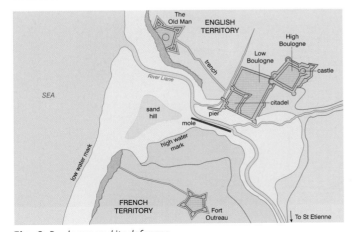

Fig. 6 *Boulogne and its defences*

Fig. 4 *James V, King of Scotland, and nephew of Henry VIII*

 Activity

Research task

Study the diagrams of the family trees of the Stuart, Valois and Tudor families. Demonstrate which links were the strongest.

 Cross-reference

The **Pilgrimage of Grace** is described in Chapter 6.

 Key term

Rough wooing: this meant using military forces to persuade the Scots that a marriage alliance between England and Scotland should be secured.

Fig. 5 *Emperor Charles V. His domination of much of Europe was to offer both support and challenge to Henry VIII*

Exploring the detail

Calais and Boulogne

Calais and its surrounding region was the only part of France to remain English following the defeat in the Hundred Years War. It provided a base for further attacks and control of the straits of Dover. It had economic importance as the basis for the export of English wool. Boulogne had little strategic importance and its castle was decaying and difficult to defend. Its importance in the early 16th century was as a focus for pilgrimage. While relics held at its cathedral had been visited by 14 French and five English kings, such pilgrimages had been outlawed by Henry VIII.

By the time Seymour was attacking Scotland, Henry had finally launched an invasion of France. The Habsburg–Valois truce had broken down and Henry decided to try to gain French territory and assert his right to at least the payment of the French pension by joining Charles V who was planning an attack on Paris. A new treaty was signed between Henry and Charles on 11 February 1543 to mount a joint attack. Very rapidly the ambitious plans began to unravel. Although his army of 48,000 men was the largest army ever to leave England until that date, it was led by two aged commanders and was encumbered by having to move at the pace at which Henry himself could travel. The real problems, however, were that not only had Charles V no real intention of mounting a serious attack on Paris, but that Henry also quickly decided to abandon any such plans and instead to achieve a swift territorial gain to prove his strength and bargaining power by taking Boulogne.

Although Henry's armies successfully occupied Boulogne, the cost was enormous. Charles V, outraged by Henry's abandonment of the joint plan, stopped his own attack and made peace with France. Freed from the double threat of the imperial and English armies, the French launched a counter-attack on England. This led to the invasion of the Isle of Wight during which Henry's flagship, the *Mary Rose*, was sunk with the loss of 500 men. In June 1546 Henry VIII signed the Treaty of Camp with the French. This gave him control of Boulogne for eight years and the French agreed to restart payments of the pension. There could be little doubt that Henry's French invasion had been a hugely expensive mistake.

> The twentieth of July, the whole navy of the Englishmen made out and purposed to set on the Frenchmen, but in setting forth, through too much folly, one of the King's ships called the Mary Rose, was drowned, by reason that she was over-laden with ordnance and had the ports left open which were very low, and the great artillery unbreached; so that when the ship should turn, the water entered and suddenly she sunk. In her was Sir George Carew, Knight and about 400 soldiers under his guiding. On the morrow after, about 2,000 of the Frenchmen landed in the Isle of Wight.

3   *Chronicles of Ralph Holinshead*

Fig. 7 *The embarkation of Henry's fleet for France. What does this painting demonstrate about the commitment to a victory in France?*

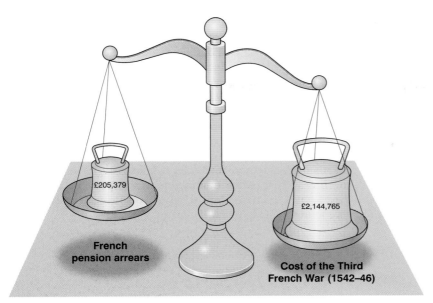

Fig. 8 *Cost v. benefit of the Third French War*

Activity

Thinking point

Why do you think Henry was so keen to capture Boulogne rather than attack the capital city of Paris?

> We are at war with France and Scotland, we have enmity with the Bishop of Rome, we have no assured friendship with Emperor Charles V, we have alienated the Protestant princes, and the war in which we are engaged is detrimental to our merchants and threatens our realm.

4 *Bishop Gardiner*

Activity

Revision exercise

1 Copy and complete the following table showing the gains and losses of Henry VIII's foreign policies against France and Scotland.

Gains against France	Losses against France	Gains against Scotland	Losses against Scotland

2 How might Henry VIII have challenged Bishop Gardiner's view that the foreign policy which he pursued in his last years was detrimental to England?

The influence of the Seymour faction and the demise of the Howards

While the events at Boulogne were significant as a mark of the importance of England in relation to the key European powers of Habsburg and Valois, in a minor way they were also significant in terms of the balance between

Fig. 9 *Edward Seymour, Earl of Hertford. He later took the title Duke of Somerset when he was made Protector of Edward VI*

Cross-reference

For a profile of **Edward Seymour** see page 121.

the Seymours and the Howards. The field of battle, especially in France, had always been a proving ground for the English nobility, which is one of the reasons why the French War had been so popular at court. Following the invasion and the capture of Boulogne, the Earl of Surrey, heir to the Duke of Norfolk, had been made Captain of Boulogne. Unfortunately for the conservative faction, Surrey, with excessive confidence in his own ability, spearheaded a bold attack on a key French fortress on 7 January 1546. Had this been successful this would have been a major triumph; instead, part of Surrey's army deserted him, and he was forced to save himself as best he could. The details of what happened reached William Paget, Henry's Principal Secretary, and other members of the reformist faction, who together were instrumental in demoting Surrey and replacing him with Edward Seymour, Lord Hertford, who had so recently proved his strength of purpose in the Scottish campaign.

Key profiles

William Paget

William Paget (1506–63) was aided in his progress by Stephen Gardiner, who employed him on a number of diplomatic missions. He survived the collapse of the Cleves marriage, having been secretary to Queen Anne. In 1543 he was made a member of the Privy Council. Paget was always prepared to position himself in support of the monarch's views, a characteristic demonstrated in the reigns of Edward, Mary and Elizabeth. He was willing to reject the views of Gardiner to be named in Edward's regency council and, in the process, gained considerable landed property.

Sir Anthony Denny

Anthony Denny, one of Henry's principal advisers, had a reputation as a scholar and patron of literature, but his greatest influence came from his position in the Privy Chamber. Denny was Groom of the Stool, a prestigious position in the Privy Chamber. He had control of the Dry Stamp, which enabled him to manage documents to be signed by Henry VIII (see page 140). As a supporter of the reformist faction he was instrumental in promoting Edward Seymour as Lord Protector following the death of Henry.

David Loades argues that Henry was unwilling to trust people:

> Henry regarded everyone around him with paranoid suspicion. Suspicious as Henry seems to have been of the motives of everyone around him, the fact remains that he chose eventually to trust men such as the Earl of Hertford, Lord Lisle and Sir William Paget rather than the Duke of Norfolk, the Bishop of Winchester or Sir Thomas Wriothesley; the reason seems to have lain in his vision of his own authority. There had not been a royal minority for over a hundred years. It was Henry's intention that the powers of the crown should be vested in the council. This was not the view of the Conservative faction. The earl of Surrey was executed precisely because he pretended a claim to the throne.

5
*Loades, D., **Henry VIII: Court, Church and Conflict**, 2007*

Activity

Thinking point

Why do you think that Henry VIII was not prepared to trust the Duke of Norfolk or Stephen Gardiner?

The final political upheaval of Henry VIII's reign resulted in the downfall of the Howards and the loss of influence of the conservative faction at a critical time when Henry was considering who should have influence during the inevitable minority of Edward. Henry's reign had been dogged by the need to secure the succession. He was always conscious of the existence of what was termed the White Rose Party: those of the White Rose were linked by potentially stronger claims to the throne than he enjoyed. Generally the attacks on these families occurred at points when the attitude of foreign powers seemed most threatening. He had at various times, as described in previous chapters, when he felt most insecure, dealt with the males of the Pole and Courtenay families who threatened his authority. Moreover, the Duke of Buckingham had been executed for his statements about his claims to the throne in 1521 when Catherine of Aragon's difficulties in producing a male heir were becoming obvious.

The crisis with the Howards occurred in 1546, when Henry was ill and Edward was far from his majority. Henry, Earl of Surrey, heir to the Duke of Norfolk, produced a new coat of arms which included reference to the arms of Edward the Confessor, the last Saxon king, and thus an apparent challenge to the Tudors' right to the throne. Such a claim was sufficient for the enemies of the Howards to attack. Both father and son were taken to the Tower of London and on 26 January 1547 the Earl of Surrey was executed for treason. Only the death of Henry VIII on the following day prevented the Duke of Norfolk from also being executed.

> ### Exploring the detail
> #### The White Rose Party
> The White Rose was the emblem of the House of York, as opposed to the Red Rose of Lancaster or Tudor Rose created by Henry VII. The White Rose Party was not a formal group, but this was an umbrella term to describe those who wanted to see a return to Yorkist rule. It could be used to describe either those who had an actual claim to the throne or their supporters.

Key profile

Earl of Surrey

Henry Howard, Earl of Surrey (1516/17–47), was the eldest son of the Duke of Norfolk; his mother was the daughter of the Duke of Buckingham, which gave him royal links on both sides. He grew up at Windsor castle as the companion of Henry Fitzroy (the illegitimate son of Henry VIII). In 1532 he accompanied Henry Fitzroy to the French court where they stayed for a year. 1536 was a significant year, not only because of the execution of his cousin Anne Boleyn, but also due to the death of Henry Fitzroy. In the same year he had his first real military experience, supporting his father in the royal army against the rebels of the Pilgrimage of Grace. He later accompanied Henry VIII's forces in the invasion of France in 1543.

The Earl of Surrey was a true Renaissance man and is best remembered for the development of a new poetic form. It has been somewhat absurdly claimed that Shakespeare's plays were written by him. It was his arrogance in the design of his coat of arms which led to his downfall and execution for treason.

Fig. 10 *The portrait of the Earl of Surrey which resulted in his execution for treason. Why were the three lions on the coats of arms so contentious?*

While the downfall of the Howards suggests that the disputes between factions dominated Henry's last few years, it would be wrong to believe that during his last two years Henry VIII was impotent and that the factions were more important than he was. Henry continued to play as significant a role in government concerns with foreign policy and

■ Key term

Dry Stamp: this replicated the signature of Henry VIII and could be used on a document and then inked over by a member of the Privy Council. It was intended to save Henry the effort required to sign a number of routine documents, but was arguably used by the Privy Council to determine policy and to change Henry's will.

■ Exploring the detail

Coats of arms

Coats of arms were important military symbols used to identify a knight and his followers in battle. They were also used on legal documents. A coat of arms belonged to an individual rather than to a family but could be passed down from father to son with a small change. Coats of arms demonstrated the lineage of the bearer, emphasising the power and significance of the family.

■ Activity

Thinking point

What problems for the government of England might be envisaged should Edward succeed as a minor?

■ Activity

Source analysis

Explain how far the views in Source 7 differ from those in Source 6 in relation to the powers of Henry VIII in the last few months of his life.

religious affairs as he had throughout his reign. Rivalries were between groups of individuals and about mundane domestic matters, but increasingly the conflicts between factions were more to do with who would determine Henry's inheritance during the period of Edward's minority. Nevertheless, access to the bedridden Henry and control of the **Dry Stamp**, which would enable members of Henry's inner circle to determine what received royal assent, were increasingly in the hands of those who favoured changes to religion.

The key people who were well placed to dominate the final months of Henry's life and to shape his instructions for the conduct of Edward's minority were Edward Seymour, Lord Hertford, who was now Lord Chamberlain of the Royal Household, and John Dudley, Anthony Denny, William Paget and Thomas Cranmer, Archbishop of Canterbury. The members of this group, who were very different characters, were linked by the desire to protect the religious changes which had occurred from the conservative faction of the Howards, and to promote an evangelical approach to religion. It was these factors which determined Henry's decision not to include Stephen Gardiner in the group of Privy Councillors who would be responsible for Edward during his minority. Henry believed that only he could control Stephen Gardiner and that he would wish to return England to Rome. Ironically, it was Henry's determination to protect the religious changes he had introduced which led him to appoint a group of ministers who would destroy the balance of the catholic Church of England which he had created.

> It was only the peculiar circumstances of the last months of the reign that produced a decisive swing in the balance of power. The Denny faction established a stranglehold on the Privy Chamber. In October Heneage, the long serving groom of the stool, was dismissed and Denny promoted to his post. Catherine Parr's brother-in-law was brought in as second Chief gentleman. As the King's health went into constant, if uneven, decline this control was brought devastatingly to bear. First power was used to exclude rivals from the court. There, literally behind closed doors, Henry's mind was poisoned against the conservatives. At the same time the King's will was doctored.

 6

*Starkey, D., **The English Court**, 1987*

> In the last months of his reign, Hertford, Paget and Denny enjoyed complete ascendancy at court and they achieved that position with Henry's full knowledge and consent. Whether the King either knew of, or consented to what happened in the last weeks of his life is another matter. Gardiner's fall from favour was a direct consequence of his defeat by Catherine over the Anne Askew affair and was certainly Henry's doing. On 26 December the King approved a will giving the reforming party complete control over the executors who were to form Edward's council.

 7

*Loades, D., **The Tudor Court**, 1986*

The group that came to dominate the Privy Council and Privy Chamber in Henry's last days used the Dry Stamp to great effect, most notably in the signing of Henry's will. While the use of the Dry Stamp was legally sound, there has been some speculation that there were in fact two wills, and that those who eventually emerged as the key advisers to Edward not only dry-stamped the will after Henry's death but also wrote it.

The consensus of opinion, however, is that the surviving will expresses Henry's last conscious intentions. This is based on the knowledge that Henry believed that, although Edward would succeed to the throne as a minor, he would inherit the supremacy with Henry's death; it would not be something which he would inherit only on his coming of age. The supremacy, like every other aspect of the crown, would therefore be vested in the council. That Henry chose not to have a single regent was the result of his suspicious nature and his fear that if one person was chosen that person would establish a separate power structure at court which would be difficult for Edward to deal with when he came of age. Of the reforming faction, Edward Seymour, as the brother-in-law of Henry VIII, and more importantly uncle of Prince Edward, was the leader of those who were left to act on Edward's behalf until he came of age.

As to the succession of the Crown, it shall go to Prince Edward and heirs of his body. In default to his daughter Mary and heirs of her body, upon condition that she shall not marry without the written and sealed consent of a majority of the members of the Privy Council appointed by him to his son Prince Edward. In default to his daughter Elizabeth upon like condition. In default to the heirs of the body of Lady Frances, eldest daughter of his late sister the French Queen.

8

The Will of Henry VIII, December 1546

Activity

Thinking point

1 Why did Henry VIII exclude the heirs of his sister Margaret from the succession?

2 What problems for the government of England were created by Henry VIII's increasing incapacity?

Signs of change by 1547

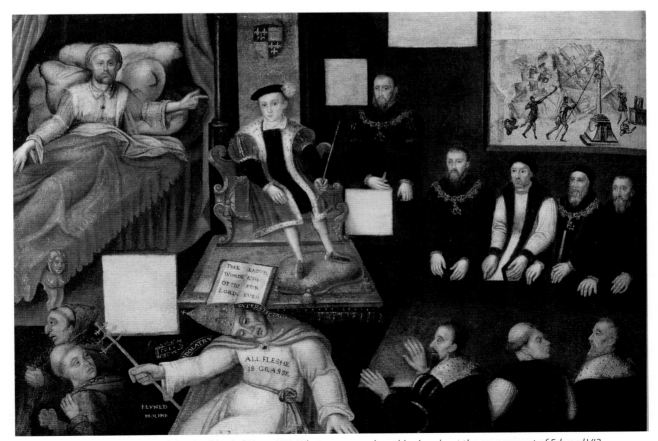

Fig. 11 *An allegorical painting of the deathbed of Henry VIII. What messages does this give about the government of Edward VI?*

I cannot choose but to love and favour you, affirming that no prince in the world more favoureth his subjects than I do you, nor no subjects or commons more love and obey their sovereign lord than I perceive you do me, for whose defence my treasure shall not be hidden, nor if necessity shall require my person shall not be unadventured. Yet I see and hear daily that the clergy preach one against another, teach one contrary to another, inveigh against each other without charity. Amend these crimes I exhort you, and set forth God's word, both by true preaching and good example, or else I, whom God hath appointed his vicar, and high minister here will see these divisions extinct.

9   *Henry VIII's last speech in parliament, 24 December 1545*

Although this speech to parliament was made more than a year before Henry's death in January 1547, it summarises a number of key elements which determined what followed. The Church of England, whose doctrine and liturgy had been created by Henry, was what he wished to preserve. It was crucial that the power and supremacy which he had established should be protected for Edward, his son and heir. For this reason disputes had to be resolved. Henry was too well aware what the consequences of division in government could be. Fear of civil war if the throne was disputed had been a cause of the desire to annul the marriage to Catherine of Aragon. The other key message conveyed by this speech is the importance of Henry himself. The potent legacy of Henry, his imposing majesty, and his imperial ambitions had to be protected. It was this legacy that Edward Seymour sought, as Lord Protector, to protect for Edward, and which was in part to prove his downfall. The power of the monarch might have been supreme but the condition of England in 1547 included a number of concerns which had the potential to become a crisis. The problems were:

- The expense of the war in Scotland and France had far exceeded what could be met from the monies held by the crown, even with the further sale of crown lands. Debasement of the coinage had begun to take place which was leading to inflation and increasing poverty.

- Maintenance of the territorial gains in Scotland and France required a large military presence on both fronts. This led to demands for more money and further debasement of the coinage.

- An increase in population put pressure on the food supply which was further exacerbated by enclosure and the conversion of arable land to pasture. The inflationary consequences of this with the impact of debasement had a potential for serious unrest.

- The pace of religious debate was gathering momentum and was going beyond the limited changes made by Henry. Protestant congregations in London and East Anglia were demanding the types of religious freedoms enjoyed in Germany and Switzerland.

On 28 January 1547, the day after the Duke of Norfolk's attainder had been passed, Anthony Denny warned Henry VIII to be prepared for the end. Thomas Cranmer was sent for, but by the time he arrived Henry was unable to make his confession, or to be given the last rites. Henry appears not to have done anything to reverse the excommunication given to him by the Pope. He seems to have died without pain and confident in what he had achieved. By his own criteria he had done his duty to God. None of his family was with him on his deathbed. Edward and Elizabeth were children, but Catherine Parr was not called and his daughter Mary was not informed that her father was near to death.

■ **Exploring the detail**

Debasement of the coinage

In Henry VIII's reign coins in circulation contained the exact amount of metal to the face value of the coin. A crown, which was worth five shillings (25p), would contain five shillings' worth of silver. As a result of the need for money to finance the wars, the Royal Mint collected in coins, melted them down and reissued them, having substituted some of the silver with a much cheaper metal, perhaps copper. After some time these coins were known as 'old brown nose', as the copper showed through. Henry VIII had more money to spend but money was actually worth less.

Henry VIII's body lay in state at Westminster for two weeks. Edward VI was proclaimed King and the government, led by Protector Somerset, Edward VI's uncle, was established. On 14 February Henry VIII was buried in the chapel of St George at Windsor Castle in the same grave as his third wife, Jane Seymour. He had asked for Masses for his soul to be said forever, but only two years later, in 1549, such Masses were made illegal by his son's government. Even when Mary became Queen and restored the relationship with Rome, the Masses for Henry were not restored. There were some rumours that during Mary's reign the bones of Henry VIII were taken out of the tomb and burned. This is not substantiated. More importantly, Henry's legacy, established by him, of the Church of England and the sovereignty of parliament, survives.

Learning outcomes

Through your study of this section you should have developed an understanding of the influence of Catherine Parr and of the conservative and reformist factions at court in the years after 1542. By examining the position and influence of Cranmer as well as the significance of the King's Book and the debates on doctrine and the Bible which opened up in the final years of Henry's reign, you will have a better idea of the state of religion in England at the time of Henry VIII's death in 1547.

You have also seen how and why Henry VIII became involved in war with the French and the Scots, and how the Seymours grew to prominence at the expense of the Howards in Henry's final years, leaving Edward Seymour in a strong position to exert his influence in the next reign.

Practice questions

(a) Explain why members of the Privy Council were able to exploit Henry VIII's weaknesses in the last months of his life.

(12 marks)

Study tip Take note of the specific period identified in the question. It is also important to link the specific individuals and their roles and positions. What was achieved by the reformist faction needs to be contrasted with what was offered by the conservative faction.

- Henry VIII was increasingly weak and members of the Privy Council were able to use the Dry Stamp and control who had access to the King.
- The Privy Council was in accord with Henry's wishes as it represented:
- the continuation of the Church of England rather than a return to Catholicism, and
- the assurance that Edward would succeed rather than another claimant.

(b) 'The last years of Henry VIII's reign were undermined by factional rivalry.' Explain why you agree or disagree with this statement.

(24 marks)

Study tip Plan your essay carefully to ensure that you have focused on the key issue of factional rivalry and have defined the context. It is important to be aware of the criteria by which Henry VIII's reign could be deemed to have been undermined. Was there a retreat back to the Roman Catholic Church? Was the power of the King in parliament eroded? Was the succession insecure?

You may suggest that Henry 'used' rather than 'was used' by the opposing factions. The conservative faction enabled him to promote an essentially Catholic doctrine while the reformist faction offered him protection for his creation of an England separate from Europe in which the King was supreme. You may also wish to suggest that involvement in foreign affairs was more undermining than factional rivalry.

Fig. 1 *An allegorical painting showing Henry with his children and his third wife, Jane Seymour*

A foreign visitor to England in 1547, who had not been in the country since 1529, would be struck by dramatic changes to key areas of policy and belief. England in 1529 had been part of Catholic Europe, with the universal Church playing a significant political, judicial, social and economic role in addition to its religious responsibilities. By 1547 the autonomous Church of England had been established: its bishops still played a political role within parliament but the Church courts, and the property, wealth, and powers of taxation of the Church and monasteries were firmly within the control of the monarch. No foreign visitor to England in 1529 could ignore the majesty of Henry VIII, but the role of monarch, which Henry had created by 1547, was significantly different: he now had power over both Church and state and controlled a more unified country with much greater legal authority than in 1529. In 1529 the visitor would have sought to influence the Privy Council which advised the monarch and, while this body was still of great importance in 1547, the visitor would have been aware that the monarch's power was strongest when exercised through parliament; the England of 1547 had, to a large extent, been created by act of parliament. In 1529 English influence had its greatest effect when rooted in diplomacy; in 1547 England was effectively at war with France and Scotland – a war on two fronts which was draining the King's financial resources and creating major economic problems, as the debasement of the coinage resulted in inflation. An observer in 1529 would have noted that Henry VIII most feared challenges from within the nobility, particularly from those whose claim to the throne was greater than his; the existence of a healthy, intelligent male heir in 1547, albeit a minor, appeared to make the Tudor dynasty more secure. The crushing of all opposition to Henry's authority, especially in the defeat of the Pilgrimage of Grace, would seem to the outsider to have cemented the control of the monarch over his kingdom. Few would have been conscious of the potential for unrest generated by the cost of the wars.

There has been much debate as to what precipitated the changes which took place during the most significant 18 years of Henry VIII's reign, but most agree that the multi–faceted role of the Catholic Church was significant. It is difficult to sustain either the view that the Church before 1529 was doomed to collapse, or the idea that Henry VIII was a fervent advocate of Protestantism. What is clear is that Henry was heavily influenced by humanism and had a view of Catholicism based on the seven sacraments including transubstantiation, but was suspicious of the worship of saints and eschewed pilgrimages. While such beliefs could have remained personal and have been contained within the existing structure of the Church, the unwillingness of the Pope to grant an annulment to his marriage to Catherine of Aragon forced Henry to respond in a series of measures which ultimately led to the break with Rome.

The relationship between Henry VIII and his ministers has also been seen as contentious. Was Henry manipulated by Wolsey and Cromwell, or was Henry the architect of the changes undertaken? While it may be tempting to absolve Henry of many of the unpleasant aspects of his reign, as he himself did, most notably through the execution of Thomas Cromwell, ultimately, Henry ensured that he got what he wanted; he used his ministers to further his desire for power and control. Wolsey had been very useful to Henry in advancing his position within Europe, but when he was unable to achieve the annulment of the marriage which had failed to produce a male heir, he was dispensed with. Thomas Cromwell was unlikely to have had a carefully crafted plan which encompassed the break with Rome, the dissolution of the monasteries and the creation of an autonomous state based on royal supremacy, but he had the ability to navigate his way to this end. At each step Henry increased his control, his power or his wealth, and by 1540 he had achieved all three. Cromwell was by this stage dispensable; indeed he was a liability. Cromwell had rejected the beliefs of Catholicism; Henry had not. Cromwell was charged with heresy and Henry was able to reassert his doctrinal principles based on a humanist interpretation of Catholicism which constituted the Henrician Reformation. The King's Book of 1543 gave the clearest statement of Henry's personal religion.

By breaking with Rome Henry placed himself and England outside Catholic Europe. The rivalry between the two major powers of France and the Holy Roman Empire for control of land in Italy had offered Henry the opportunity for power brokering and potential allies. Although Henry was excommunicated by the Pope and effectively condemned to hell for eternity, neither Francis I of France nor Charles V was unwilling to overlook Henry's lack of orthodoxy if it suited their own interests. The fear of a joint invasion of England was very real in the late 1530s but did not materialise. Much more significant was the individual relationship which Henry was able to broker with one or other of the two main powers. Charles V's support for his aunt was one reason why the Pope was unwilling to grant an annulment of Catherine and Henry's marriage; at the time the Pope was a virtual prisoner of Charles V. The recognition given to Anne Boleyn as the Marchioness of Pembroke as a result of her visit to the French court in 1532 is believed to have given the go–ahead to Henry's marriage to his mistress. Charles V was, by the early 1540s, willing to ally with England to attack France. On his deathbed Henry VIII was still effectively at war with France; deserted by Charles V, he was no nearer to achieving his ambition to recapture the land once owned by England in France than he had been in 1509.

Henry used the law – and although he executed wives, ministers and nobles, he tried hard to set his actions within a legal framework. The wealth accrued by the dissolution of the monasteries could have freed him from the need to raise taxation and therefore to call parliament, but all the major steps undertaken were achieved through act of parliament. It is difficult to argue that the Henrician Reformation transformed the role of parliament – this did not happen until the 17th century – but it is clear that the monarch was strongest when he acted through parliament. Members of parliament, both Lords and Commons, ultimately gave their support to the break with Rome, the creation of the royal supremacy and the dissolution of the monasteries. As with Cromwell, it is unlikely that they were supporting a master plan for the creation of an autonomous state. Most members of parliament acted in their own interest and the interest of their localities. The financial power of the Roman Catholic Church was a concern to some; others, who were well educated, were critical of the corrupt practices of the Church. While Henry was able to gain overarching powers, and in the short term wealth, through the break with Rome and the dissolution of the monasteries the longer–term beneficiaries were the nobility, gentry and merchants who bought property from Henry and gained with it power and local influence.

Not all decisions taken by parliament received unequivocal support from within the Houses of Lords and Commons, but increasingly Henry made dissent very difficult through the use of the laws of treason. Only those prepared to die for their beliefs were willing to stand out against what the King was doing. Sir Thomas More and the Carthusians were obvious examples. Those who participated in the Pilgrimage of Grace were others. The widespread actions taken by different groups in the north of England sought not to challenge Henry VIII himself but to protect the monarch from the advice of those who they felt were misleading him. It was not in Henry's interest to take heed of their intentions. The execution of Aske and the crushing of the rising in early 1537 demonstrated that Henry saw the rising as a treasonable challenge. This, and support for the Statute of Wills, prevented any further widespread dissent for the remainder of his reign.

Henry VIII was dependent on support from parliament, from his chief ministers and from his Privy Councillors. Faction was a consistent feature of his reign; different interest groups gained the ascendancy at different times. Thomas Wolsey had been very careful to reduce the power and influence of the nobility during his period as chief minister but was brought down by the alliance of the Howards, Boleyns and Thomas Cromwell. Thomas Cromwell was swift to distance himself from the Boleyns following Anne's disgrace, but was himself brought low with the support of the conservative faction. All these developments were supported by Henry VIII and in the 1540s he proved himself adept at creating tension between the two rival groups, allowing his own needs and the future of the Tudor dynasty to be paramount.

The main factor which underpinned the most important developments of Henry VIII's reign was the need to secure the inheritance. It may be an apocryphal tale that Henry VII on his deathbed charged his only surviving son with the continuation of his dynasty. Nevertheless, the 'King's Great Matter' was the need to achieve a legitimate male heir. The charges placed against Anne Boleyn were rooted in her failure to provide a live male child. The abortive marriage to Anne of Cleves had been based on the attempt to provide another male child; it was not forgotten that Henry had been the second son and that Arthur had died on the brink of adulthood. It is uncertain whether Henry realistically believed that Catherine Howard would have his child, and Catherine Parr may have been deemed to be too old. However, the last years of Henry's reign were as much about securing the Tudors as the break with Rome had been. That Edward was likely to inherit the throne as a minor exercised Henry. He had managed to remove all credible alternative claimants to the throne, beginning with the Duke of Buckingham and concluding with the Earl of Surrey as late as 1547; but in 1547 Henry not only had the Tudor dynasty to secure, but also the autonomous state which he had created, based primarily on his role as head of the Church of England.

Glossary

A

Acts of Attainder: acts of parliament which declared a person guilty of treason without a trial, after which the crown would acquire all that person's possessions. The person could be executed or allowed to live. A noble's title would revert to the King.

C

chantry: chantry chapels were where Masses were said for the dead. Chantry also refers to the money which was invested, either by an individual or a group of people, to pay for the priest to say Masses.

clergy: term used to describe all those who were priests in the church; it could refer to a parish priest or to an archbishop.

commons: people who were not members of the nobility or gentry. This was a term which could be used to describe those who owned no property, and also those who owned significant amounts but did not have a title or an inherited role in the government of England.

D

doctrine: the teachings of the Church and its beliefs.

E

Eucharist: the Christian sacrament in which bread and wine are consecrated and consumed, in commemoration of the Last Supper; also known as the Mass.

Evangelical: a person who preached the gospel; in particular how the death of Christ on the cross removed the fear of death for believers.

F

faction: a group of courtiers who came together either to oppose the views of another group or to influence the King to ensure that their ideas and the policies they favoured were put into practice.

Fifteenths and Tenths: the standard form of taxation granted by parliament to meet specific needs, usually relating to defence. Originally they had been based on the value of movable goods but by the 16th century were a fixed amount to be paid by each borough and settlement.

G

Groom of the Stool: The Chief Gentleman in the King's Privy Chamber who was in charge of the close–stool.

H

heresy: beliefs which contradicted the established doctrine of the Church of Rome.

Holy Roman Emperor: the elected monarch who ruled over the states which made up the Holy Roman Empire. The Empire was based on territories which had been held in the 9th century by Charlemagne and was seen as the successor to the western Roman Empire. The individual princes and dukes of the states in what are now Germany, the Netherlands and Austria elected the Emperor. Charles V was Holy Roman Emperor between 1519 and 1556, having succeeded his grandfather Maximilian I to keep the Empire in the control of the Habsburgs.

humanism: an intellectual movement which sought to return to the original Greek texts of the Bible to further the understanding of the Scriptures. There was also a focus on Latin and Greek literature. The leading humanist was Erasmus.

J

justices of the peace: Unpaid members of local government appointed by the King and responsible for implementing royal proclamations and ensuring that criminals were brought to justice.

L

laity: term used to describe those people who were not the clergy. This included both nobility and the commons when used in a religious context.

liturgy: the established services of the Church. The term was also used to refer to the language of the services and their rituals, such as the actions of the priests and congregation during the service in crossing themselves.

Lutherans: followers of Martin Luther who, like him, were classed as heretics for challenging the teachings of the Roman Catholic Church. Most significantly, they believed that people would go to heaven when they died owing to their faith in Christ, who alone had saved them by his death, not because they had done good works while on earth.

M

Mass: the most important service of the Roman Catholic Church. The high point of the service was the elevation of the bread and wine, which then became the body and blood of Christ. Henry VIII was said to observe four Masses each day.

monastery: a collective term which can be used to describe religious houses of monks, nuns and friars. The monasteries were based on a place of worship and provided accommodation for monks and nuns; they also offered help for the poor. Most monasteries had extensive land holdings, many of which were located some distance from the main settlement.

P

patronage: Henry was able to secure support by granting positions through which the recipients could increase their wealth. Alternatively he would give land or even gifts such as gold or silver plate.

Privy Chamber: the innermost private room of the King's apartments. Only those who were closest to the King and those who looked after his bodily needs were admitted. It was staffed by men.

Privy Council: the group of councillors who advised the King. The majority of them were either members of the nobility or the Church, but increasingly commoners such as Cromwell were members of the Privy Council.

purgatory: when people died – unless they were either spiritually pure, having committed no sins and so progressed straight to heaven, or were totally wicked and went directly to hell – they would spend time in purgatory. Time spent in purgatory could be reduced by good works done during a person's life or by prayers said for their soul. There is no reference in the Bible to purgatory.

R

regent: a person who ruled the country until the King or Queen reached majority, which was usually at the age of 18. The regent was generally a senior member of the royal family.

royal assent: for an act of parliament to become law it needed to be agreed by the King. This was demonstrated by the monarch's signature and the attachment of the seal of state.

royal supremacy: Henry VIII became the Supreme Head of the Church of England, replacing the Pope as the person responsible for religious law and for the protection of his subjects' souls.

T

temporal: a term used to distinguish between members of the House of Lords. A temporal lord was one who had access to property and a responsibility in local government; a spiritual lord was the term used for a bishop, archbishop or abbot.

transubstantiation: the term used for the transformation of the bread and wine into the body and blood of Jesus Christ.

treason: a crime, punishable by death, in which a challenge is made to the authority, or person, of the monarch.

V

Vicegerent: a position created for Thomas Cromwell. The position gave Cromwell the authority to act on the King's behalf in religious matters.

Bibliography

Books for teachers and for stretching the most able

Bernard, G. W. (2005) *The King's Reformation*, Yale University Press.

Cook, D. (1980) *Documents and Debates: Sixteenth–century England 1450–1600*, Macmillan.

Cressy, D. and Ferrell, L. A. (1996) *Religion and Society in Early Modern England*, Macmillan.

Duffy, E. (1992) *The Stripping of the Altars*, Yale University Press.

Haigh, C., ed. (1987) *The English Reformation Revised*, Cambridge University Press.

Haigh, C. (1993) *English Reformations*, Clarendon Press.

Hoyle, R. (2003) *The Pilgrimage of Grace*, Oxford University Press.

Marshall, P. (2003) *Reformation England 1480–1642*, Arnold.

Moorhouse, G. (2003) *The Pilgrimage of Grace*, Phoenix.

O'Sullivan, D. and Lockyer, R. (1993) *Tudor England 1485–1603: Sources and Opinions*, Longman.

Rex, R. (1993) *Henry VIII and the English Reformation*, Macmillan.

Books for student use

Anderson, A. and Imperato, T. (2001) *Tudor England 1485–1603*, Hodder & Stoughton.

Dawson, I. (1993) *The Tudor Century*, Nelson.

Ellsmore, S., Hudson, D. and Rogerson, D. (2001) *The Early Tudors*, John Murray.

Fellows, N. (2002) *Disorder and Rebellion in Tudor England*, Hodder & Stoughton.

Fletcher, A. and MacCulloch, D. (2004) *Tudor Rebellions* (fifth edition), Longman.

Lockyer, R. and O'Sullivan, D. (1997) *Tudor Britain*, Longman.

Murphy, D. *et al.* (1999) *England 1485–1603*, Collins Educational.

Newcombe, D. G. (1995) *Henry VIII and the English Reformation*, Routledge.

Palmer, M. D. (1983) *Henry VIII*, Longman.

Pendrill, C. (2000) *The English Reformation*, Heinemann.

Randell, K. (2001) *Henry VIII and the Government of England*, Hodder & Stoughton.

Randell, K. (2001) *Henry VIII and the Reformation in England*, Hodder & Stoughton.

Articles

Fellowes, N. 'The Pilgrimage of Grace', *History Review*, September 2000.

Davies, C. S. L. 'The Pilgrimage of Grace', *Early Modern History*, April 1992.

Hutton, R. 'Majesty with Menace', BBC, available at bbc.co.uk/history/british/tudors/majesty_menace_01.shtml

Television and fiction

Starkey, D. *The Six Wives of Henry VIII* (DVD), Channel 4.

A Man for All Seasons (DVD), 1966.

Henry VIII (DVD), 2003.

Gregory, P. (2001) *The Other Boleyn Girl*, HarperCollins.

Sampson, C. J. (2003) *Dissolution*, Macmillan.

Websites

www.activehistory.co.uk

www.learningcurve.gov.uk

www.bbc.co.uk/history

www.schoolhistory.co.uk

www.historylearningsite.co.uk

Acknowledgements

Author acknowledgements:

The author would like to thank her parents for encouraging her interest in History, in general, and the Church of England in particular.

The author and publisher would like to thank the following for permission to reproduce material:

Source texts:

p15 Rosman, D., *From Catholic to Protestant: Religion and the People in Tudor England*, Routledge, 1996. Reprinted with permission of Cengage Learning Services Ltd; p16 Murphy, V., in MacCulloch, D., (ed.) *The Reign of Henry VIII: Politics, Policy and Piety*, 1988. Reprinted with permission of Palgrave Macmillan; p19 Chaucer, G., *The Canterbury Tales*; p20 Lord Herbert, *Life and Reign of King Henry VIII*, 1649; p21 (top) Fish, S., *A Supplication for the Beggars*, 1529; p21 (middle) Melton, W., 1510; p21 (bottom) Duffy, E., *The Stripping of the Alters: Traditional Religion in England, 1400–1580*, Yale University Press, 1992. Reprinted with permission of Yale University Press; p29 (top) Foldyngton, T., 1530; p29 (middle) Mason, J.; p25 (middle) Dickens, A.G. and Elton, G. R., *Renaissance and Reformation 1300–1648*, Macmillan, 1968. Reprinted with permission of Palgrave Macmillan; p25 (bottom) Duffy, E., *The Stripping of the Alters: Traditional Religion in England, 1400–1580*, Yale University Press, 1992. Reprinted with permission of Yale University Press; p26 Foxe, J., Book of (Protestant) Martyrs, 1563; Sheils, W. J., *The English Reformation 1530–1570*, 1989, Longman; p37 (top) Dickens, A.G., quoted in Hurstfield, J. (ed.), *The Reformation Crisis*, 1965; p37 (middle) Cross, C., *Church and People 1450–1660*, Fontana, 1976; p37 (bottom) Duffy, E., *The Stripping of the Alters: Traditional Religion in England, 1400–1580*, Yale University Press, 1992. Reprinted with permission of Yale University Press; p39 Starkey, D., *Six Wives: The Queens of Henry VIII*, Chatto & Windus, 2004. Reprinted by permission of The Random House Group Limited; p43 (middle) *The Bible: Leviticus 20 v 21*; p43 (bottom) *The Bible: Deuteronomy 24 v 5*; p44 (top) Ives, E., *Anne Boleyn*, 1986; p44 (middle) Murphy, V., in MacCulloch, D., (ed.) *The Reign of Henry VIII: Politics, Policy and Piety*, Macmillan, 1996; p45 (middle) *Letter from Henry VIII to Anne Boleyn*, 1526; p45 (bottom) *Letter from Henry VIII to Anne Boleyn*, 1527; p46 (top) Pole, R., quoted in Bernard, G.W., *The King's Reformation*, Yale University Press, 2005. Reprinted with permission of Yale University Press; p46 (middle) Bernard, G.W., *The King's Reformation*, Yale University Press, 2005. Reprinted with permission of Yale University Press; p49 Cromwell, T.; p50 *The Submission of the Clergy*, 1532; p54 Pope Eleutherius (2nd century AD); p55 *Act for the Restraint of Appeals*, 1533; p57 (middle) *Act of Supremacy*, 1534; p57 (bottom) Bernard, G.W., *The King's Reformation*, Yale University Press, 2005. Reprinted with permission of Yale University Press; p61 (middle) More, T; p61 (bottom) Elton, G. R., *England under the Tudors*, Methuen, 1956. Reprinted with permission of Taylor and Francis Books UK; p62 Smith, A. G. R., *The Emergence of a Nation State 1529–1660*, Longman, 1998. Reprinted with permission of Pearson Education Limited; p64 Knowles, D., Bare Ruined Choirs, Cambridge University Press, 1959; p67 (top) Layton, R., 1535; p67 (middle) Tregonwell, J., 1535; p72 *Act for the Dissolution of Monasteries*, 1536; p73 *Surrender of Furness Abbey*, 1537; p74 Sherbrooke, M., extracts taken from http://www.cistercians.shef.ac.uk/roche/history/spoilation/sherbrook.php; p76 Elton, G. R., *England under the Tudors*, Methuen, 1956. Reprinted with permission of Taylor and Francis Books UK; p78 Moorhouse, G., *The Pilgramage of Grace*, Pheonix, 2003. Reprinted with permission of The Orion Publishing Group Ltd and Aitken Alexander Associates; p79 James, M. E., 'Obedience and Dissent in Henrician England: The Lincolnshire Rebellion 1536', *Past and Present*, 48, 1970; p80 (top) extract from the Lincoln Articles, 1536; p80 (bottom) extract from the Pontefract Articles, 1536; MacCulloch, D. and Fletcher, A., *Tudor Rebellions*, Longman, 2004. Reprinted with permission of Pearson Education Ltd; p87 Elton, G. R., *England under the Tudors*, Methuen, 1956. Reprinted with permission of Taylor and Francis Books UK; Scarisbrick, J., *Henry VIII*, Methuen, 1988; p97 Cranmer's Preface to the Great Bible, 1539; p99 from the trial of John Lambert, 1538; p101 Graves, M. A. R., quoted in Dawson, I., *The Tudor Century*, Longman, 1993. Reprinted with permission of Pearson Education Limited; p105 Williams, P., quoted in Dawson, I., *The Tudor Century*, Longman, 1993. Reprinted with permission of Pearson Education Limited; p106 Beckinsale, B. W., quoted in Dawson, I., *The Tudor Century*, Longman, 1993. Reprinted with permission of Pearson Education Limited; p107 Doran, S., *England and Europe*, Longman, 1996. Reprinted with permission of Pearson Education Limited; p110 (middle) letter from Thomas Cromwell to the King's representative in Germany, 1539; p110 (bottom) Loades, D., *Henry VIII: Church, Court and Conflict*, National Archives, 2007; p113 (margin) Letter from Cromwell to Henry VIII, June 1540; p113 (bottom) Bernard, G. W., *The King's Reformation*, Yale University Press, 2005; p115 (middle) Pendrill, C., *The English Reformation 1485–1558*, Heinemann, 2000. Reprinted with permission of Pearson Education; p115 (bottom) Scarisbrick, J., *Henry VIII*, Methuen, 1988; p119 Wilson, D., *In the Lion's Court: Power, Ambition and Sudden Death in the Reign of Henry VIII*, Hutchinson, 2001. Reprinted with permission of The Random House Group Limited; p121 Elton, G. R., *England under the Tudors*, Methuen, 1956. Reprinted with permission of Taylor and Francis Books UK; p122 Udall, N., quoted in Loades, D., *The Tudor Court*, Headstart, 1986; p124 (middle) Ridley, J., *Thomas Cranmer*, Clarendon Press, 1962. Reprinted with permission of Oxford University Press; p124 (bottom) Rex, R., *Henry VIII and the English Reformation*, Macmillan, 1993. Reprinted with permission of Palgrave Macmillan; p126 Guy, J., *Tudor England*, Oxford University Press, 1988. Reprinted with permission of Oxford University Press; p126 quoted in Dickens, A. G., and Carr, D., *The Reformation in England*, 1967; p132 Scarisbrick, J., *Henry VIII*, Methuen, 1988; p133 Morrill, J., *The British Problem 1534–1707*, Macmillan, 1996. Reprinted with permission of Palgrave Macmillan; p136 Chronicles of Ralph Holinshead; p137 Bishop Gardiner; p138 Loades, D., *Henry VIII: Church, Court and Conflict*, National Archives, 2007; p140 (middle) Starkey, D., *The English Court*, Longman, 1987. Reproduced with permission of Curtis Brown Limited, London on behalf of David Starkey; p141 the will of Henry VIII, December 1546; p142 Henry VIII's last speech in parliament, 24 December 1545.

Photographs courtesy of:

Aidan McRae Thomson 10; Ancient Art & Architecture Library 31 (bottom), 94 (top); Ann Ronan Picture Library 95; Bridgeman Art Library [The] 53; Bridgeman Art Library [The]/His Grace The Duke of Norfolk, Arundel Castle 78; Bridgeman Art Library [The]/Wakefield Museums and Galleries, West Yorkshire, UK 81; British Library [The]/HIP/TopFoto 107; Edimedia 22, 24, 39, 115, 116, 121 (both), 125, 139, 141, 144; Literature Archive [The] 28 (top), 83, 89, 98; Mary Evans Picture Library 26, 59, 127; Nirvaan Ghosh 135 (top); Photo12 88; Royal Collection 136; Topfoto 6, 14 (bottom), 16, 55 (both), 65, 100; World History Archive 3, 19, 28 (bottom), 29, 30, 31 (top), 32, 33, 43, 45, 48, 49, 52, 54, 56, 57, 61, 70, 73, 94 (bottom), 104, 110, 112, 113, 130, 132, 135 (bottom), 138.

Cover photograph: Courtesy of Richard Lea–Hair/Historic Royal Palaces/newsteam.co.uk

Photo research by Unique Dimension, www.uniquedimension.com

Special thanks to Jason Newman, Ann Asquith and Dora Swick

Index